P9-DGQ-434

I Think I Don't Remember

ART BUCHWALD

I THINK I DON'T REMEMBER

Illustrated by
Steve Mendelson

G. P. PUTNAM'S SONS   NEW YORK

G. P. Putnam's Sons
Publishers Since 1838
200 Madison Avenue
New York, NY 10016

Copyright © 1985, 1986, 1987 by Art Buchwald
Copyright © 1987 by Los Angeles Times Syndicate
Illustrations Copyright © 1987 by Steve Mendelson

All rights reserved. This book, or parts thereof,
may not be reproduced in any form without permission.
Published simultaneously in Canada by
General Publishing Co. Limited, Toronto

Library of Congress Cataloging-in-Publication Data

Buchwald, Art.
I think I don't remember.

I. Title.
PS3503.U1828I25   1987   814'.54   87–13920
ISBN 0-399-13325-9

Printed in the United States of America
1   2   3   4   5   6   7   8   9   10

*To my wife, Ann, to my friend, Jeannie Aiyer,
and to my assistant Cathy Crary, all of whom played a
marvelous role in getting this book to bed.*

Contents

CONTENTS

CONTENTS

LIST OF ILLUSTRATIONS

Introduction

M ANY years ago there was an emperor who loved new clothes. While he looked good in everything, the cloth he preferred was Teflon.

Everyone admired the Emperor when he walked about the grand white palace he lived in with his most gracious wife, an empress who, if it can be believed, possessed a wardrobe even more beautiful than the Emperor's.

One day three tailors came to the palace and announced they were from the haberdashery firm of McFarlane, North, and Poindexter.

"We wish to make you the most beautiful suit that any emperor has ever worn," one of the tailors said.

"It must be made of Teflon," the Emperor said. "It's the only fabric that suits me when I'm sitting on the throne."

"Do not worry," the second tailor spoke. "This is Teflon the likes of which no one has ever seen. It is woven of Persian thread and Contra trimming. The peculiar quality of this cloth is that no matter where you go nothing can penetrate it."

"I like that. How much do you want for this suit?"

"Twenty-four million dollars, if you say the money is for humanitarian reasons."

"I shall do it. Start at once," the Emperor cried.

"We will make it covertly, so no one in the land finds out you have ordered a Persian-made suit, particularly while the Persians are holding your loyal subjects as hostages."

A few weeks later the Emperor sent his chief of staff to find out how his suit was coming along. The chief discovered the tailors working at an empty loom. He was perplexed as to where the suit was. When the tailors insisted he was short-sighted, the chief said gruffly, "I see it but I don't see it. If anyone asks, I will say I may have seen it but I never knew about it."

One of the tailors said, "Good Teflon affects people that way."

After the chief reported back that he liked what he saw, other loyal followers of the Emperor visited the tailor shop to inspect the cloth. Each one saw nothing but they could never admit this for fear that the Emperor would consider them disloyal.

With every passing day the Emperor became more excited about his Teflon suit. He dreamed that once he put it on he would do wonderful things for his country such as launch great rockets into the sky, cut taxes down to nothing, and get the poor to shape up and fly right. He promised the Empress that as soon as the suit was delivered they would travel across the land spreading charisma far and wide.

Finally the big day arrived. The suit was delivered by McFarlane, North, and Poindexter. The Emperor immediately tore off all his clothes and put it on.

"Beautiful, magnificent, gorgeous," said every person in the white palace, not one admitting there was nothing there.

The Emperor, who felt no cloth or weight, did not want to look dumb in front of the staff so he said, "It fits like a glove."

"That is the beauty of Persian Teflon, you cannot feel it when you wear it," said one of the tailors.

Convinced, the Emperor walked into his rose garden to smell the flowers.

"Oh my God," a scribe said. "The Emperor has no clothes! Sir, do you realize that you are completely naked?"

The Emperor replied, "You obviously don't recognize good Teflon when you see it."

"Can you tell us what happened to your pants?" another scribe asked.

"No," the Emperor said. "I'm saving that for the third act."

Let Them Eat Cake

WHEN White House envoy Bud McFarlane went to Iran, he delivered a Bible and a chocolate cake.

I found the secret place that makes chocolate cakes for pro-terrorist regimes.

The baker was putting icing on one in the shape of a beard.

"Who is that for?" I asked.

"The Ayatollah Khomeini. The White House is going to pick it up in an hour."

"Does Khomeini eat cake?"

"The CIA swears he's a chocaholic. Once he gets his teeth into this we'll have him on his knees."

"What is this Bible doing here?"

"It's autographed by President Reagan and is part of America's new carrot and stick diplomacy. The Bible is the carrot and the cake is the stick. We're hoping to use both to bring our hostages out of Lebanon."

"From a diplomatic point of view it can't miss."

"It won't," the baker said. "As soon as we deliver the Bible, the cake, and enough spare parts for one hundred F4 fighter planes, the Iranians will be eating out of our hands."

"I thought we had a policy against giving cake to countries which support terrorism."

"We do and we don't. It's all right to give out cake if we deliver it with spare parts."

"What happens when the Iranians run out of spare parts? Does that mean their people will kidnap new hostages?"

"Probably, unless we give them the equipment before they grab more Americans."

"Then they won it all. Doesn't that make us patsies for terrorism?"

"Don't ask me. I just make chocolate cakes."

"Who are you making those cakes over there for?"

"That one is for Gadhafi. We're going to send it over to him with three hundred fifty ground-to-air missiles in hopes he'll cut his worldwide death squads in half."

"Suppose he takes the missiles but not the cake?"

"We'll be disappointed but we'll continue our 'quiet diplomacy' anyway. This chocolate cake goes to Vietnam with sixty tanks, this one to Cambodia with three hundred thousand bazookas. The Black September cake with white icing goes to Syria. There are hundreds of countries whose leaders are praying that McFarlane is going to show up at their place with a Bible and a cake."

"I don't blame the dictators around the world for wanting a piece of the cake," I said. "After all, you don't just get chocolate, but U.S. flamethrowers as well. Will this good-neighbor terrorist policy send a message around the world?"

"Definitely. The more hostages a country holds, the more cake and spare parts it can demand from America."

"Whose bright idea was this, anyway?"

"The President thought of it. One night he was having a state dinner and the chef served a chocolate layer cake. The President licked the knife and said, 'If our enemies could taste this cake they would never resort to terrorism again.' Thus another Reagan doctrine was born."

How Suite It Is

THERE have been recent reports that President Reagan's attention span is getting shorter and he keeps wandering away from the subject at hand.

One article written by Martin Tolchin in *The New York Times* reported that Congressman Robert Michel, the House Republican leader, urged the President to support a federal health-insurance program for catastrophic illness. Mr. Reagan responded to the request by telling a story about a welfare family living in a plush hotel in New York at enormous cost to the taxpayer. When it was pointed out to the President that health insurance is not a welfare program, Mr. Reagan is said to have repeated the story again.

Before anyone comes to any conclusions that the President has changed since the Republicans lost the Senate and the United States lost the Contra money in Switzerland, let me add that the story of a welfare family living in a plush hotel in New York has been bugging Mr. Reagan for six years.

White House sources say the President is obsessed with finding this family and showing them up for what they are—liberal chiselers feeding at the government trough.

The problem Mr. Reagan has in producing the family is that he heard the story about them second hand. He can't remember who told it to him, and so he has been forced to instigate a search himself. It's taken up a great deal of his time.

They say the President will sit in his Oval Office late at night studying a map of Manhattan. Then he'll pick up the phone and speak to FBI Director William Webster.

"Bill, did you find them yet?"

"No, Mr. President. But we're thinking of organizing a sting operation and offering free rooms in the Ritz Carlton to anyone now on welfare. We think that way we could smoke them out."

"What about the Plaza, Bill?"

"We've got every room wired and we're giving lie detector tests to anyone who gets on the elevator."

"They have to be somewhere," the President protests. "A welfare family can't just disappear amongst eight million people in a city like New York."

Mr. Webster says, "The FBI swat team is raiding Mrs. Helmsley's Palace tomorrow."

"Be careful, Bill. A welfare family which lives in a deluxe hotel can be very dangerous."

The President hangs up and buzzes the Air Force command center. "Any photos of the welfare family which is living off the fat of the land?"

"No, sir. Today's satellite pictures show nothing but a string of muggings and a dozen city commissioners being paid off by contractors."

Howard Baker comes in. "Mr. President, do you want to check over this trillion-dollar budget?"

"Howard, if you were a welfare cheat, what fancy hotel would you hole up in in New York?"

"How about the Hilton?"

"That's a thought. Why don't we stay there the next time we're in the city? Then, while I'm taking a nap, Pat Buchanan can hold you up on his shoulders and you can peek over the transoms."

"I think you ought to read this latest Senate report which tells how badly you fouled up on the Iran business."

"What I'd like to do," says Mr. Reagan, "is drag the entire family on television and show the American people what kind of welfare bums are living in our best hotels these days."

"That's fine, sir. Now what do you want to do about the Contras in Nicaragua?"

"Fly them up here and have them search the Waldorf-Astoria room by room."

Speak Up for Irangate

THERE are many citizens in the country who insist that the Iran-Contra operation is no big deal. Unfortunately, they are unable to put their thoughts into words. Perhaps I can be of help. Repeat after me:

"I'm keeping an open mind on Irangate until all the facts are in and the blame is placed on Jimmy Carter where it belongs."

"There are a lot more good people in Iran who need spare parts than there are bad people who want to cut off our legs."

"The United States will not trade arms for hostages, but that doesn't mean we shouldn't give it the old school try."

"Ollie North will always be a national hero because he showed us that patriotism and immunity are the same thing."

"What would you have done if you were President and Congress said you couldn't give any money to the Contras? You would have done what Reagan did—he screened *Rambo* for the seventeenth time."

"Poindexter is innocent until proven guilty, but if it turns out he did something wrong he deserves a much better price for his book."

"The President had no idea what was going on in his own White House, and we should all be grateful for this."

"I believe that when you get two Israeli arms dealers, one Iranian joker named Ghorbanifar, a Saudi promoter named Khashoggi, a Marine hotshot called North, plus the head of the CIA, and you issue each of them a Swiss bank account number, something is bound to go wrong in Nicaragua."

"People complain because we delivered a chocolate cake and a Bible to the ayatollahs in Tehran. It was a lot cheaper than sending them a dozen roses."

"Bush had nothing to do with Irangate, but I can understand his wanting to back away from the President. After all, he is the only Republican presidential candidate who isn't better off today than he was four years ago."

"I'm not for perjury per se, but I would rather have it committed by our side than theirs."

"What Irangate boils down to is credibility. We have to choose between those who are telling the truth, those who are lying, and those who are taking the Fifth Amendment. Personally I trust people who take the Fifth, because they're officers and gentlemen."

"The thing that gets me the maddest is when they call Irangate another Watergate. Show me a moderate Iranian who was involved in Watergate."

"The worst part about the Iran scandal for conservatives is that it turns people's attention away from the real issues of the country, which are prayers in school and confiscating *Playboy* from the blind."

"The fact that the money from Iran arms sales has never been accounted for doesn't mean that it didn't go to orphans in Costa Rica."

"Look at it this way. By letting them sample our Hawk missiles we create a new hardware market in Iran. Once they stop burning Americans in effigy we'll have another generation of satisfied consumers."

"I ask you, what would you rather have in the White House—a weak President who had no idea what his staff was doing, or a strong leader who knew everything that was going on, but had no idea what *anyone* was doing?"

Never Again

HOLLYWOOD is not the swinging place it was in days of yore. The fear of AIDS has made it the anti-bundling capital of the world.

The other night I was at a dinner table in Beverly Hills which was graced by the most beautifully turned-out men and women in California. I was surprised when they immediately declared where they stood on the matter of seeking out a love mate.

Idra Darkeyes announced that she was not only against having a long-term love affair, but was fearful of participating in one-night stands as well.

Clark Ablebody said he couldn't care less about making it with women, nor was he interested in how they felt about not making it with him.

The lady, whose name was Sue, said she'd rather be pushed over a Malibu cliff than bundle with a man. Her date said he wouldn't do it even if two uniformed policemen held him in a chokehold grip.

"Do they still do it back East?" my host asked me.

"No," I said. "We haven't done it since James Watt destroyed the environment."

"What do you do in the East in place of sex?" my hostess inquired.

"We study the Tower Commission Report. The feeling back home is that it's much better to read about White House erotica than create your own."

"I don't know anybody out here who does it anymore," Clark said.

"But," I protested, "if you people in California are so determined not to do it, why does everyone always dress up as if they want to?"

Sue said, "You have to pretend or they will think you have lost your sex appeal."

"But you're provoking others with your flirting."

"Just because you don't do it doesn't mean that you can't look as if you would."

The host said, "People don't need a sex drive to be attractive. You see these custom-made jeans I'm wearing? Cost me eight hundred dollars. To look at me you would think I'm the son of Casanova. What no one knows is you will have to drag me along the freeway behind my BMW before I'll fool around."

"Does this mean that you're abstaining from your wife?" I asked.

"Especially my wife. Who knows where the vegetables she buys were grown. If you stay away from people like your wife you will live a lot longer."

My host's wife said, "I feel the same towards him."

I said, "Is the table unanimous on California celibacy?"

Idra said, "Of course we are. Women are just not into sex anymore, and happily men feel the same way. The struggle at the door is over. Now when you have a date, it's a race to see who can get home first to watch David Letterman."

Clark said, "I met a girl the other night who said she would bundle if the circumstances were right."

"What did you do?" the hostess asked.

"I reported her to the Surgeon General."

The host turned to me and said, "Do you find us peculiar?"

"No. I find you right on target. What I admire about you is that for people who have no interest in making love, you wear a helluva lot of perfume."

Ollie and Fawn

THE producer came into my office and threw the script down in disgust.

"It doesn't work," he said. "Who is going to believe the name Ollie for a Marine hero who worked in the White House?"

"I got the name from Laurel and Hardy. It sounded different."

"And 'Fawn.' You want me to think there is a beautiful, long-legged girl named Fawn who is involved with a bunch of cowboys in the National Security Council?"

"We need some sex appeal. You're not going to get men turned on from John Poindexter stuffing tobacco in his pipe," I told him.

The producer said, "Look, I hired you to write a movie script about a president of the United States who used to be a movie star and becomes one of the greatest communicators in history, until one day he forgets where he parked his car. The story line is simple. While the President is shaking hands with Icelandic freedom fighters in the Rose Garden, his staff is stealing everything that's not bolted down in the White House. I don't see that in these pages. I want more sleaze and slime.''

I said, ''I have to flesh out the characters before I develop it. To begin with, I don't know what to do with Ollie's friend who flies all the arms to Iran. The scene as it plays now is flat, even when he is met by three ayatollahs and they hold hands and dance around the control tower.''

''Why can't you have Fawn sipping a drink with Bud at the Tehran airport bar as the piano player sings 'As Time Goes By'?'' the producer asked.

''What would she be doing at the airport in Tehran?''

''She's waiting for Ollie because she thought he was on the plane.''

''But Ollie isn't on the plane. He's speaking at a Contra fund-raiser in Dallas, Texas. What does Fawn do when Ollie doesn't show up?'' I protested.

''She flies back to Washington and makes out more travel vouchers for Ollie.''

''What is Mr. Reagan doing?'' I asked.

''He's trying to remember what he was doing on the day he was sworn in as the fortieth President of the United States.''

I shook my head. ''I don't know if I can write this. It's believable and at the same time there are holes in it. For example, I'd like to work the CIA into it, but I haven't figured out if they are on our side or theirs.''

The producer said, ''Write that at the beginning they're on our side, and then later on in the picture they wind up on their side.''

"I have some good business in the film. The first thing I'm going to have Ollie do is declare war on Panama and nuke the canal. Then I want him to personally take a U.S. atomic submarine up the Neva River and shell Leningrad. After that I have him going to France and kidnapping the entire French parliament. Then he flies in a hang glider and carpet bombs the Philippines with Imelda Marcos's shoes."

The producer said, "It's not bad. Can't you get him to assassinate somebody?"

"I don't want Ollie to do anything that's against the law because he's the national hero in my picture."

"The movie is shaping up," the producer said. "Have you got anything in the script about Ollie taking the Fifth?"

"With all the things I have him doing—he doesn't have time to take the Fifth."

"One more question," the producer said. "Where is Fawn while Ollie is making mischief around the world?"

"I have her doing what any American woman would do. She's home shredding papers for her man."

All-American Boy

IT's hard to believe Lieutenant Colonel Oliver North was able to do all the things he is said to have done in the last few years. The mind boggles at how he kept all those balls in the air.

I can just imagine a simple day in the life of this gung-ho Marine.

"Fawn, I have to go to China tomorrow to pick up some guns for the Contras. Book me on a Pan Am flight to Beijing. . . . Hold it a minute. I just found a note here that the Poles will see me on my request for the land-to-air missiles we're trying to buy. Fix my ticket so I can stop in Warsaw on my way back from Beijing."

"But, Ollie, you can't go to China tomorrow. You're scheduled to brief all the contributors of the Freedom-Fighting Foundation at the Kennedy Center."

"I'll talk to them at breakfast and fly to China in the afternoon."

"You're booked in Miami in the morning to address the anti-Castro Cubans. You were going to do that on your way to Grenada. The anti-Castro meeting is important because they're trying to raise money to invade Cuba."

"I'll do that after Poland. By the way, I have to stop off in Geneva to arrange financing for arms we're giving Iran."

"Ollie, you didn't tell me about any arms for Iran."

"I'm flying them in with Bud McFarlane after I meet with a Saudi Arabian, an Iranian, and an Israeli businessman in Jerusalem."

"You want to fly from Geneva to Jerusalem?"

"Yes, because that's my takeoff point for Tehran."

"Didn't you promise to race in the America's Cup in Australia this weekend?"

"I haven't forgotten. What time is my briefing with the President?"

"It's Friday at two o'clock."

"I'll be back for that unless I go underground in Italy to infiltrate the Red Brigade."

"What are you going to tell the President?"

"I'm not telling him anything. He just wants to be assured everything will be all right."

"Ollie, did you know you were scheduled to rewire the entire U.S. Embassy in Moscow on Friday?"

"Don't worry, Fawn. I'll take the red-eye back from Tehran."

"You have a PTA meeting on Friday and your wife said she'll kill you if you miss it."

"It seems to me I'm also conducting the National Symphony Orchestra that night."

"That's next week. This week you're slated to give the definitive lecture on brain surgery at the National Academy of Sciences."

"Wasn't I supposed to ride a horse in the Kentucky Derby?"

"No they scratched you when they heard you were going to race in the Indianapolis 500. Ollie, you're doing too much."

"Fawn, whoever heard of a Marine doing too much? We have wars to win, Communists to kill, and presidents to save. If I don't keep this whole thing together, who will?"

"You're so strong, Ollie. Is there anything else you want me to do?"

"Maybe I'll test Star Wars after lunch."

"Ollie, the Supreme Court is on the other line. They want

to know if you'll write the majority decision on 'The People Versus Gambino.' "

"Okay, but tell them to get the transcript over pronto. I have a yen to parachute into Libya and give Gadhafi a piece of my mind."

Coming Attractions

PRESIDENT Reagan has had a great deal of difficulty with the history of World War II. His first gaffe was to believe that German and American soldiers were buried in the same cemeteries in Germany, and could presumably be honored at a combined ceremony. His second one was to say that very few of today's Germans remember the war and certainly none of the adults now living participated in any way. Finally, he really flunked the course when he said that the soldiers buried at Bitburg were just as much victims of the war as people who died in the Holocaust.

What are we to make of the President's blunders?

There may be clues in a book titled *The Films of Ronald Reagan,* by Tony Thomas, published by Citadel Press (1980).

Despite being under contract to Warner Brothers, Mr. Reagan did not play in as many World War II movies as one might think. Yet his view of the war and the Nazis could easily have been formed by the ones he did appear in.

In 1941 Ronald Reagan went into action for the first time in a film called *International Squadron*. His role was that of a daredevil American stunt pilot who ferries a bomber to the RAF in England. Once there, he witnesses a child killed in an air raid and joins the RAF to get even with the Nazis. But Reagan doesn't take his flying job seriously, and while he's messing around with a French pilot's girlfriend, he misses a mission. His best American friend substitutes for him and is killed.

This sobers him up as far as World War II is concerned. He decides to atone for his tacky behavior by knocking out the French pilot and taking *his* mission. After shooting down several German fighter planes in a smashing dogfight, Reagan dies a fiery heroic death. The important thing to remember is, while there was lots of talk of German bad guys, Reagan never got to meet one personally in the film.

To my knowledge, the only time Ronald Reagan ever came face-to-face with the Nazis was in *Desperate Journey,* made in 1942. He co-stars with Errol Flynn as part of the crew of an RAF Flying Fortress. In the film Reagan plays a brash, amusing, irreverent but very brave Yank.

After the RAF plane drops its bombs on Germany, it is shot down and the crew is rounded up by a German major (Raymond Massey). The German military personnel in *Desperate Journey* are portrayed not so much as villains as they are bumblers and idiots. (The picture was the *Hogan's Heroes* of its time.) In Reagan's big scene he is being debriefed alone by the major, who thinks the Yank will tell him everything he wants to know about the mission. Instead Ronnie knocks out Massey, *and then sits down and eats the major's breakfast*.

After this hilarious scene, Reagan and the crew find it a

breeze to escape, and make their way across all of Germany, blowing up half the country with violent acts of sabotage. In a slam-bang finish they manage to steal a German bomber and take off for England with Errol Flynn at the controls. Having wiped out Germany, Flynn turns to Reagan and says, "Now for Australia and a crack at the Japs."

That, as far as I know, was Ronald Reagan's only Hollywood action in the European theater during World War II. He did serve honorably in Burma in *The Hasty Heart,* and in the Korean conflict in an MGM film titled *Prisoner of War,* which was so bad that it apparently hastened Mr. Reagan's decision to go into politics. The President's finest hour was *Hellcats of the Navy,* in which Reagan was cast as a Naval commander of a sub in the Pacific that wreaks havoc on the Japanese fleet. Not only did Mr. Reagan win the war, but he also won the girl, a nurse played by Nancy Davis, who is now our first lady of the land.

I detail the films in which Mr. Reagan starred for only one reason. It appears that the President's Hollywood war record, while distinguished, certainly did not prepare him in any way or shape for the fortieth anniversary of the end of hostilities with Nazi Germany. It also might explain why Mr. Reagan is so ignorant of World War II history. Even a bit part in *The Battle of the Bulge* would have made him realize that visiting a German military cemetery where SS soldiers are buried is just not the right thing for an American president to do.

The Electronic Church

"LORD, listen to me. This is the Reverend Shorty Beans, broadcasting on Channel 83, from the Electronic Church of the Tender Wallet in Boosterville, Virginia. This is not a test. I'm up to my cowboy boots in trouble.

"Somebody's trying to take my flock. I suspect it's that garden snake Reverend Jimmy Haggard, the one who takes Mastercharge and VISA to heal arthritis sufferers. He wants my ministry so he can cash in on my late-night listeners. God, I need You to come up with a poison-pill defense against this diabolically hostile takeover.

"Lord, don't listen to the stories about me committing a sexual transgression with my secretary in the TV control room. This is just the Devil's blackmail put out by Haggard to hurt my Neilsen ratings. You know and I know that there is less hanky panky in the Church of the Tender Wallet than in any TV pulpit in the land.

"Haggard is putting out the word that I've sinned in church business administration. He can go to hell. Last year we grossed one hundred million dollars, of which You got two. Sales of my wife Barbie's gospel album have soared through the roof. The condos on the Red Sea Golf Course are finished, the Cain and Abel amusement park is SRO, and we're adding another wing to the twenty-five-story Sodom and Gomorrah Motel.

"Haggard can't come close to our numbers. Ask him how many Sea of Galilee hot tubs he sold last month. He almost put his church into bankruptcy.

"Lord, we're willing to make any changes You want in order to cut expenses. You tell us how many on-camera faith healers to fire, and we'll do it. Barbie is starting to save money already. She's dumped the entire symphony orchestra that always accompanies her spiritual version of 'If I Was a Rich Man.' And we've cut back on the fireworks display we set off every time a pledge of five thousand dollars lights up the telethon board.

"And get this—I decided to take a salary cut. I intend to say today on the air that I will accept no more pay from the Church of the Tender Wallet than Lee Iacocca takes out of Chrysler Motors.

"Haggard has no right to bad-mouth me, Lord. He's Satan's hatchet man. If You allow him to take over our TV show, the ratings will plummet to zero. He'll drive every viewer from our channel to *Miami Vice*.

"Lord, I've got a great ploy to stop the takeover. I'm going to announce that if the listeners don't give me eight million dollars to prevent Haggard from grabbing my church, You are going to take me home. It's going to be 'bye-bye' Reverend Shorty, because I'm going to that big cathode-tube cathedral in the sky.

"If that fails, I will go for broke. I shall say that if my congregation doesn't raise the money, I'm going to do something desperate. I'm going to run for president of the United States.

"I know what You're saying, Lord. Where do I come off running for president? It's very simple. I have all the qualifications any candidate has this year, not to mention my own TV network. I'm going to tell my flock a vote for me is a vote for You—and if You don't mind, Lord—I'm going to reveal that I have Your endorsement. And if this doesn't do the trick I will bring up my war record.

"You don't have to make any personal appearances for me, Lord. By the same token You don't have to make a big deal of it if You are not going to be there.

"I think I've covered everything. We're only three minutes to air time. What I'm asking from You, Lord, is to help me stop the Devil's takeover of my ministry. If this means a Holy War, Thy will be done. Trust me Lord. I will always keep one eye on You and the other on the bottom line."

Where Were You?

No matter what Ronald Reagan says in order to win back his popularity, he will never convince the American people of his innocence about Iran until he remembers what he was doing on August 8, 1985. Not only did President Reagan insist that he could not recall what he was doing then, but he challenged every man, woman, and child in the United States to remember what they were doing on that day.

Mr. Reagan has taken the position that as president he has the authority to forget anything he wants to. Privately he is going bonkers trying to remember what he was doing on that August date.

The other night at dinner he said to Nancy, "Wait a minute, it's coming to me. I know what I was doing. I was windsurfing on the Potomac with George Shultz. I remember it because he showed me his tattoo.''

Nancy said, "I saw the tattoo too. But that was August 7th, Ronnie."

"Darn, I know I was somewhere, doing something. It's on the tip of my tongue."

"Ronnie, you're fretting too much. People don't care where you were on August 8th. They want you just as long as you will be their Teflon president."

"How can I be a Teflon leader when I don't know my own whereabouts?"

"Many presidents did not know where they were during their terms in office. But that didn't stop them from getting into the World Almanac. History will remember you for what you forgot."

"Nancy, it's weird. I can't sleep in the afternoon trying to recall what I did on August 8th."

"Doesn't your staff have some record of that date?"

"They can't even remember what Donald Regan was doing that day."

"The date couldn't have been an important one or someone would have remembered seeing you."

"Suppose I was on a secret mission with Bud McFarlane and Ollie North flying arms in dense fog over Iran."

"You wouldn't do that."

"I would if I was still working at Warner Brothers."

"If I know you, Ronnie, you were probably doing nothing more than holding a photo opportunity session on the White House lawn."

"Why don't I call Sam Donaldson and ask him if he shouted at me in the Rose Garden on August 8th?"

"It wouldn't mean anything. Sam shouts at you every time

he sees you. Ronnie, you have a lot to remember now without trying to recall what you were doing two summers ago.''

''But, Nancy, my whole credibility depends on it. How can a president maintain his popularity if he has no idea what he was doing in the heat of 1985?''

''Ronnie, all the people want to know is when you okayed the arms for Iran.''

''It's not that easy. I'll bet there isn't one person in this country who can remember when he okayed an arms shipment to Iran.''

''It doesn't matter. What matters is where you keep the button and how you push it.''

''What button? I don't know anything about a button. Have I got a button here somewhere?''

''Ronnie, I wrote it all down on your shirt cuff. The button is under the dining room table next to your foot. You step on it once to launch an all-out missile attack on the Soviet Union, and twice when you want the butler to clear the table. Can you remember that?''

''Of course. That's something that stays in a president's mind forever. What butler?''

The Story of a Bike

THE trouble in the Defense Department (and who says there is any trouble in the Defense Department?) is that as our weapons become more sophisticated, they take longer and longer to produce. Consequently, the person in the Pentagon who originally came up with the idea is no longer there, and the project has gone through dozens of teams and many different lives before it is ready for combat.

Take the SCM Mark 89. Back in the 1950s the Army wanted a scout-car motor vehicle, which, in effect, was a motorcycle with a sidecar.

The idea for a new scout bike was thought up by Lieutenant Harold Doggett, who is now a retired general in Sarasota, Florida.

"Do you remember being the project officer on the SCM?" I asked him on the phone.

He thought hard. "Seems to me I had something to do with it. The scout bikes from World War II were obsolete and I went to the Harley-Davidson people and asked them to come up with a design. When I left we were haggling over the price. They were asking five hundred dollars for each one and I was trying to knock them down to four-fifty."

"Then you left before it got off the drawing board?"

"Yes, I did. I turned it over to a Major Art Hammond, and that's the last I heard of it. I believe he's out in Sun City, Arizona."

I tracked Art Hammond down.

"Sir," I said, "I understand that you were involved with an SCM scout motorbike which the Army was building."

"That wasn't a motorbike. The only SCM I remember was an eight-thousand-dollar, four-wheel-drive, semi-personnel carrier. I stayed with it for three years and then I was transferred to Hawaii."

"You don't remember who took charge of the project after you?"

"Colonel Jeffries or Joffrey. Not too sure of the guy's name, but he wound up heading the Lackadaisical Defense Company, which was going after the contract."

Jeffries was also retired when I found him on his boat in the Chesapeake Bay. He recalled the SCM well. "We never did go into production with the SCM because the Army decided that instead of a semi-personnel vehicle it wanted an all-weather tank. So we tore up the plans and started from scratch. Then I retired from the service and Brigadier General Tommy Wuggenheimer headed the project team. He was really hot on the SCM and had Congress convinced that the Army couldn't do without it. Wuggenheimer insisted the SCM have radar on top of it and the capacity to float on water. We told them we could build it for $500,000 each, and they were about to sign the order when Wuggenheimer was sent to Vietnam and replaced by Lieutenant General 'Swede' Ruffles.

"Swede was the top helicopter pilot in the Army and he decided the SCM would have to fly. So he brought in a helicopter company as a co-contractor and we worked for ten years trying to get the thing off the ground. We were up to $2,500,000 when Swede was relieved by General Archie Toland, an engineer, who not only wanted the SCM to carry airborne personnel, do the work of a tank, and have the ability of a helicopter, but also perform as a bulldozer. We said it could be done for ten million dollars each.''

"In all the years you worked on the SCM, did anyone ever mention that originally it was supposed to be a scout bike with a sidecar to transport a lieutenant and his aide?''

Jeffries said, ''What would the Army want with a motorcycle that could only transport two people?''

Crime and Punishment

As part of the Justice Department's unending war against corporate crime, a new facility has just been built to deal with serious offenders.

I was taken on a tour by an assistant attorney general for corporate crime, who was quite proud of the place.

He showed me into the receiving area, which was beautifully furnished with leather chairs and couches, and a TV set.

"This is where we ask the defendants to wait while we are negotiating a plea-bargaining session with their lawyers.''

"It's nice of you to provide a waiting room for them.''

"Just because a man has committed a corporate crime is no reason why he can't be comfortable.''

"How long do you keep him in the pen?''

"It depends. If the guy wants to plead guilty and go along with the Justice Department's recommendations on punishment, we'll let him out in a couple of hours. But if he's going to play hardball and try to get off lightly, we'll keep him in here until he misses his business lunch."

"I had heard your corporate criminal division was tough, but I never thought you'd make someone miss a business lunch."

All the leather chairs were taken. "Is that man in the pin-striped suit over there a white collar criminal?"

"No," he replied. "That's his lawyer. The other fellow in a pin-striped suit is the criminal. The toughest thing about prosecuting corporate crime is you can't tell the defendants from the lawyers."

My guide pointed to a large sign on the wall. "That's our rate card for each white collar crime. We put it up there so the defendants can study it while waiting to see a Justice Department attorney."

"The rates seem very reasonable," I said.

"We try to keep them low so that we don't have to go to trial," he said. "It's to our advantage to settle out of court and save the taxpayer money."

"What did that guy reading *The Wall Street Journal* do?"

"He's a contractor and we have five hundred forty counts against him for overcharging the Defense Department ten million dollars for missile parts."

"He doesn't seem very worried."

"He better be. We're going to fine his company five thousand dollars."

"Will he pay it?"

"He will if he doesn't want a long drawn-out trial with a lot of publicity. We don't fool around here."

"Okay, so let's say he agrees to pay the five thousand dollars. Then what happens?"

My guide led me into a quiet, carpeted room. "After the defendant agrees to plead guilty and pay his fine, we bring him in here and make him swear on this Bible that he will never do it again."

"Do what again?"

"Commit a corporate crime."

"And that's it?"

"Not by a long shot," he said. "Over here is where the real punishment is meted out. You see this wooden block? Well, every person who pleads guilty has to put his hand on the block. Then the Attorney General or one of the assistants slaps him on the wrist."

"Is it painful?"

"Put your hand up here and find out for yourself."

I did and he slapped my wrist as hard as he could. "Did it hurt?" he asked me.

I thought about it for a moment and then said, "Ouch."

Testing—Testing

THE testing of baseball players for drugs has begun.

"Well, ladies and gentlemen, this is Dan Sundergard of WFLY Radio, and we are in Florida at the baseball training camp stadium of the Doppler Snail Darters. They are playing an exhibition game against the Windemere Dumplings. Leading the lineup for the Snail Darters is Brian Smirk.

"Brian steps up to the plate, tips his cap, takes a practice swing, and the umpire hands him a specimen bottle. Smirk is shaking his head to indicate that he doesn't want to be tested, but the umpire vehemently insists. Hold it. Max Fury, the Snail Darter manager, has just jumped out of the dugout and is having a tantrum. He is cussing and throwing his hat on the ground. The umpire is telling him to get back to the dugout. But Max is too incensed to pay any attention. Wait a minute—Fury has grabbed the specimen bottle and thrown it at the Windemere bench. It's broken into a thousand pieces. The umpire is now tossing Max out of the game for interfering with the testing of a baseball player when he is at bat.

"Things have settled down. Smirk is back at home plate. The umpire gives him another specimen bottle. This time Brian does not flinch. He jogs behind the backstop where no one can see him and . . . Let's pause now for a commercial.

"Welcome back to Doppler stadium. Smirk is returning to home plate. He hands the specimen bottle to the umpire, who raises it up to the sun. Everyone in the stadium is holding his breath. Here comes the decision from the umpire. He is spreading out his hands in a sweeping gesture. SMIRK IS SAFE! The test has come up negative! The crowd is going crazy. All the Doppler players are swarming around Smirk hugging and kissing him. Now he is riding on their shoulders waving to the fans. Just a second, Tap Chewing, the Windemere manager, is arguing with the umpire that Smirk's specimen was positive and not negative. The umpire has turned his back on Chewing, who seems to be threatening to take the test to the Baseball Commissioner on appeal.

"The umpire has told everyone to get off the field so the teams can play ball.

"Monarchy throws a fast-breaking ball which Smirk connects with and there it goes over the second baseman's head . . . back to the wall. Brian has a triple! The third-base umpire hands Brian another specimen bottle to make sure he hasn't used any drugs while running from home plate to third. Smirk is going behind a billboard . . . And now it's time out for another commercial.

"Here comes Brian back to third with his specimen. The umpire is taking out his test kit. Hold it! He is looking at Smirk strangely. Now his thumb goes up in the air. Smirk is out. Smirk is out! This is the first time a major-league player has ever been tested safe at home and then called out at third.

"Smirk is jumping up and down on the umpire's test kit. The Doppler third-base coach is throwing sand into the umpire's face. But nothing will change the umpire's mind. In baseball, test tubes don't lie.

"There goes Brian walking toward the dugout. Maybe our man on the field, Simple Semple, can have a word with him."

"What happened, Brian?"

"It was a bad call. I was clean for the entire triple."

"What was that white stuff you were sniffing when you slid into third?"

"That was lime from the baseline."

"Do you think it was the lime that made your test positive?"

"Beats me. I don't even know what the test for lime is."

"Do you believe the Baseball Commissioner is out of line with this testing of baseball players?"

"Damn right. There is nothing wrong with testing us once. But when they test us at every base they've gone too far."

PR for Imelda

ALMOST every public relations firm in America is after the Imelda Marcos account. Myron Steaknife told me why. "Mrs. Marcos has a distorted image in the U.S., but fortunately she has enough money to change it. I'm making a presentation next week. What do you think of it?"

Myron opened a large folder. "The way I see it, Imelda owns half of all the real estate in New York, and Leona Helmsley owns the other half. I want Imelda to move to New York and personally advertise her real estate properties in the same manner that Leona does hers.

"I see Imelda in a full-page photo stretched over the top of a piano saying, 'Leona is wild about Harry and I'm wild about Ferdinand. If you really want to have a ball come to the Golden Casa for a lovers' weekend. We feature free breakfast, free ice, free movies, and free elections.'

"I have another based on Mrs. Helmsley's ad in *New York* magazine. It shows Leona standing in the dining room of her Palace Hotel saying, 'It's the only palace in the world where the Queen stands guard.' "

Steaknife said, "We'd show Imelda singing into a microphone on the balcony of her hotel. The copy would read, 'Leona Helmsley has no idea what it takes to guard a palace. Would you believe even a company of crack troops and a dozen tanks isn't enough?' "

"Why the ads?"

"I want the public to think of Mrs. Marcos as an astute businesswoman instead of someone who keeps shoving pesos in her Calvin Klein jeans. The fastest way to do this is through advertising. I also have a brokerage firm interested in signing up Imelda for a commercial. She would stand in front of the plane she arrived on from the Philippines and say, 'Hello, I'm Imelda Marcos and my husband and I made money the old-fashioned way—we smuggled it out of the country in a trunk. If you expect to be overthrown soon, call me at this toll-free number, and for a fee I'll advise how to keep your loot with the blessing of President Reagan.' "

I said, "You think that will help Imelda's image?"

"It can't hurt it. I want to persuade the country that Imelda was not one of these dictator's wives who spent all her time in Paris buying clothes with her country's Fresh Air Funds. I'm going to show that there were a lot worse spendthrifts kicked out of their countries."

"You're not talking about Mrs. Duvalier?"

"Let's just say I'm talking about anyone who knows anything about voodoo economics."

Steaknife said if Imelda doesn't want to go head-to-head with Leona Helmsley, or do brokerage commercials, she could always venture into the jewelry business. "She has enough diamonds to light up the Statue of Liberty for a week," he said.

"That's a lot of diamonds."

"Just because a person is a head of state's wife doesn't mean she can't own a few nice things."

"Your entire presentation seems to be built around getting Mrs. Marcos a job."

"Every woman has to fulfill herself," he said. "Since Imelda owns shopping centers, art treasures, stocks, and chests full of gold bullion, she doesn't have to lift a finger for the rest of her life. But when you've been married to someone like Marcos you have to keep occupied in your spare time. There is just so much polo Imelda can play with Ferdinand."

"This is a pretty good presentation," I told him. "Do you think Madame Marcos will go for it?"

"I don't see why not. If she doesn't want to do it, I have a book contract for her to sign. A publisher wants her to write *Hawaii on $750 Million a Day*."

Happy Hour

IT was Happy Hour at the OK Corral Saloon on Capitol Hill. The place was jammed with its usual five o'clock crowd when the tall lobbyist with the white hat strode up to the bar and said, "Drinks on the house for everybody."

We filled up and then turned to the stranger. "And what victory might we be toasting?" someone asked.

"Congress has said goodbye to the 1968 Gun Control Act. I'm with the National Hair-Trigger Association, and this is a great moment for my people."

"I didn't know the hair-trigger manufacturers had their own lobby."

"Ah yes. We've always had a strong interest in a weak gun law. The easier it is to buy guns the more hair-triggers we're going to sell. I was given a million dollars to make sure the people's representatives would vote the American way. Fill up, everybody. This is the last of my money."

He started to sing, "A gun for me and a gun for you. And a gun to shoot your neighbor too."

All of us have seen lobbyists celebrate when they got a bill through, but it was nothing compared to this.

"How come the police departments were against you people weakening the gun bill?" Tom the bartender asked.

The stranger said, "Cops don't know anything about guns. All they run up against are the criminal elements who use weapons to commit robberies. They never see the law-abiding people who buy their handguns to hunt and fish."

"Fish?"

"Don't tell me you never shot a fish with a thirty-eight? The important thing to remember is that under the old law you couldn't even bring a gun from one state to another. Dealers were responsible for keeping records of who bought handguns and ammunition. Do you know what this meant for thousands of gunshop owners?"

"What?"

"It meant *paperwork*. These good merchants used to have to stay up all night long trying to remember who bought a gun and who bought ammunition. We got all that red tape eliminated and from here on out you're going to see a boom in the sale of every type of firearm. Drink up, friends, the Constitution is alive and well in the hair-trigger lobby."

"How did you get Congress to knuckle under to a weak gun-control law?"

The stranger winked. "Let's say we just sent the legislators a message. If they didn't vote to reform the 1968 act we would send our people into their districts and riddle them with innuendos. On the other hand, if they promised to be good boys and support us we would make a donation to their favorite political charity. One more for the road, men. Then I must make the rounds of the halls of Congress to drop off some goodies to those who backed our bill, and mark a red X on the doors of those who lost their nerve."

The man plunked one thousand dollars on the bar. I raised my glass. "To good sport," I said.

We drank.

Someone shouted, "Death to all gun laws!"

The stranger wasn't drinking. He said, "We can't have that. The threat of stronger gun-control bills keeps the National Hair-Trigger Association alive. Our members would refuse to provide us with money if they thought the battle was all over.''

"And how do you keep the threat going?" I asked.

"By putting out the word to our members that the law-enforcement people are mad as hell at us and aren't going to take it anymore.''

The man exited through the swinging doors.

"Who was that stranger who was just here?" someone asked.

"That was no stranger," the bartender replied. "That was the leader of the PAC."

Football Injuries

I am sure most of you have noticed that more and more football players are getting hurt these days and doctors are trying to find out why.

Dr. Frederick Pickett has been doing a study, and his conclusion is that the players' injuries are not coming from the other side.

"There was a time when someone on the team made a good play and his teammates patted him on the bottom," Dr. Pickett said. "This is no longer the case. Let me show you these tapes." He pushed a button and up came a linebacker from the Redskins sacking a Chicago Bear.

"Now watch this," Pickett said. Six burly Redskin defense men jumped on their own linebacker and started to pound and kick him.

"Are they mad at him?" I asked.

"No," said Dr. Pickett, "they're just congratulating him on the good play."

"But he isn't getting up."

"That's what makes football interesting. You can be hurt by either side."

The Chicago Bear quarterback faded back, threw the ball, and as the tight end caught it he went over for a touchdown. The entire Bear team ran across the field, knocked down the end, then punched him senseless. The tight end, to the cheers of his own bench, was taken off the field on a stretcher.

Pickett said, "The most dangerous place for a player to be is anywhere near the goal line, particularly if he's the one making the touchdown. I've had players tell me that they live in fear of scoring because they can't take the physical abuse from their teammates. One wide receiver confided to me, 'I have to run to catch the ball, and then I run twice as far so the guys won't break all my bones.' "

"Why do the players do it?"

"To show team spirit," Pickett said. "Those three-hundred-pound guys will slam-dunk a two-hundred-pound quarterback to prove they want to win the game. I have even seen an offensive lineman jump up and down on his running back's chest only because the fullback made a first down. We're not talking about bodily harm committed by the opposition— we're talking about the violence between one teammate and another."

"Can't the officials stop it?"

"The referee can't call a personal foul on one member of

a team for beating up on his fellow player. Watch this tape. The Cleveland cornerback has just intercepted a pass and scored. Look what his teammates are doing to him.''

"I can't look. It's too horrible," I said. "Why are they kicking him in the groin?''

"Because he's the best pass interceptor in the league.''

"Does your research indicate that most of the football injuries are caused while players are celebrating a good play by one of their own?''

"Yes. Players like to hit their buddies hard, and keep them on the ground to show how much they respect them.''

Pickett continued, "I'm going to show you something else. This is the end of a playoff game last year and the fellow chewing gum is the coach. They just won. Now here comes his team.''

"They threw the coach over the goalposts," I said.

"Yes, but worse than that they failed to catch him when he came down. The coach spent all of the winter and spring in traction. The medical lesson I now preach is that if you want to survive in football, don't do anything to call attention to yourself on the field.''

Yelling for News

THE young man came into the office to apply for a job as White House correspondent for *The Daily Quagmire*.

The veteran bureau chief said, "Tell me about yourself."

"Well, sir, I was a reporter for the Harvard *Crimson,* and I wrote a textbook on economics while I was in college—"

"I don't care what you wrote, boy. Can you yell?"

"I beg your pardon?"

"Let me hear you shout. Shatter those wineglasses over there."

"What do you want me to yell, sir?"

"Yell, 'Mr. President when are you going to tell all you know about the Iran affair?' "

"You want me to yell that?"

"You damn well better if you expect to be a White House correspondent."

"MR. PRESIDENT, WHEN ARE YOU GOING TO TELL ALL YOU KNOW ABOUT THE IRAN AFFAIR?"

"The glasses didn't even crack. You're going to have to practice a lot. Let me give you a little advice, son. Covering Ronald Reagan is no piece of cake. With other presidents you asked questions respectfully and you got quiet answers in return. This president is different. You don't talk to him, you shout. You have to break the sound barrier to find out if Reagan is going to get an arms deal with the Russians."

"I can yell with the best of them, sir."

"I'm not talking about ordinary yelling. I'm talking about getting through to the President when he steps off the helicopter with the engines roaring and the dog barking. I'm talking about shouting to Ronald Reagan when he's on an aircraft carrier in the Mediterranean and you're on a tanker three thousand yards away. And I'm talking of asking a question about his prostate from the sidewalk when the President's in his pajamas peering out of the twenty-fourth-story window of Bethesda Naval Hospital."

"I know I can do it. I used to yell *all* the time when I attended Harvard football games."

"You're a sad sack compared to some of the White House greats. Have you ever seen Sam Donaldson, the finest presidential shouter of all time?"

"No, but I've *heard* him on television."

"Sam has a way of getting the President's attention that is a joy to watch. Whenever the President sees Sam he automatically cups his ear. Study Donaldson's technique, son, and you'll go far in the White House correspondents' business."

"Gosh," the young reporter said, "I never dreamed I would be yelling in the same reporter pack as Sam Donaldson."

"Don't let Sam fool you. He may seem like a nice fellow but he'll bust your eardrum before he'll let you yell a question to the President."   ·

"Maybe I should bring a megaphone to work."

"They won't permit it. When it comes to interviewing Ronald Reagan the only things you can use are your vocal cords."

"I'll gargle every day," the young man said.

The bureau chief said, "Come with me." He took the

young correspondent into a soundproof room with a tiny photo of Ronald Reagan in the distance. "This is where we practice yelling at the President. Now let's hear you shout."

"Here I go. MR. PRESIDENT, WERE YOU INVOLVED WITH THE LAUNDERING OF THE ONE-TRILLION-DOLLAR BUDGET? How is that?"

"Not very good," the chief said.

"What's wrong?"

"You should have also said, 'AND I INTEND TO SHOUT A FOLLOW-UP QUESTION!' "

Hospitality Suite

I was walking through National Airport when I saw a sign: WELCOME SPECIAL PROSECUTORS.

"Is there a convention?" I asked the lady at the booth.

"No, we're a volunteer organization which provides hospitality and doughnuts for special prosecutors who have been assigned to root out wrongdoing and evil in the executive branch of government."

"I didn't know there were so many prosecutors arriving."

"We expect over ten thousand before the year is out. These people are serving their country as well as our boys in Honduras and we want to keep their morale high."

A man came up to the counter. "I'm a special prosecutor. Could you tell me where I can find a room while I'm investigating high crimes and sleazy misdemeanors complicated by unbelievable conflict of interest?"

"We can put you in a hotel until we get the permanent barracks on the Mall completed."

The man said, "You're building a barracks on the Mall for special prosecutors?"

"We have to," the lady replied. "The hotels in town can't house all of them, and if Ollie North and Poindexter ever spill the beans we could have special prosecutors sleeping in the streets."

"Okay, I'll take the room."

"Would you care to go to a Special Prosecutors' Get Acquainted Dance?"

"You hold dances?" the man said.

"It's a chance for all the prosecutors to get together, let their hair down and trade stories about who is committing perjury. Our hostesses have all been cleared by the FBI."

"How much is it?"

"It's free because it is sponsored by the Daughters of Watergate. They were responsible for special prosecutors in the first place."

I said to the gentleman, "Welcome to Washington. Why doesn't the Justice Department do the work instead of the special prosecutor?"

"Because Justice is not equipped to find wrongdoing in the administration. They don't have the staff, the resources, or the stomach for the job. All the Attorney General has to do is question someone on wrongdoing and everyone in the White House starts bolting for his shredding machine."

"Does this mean the Attorney General is covering up for the administration?"

"That's what they pay me to find out."

The lady behind the counter asked the special prosecutor if he wanted a cup of coffee.

He thanked her. "I'll remember this when I'm far away in the trenches of federal court."

The lady said, "This is the address of our Special Prosecutors' Hospitality Suite downtown where you can take a shower and have your suit pressed while you're waiting for General Secord to talk."

The man answered, "I'm very grateful for all you've done for me. My wife said no one in Washington would speak to me."

"*We'll* speak to you," she assured him. "It's the ones whose lawyers told them to clam up who won't talk."

I said, "One question. Why would someone want to be a special prosecutor?"

He replied, "Some do it because they are bored with their jobs—others because they are bored with their wives. I do it because investigating Donald Regan keeps me young."

A Lousy $14 Million

As everyone knows, I'm very generous about financing revolutions in Central America. So when a White House lobbyist asked for my help in the administration's efforts to wrest fourteen million dollars out of Congress to support our Nicaraguan freedom fighters, I told him, "I not only support Mr. Reagan, but assure the President he doesn't have to go to Congress. Just charge the fourteen million to my VISA credit card."

"We don't want you to put up the money," he said. "All we're asking you to do is stand behind the President in the Oval Office when he says, 'The Sandinista government is the greatest threat to mankind since the world began.' "

"I'll be there," I told him. "But why don't you let me pick up the tab as well? It's only peanuts and this way the President won't have to beg Congress on his knees."

He said, "It's no longer a question of money with Mr. Reagan, but of honor. The President has put his reputation on the line over Nicaragua. If he loses the fight on this one, we will be sending a message that any government in the Western World can stomp on us."

"I'll tell you what. I'll give the money anonymously," I said. "Then when the Contras overthrow the Sandinistas, you can pay me back."

"It will take more than fourteen million dollars to bring down the Sandinista government."

"Then why doesn't the President ask the members on the Hill for the exact sum needed to wipe them out?"

[63]

"Because it might cost a billion dollars before we're through, and we know Congress won't go for *that*."

"That is a lot of coffee beans," I admitted. "I'm curious. How did you arrive at the original fourteen-million-dollar figure?"

"It seemed like a nice compromise between nothing and a billion. You can't even buy a used American fighter plane for that kind of dough, and we felt Congress would consider it chickenfeed. But word leaked out that once we used up the fourteen million dollars we would go back to ask them for more. If we had known how much trouble we were going to have, we would have asked for the full amount. Then if we were rejected it would look as if Congress was voting against the money and not the President on his Central American policy."

"I can see where you blew it. By asking for such a meager sum you tipped them off that Mr. Reagan was making them stand up and be counted as to where they really stood on Communist subversion in Nicaragua."

"There may be something to that," he admitted. "But our main concern now is public support for the President in what he's trying to do down there."

I said, "Look, I can't give you a billion dollars because I'm thinking of buying CBS. But if the President wants ten or twenty million for the freedom fighters until Congress sees a light at the end of the tunnel, I'll send my kid over with a check."

"It won't be necessary," the White House man said. "At the moment we just need people of your high caliber to come out and support us."

"You've got it," I assured him. "Who else have you lined up?"

"The Pope has come out for President Reagan's Nicaraguan policy."

"I read the Pope denied it," I said. "Who is lying?"

"Neither one. Let's just say the Pope's support got lost in the translation."

Raising Funds

ACCORDING to the House and Senate committees investigating the Iran-Contra affair, most of the money raised for the Contras came from private sources. This is how the fund-raisers operated.

"Would you care to make a contribution to the Low Channel Freedom Fighters Foundation?"

"What do you do?"

"We perform deeds of mercy in the hills of Nicaragua, while Congress ignores the Communist threat from Russia and Cuba."

"Will this money go to kill Sandinistas?"

"What a question. Every thousand dollars is used to replenish needed food supplies in the boondocks."

"How can I be sure the funds are going where you say they are?"

"We send you the tops off every six-pack of Coors Beer

that is delivered to the countryside. In that way it makes the war much more personal."

"If I give to the Contras will I get to meet President Reagan?"

"It goes without saying. The White House is open day and night to anyone who supports the Foundation. We have our own man there and he will arrange for your picture to be taken with President Reagan, or the entire Cabinet, if it's in session. The President is very interested in this project although he's not sure what we do."

"Do I get to meet the Vice President too?"

"You don't even have to ask. The Vice President is more anxious to meet you than you are to meet him. Of course later he'll deny he saw you, but it will be a moment you'll never forget."

"Besides meeting the President and Vice President, what else do I get for my money?"

"You will be personally briefed by a U.S. Marine officer named North who knows about everything that takes place in Central America, and any other hot spots in the world. He'll tell you which Contras require bread, what ones are out of beans, and who needs Rolaids. We want our donors to know where every nickel is going."

"If I contribute will I become part of what you're doing?"

"You are a part of it now. Your check makes you a benefactor in this war or any other war in the hemisphere."

"Is there anything else my donation entitles me to?"

"If you would like to go down and kill some Sandinistas in the bush I can arrange it."

"I'd rather have my money do my talking for me. Say, are you really sure none of it is for guns?"

"Would the President of the United States get involved with a foundation that is trafficking in arms?"

"Maybe he doesn't know."

"How can the President not know what is happening in his own White House?"

I said, "Mr. Reagan doesn't know a *lot* of things. That's why he's such a good president."

"Did I tell you that your contribution is tax deductible?"

"Why is it tax deductible?"

"We inform everyone the money is going for Kleenex and Alpo dog food. What we do after that is nobody's business."

"That's fantastic. Put me down for five thousand dollars."

"Thank you. Here's a pass for the Oval Office. Just tell the President's aide you made a contribution to our Foundation and he'll usher you right through without waiting."

Country Number Ten

I N the Iran-Contra congressional hearings it has been decided to refer to countries that were asked to make donations to the freedom fighters by numbers. Thus, to protect their identities, we have country number one, country number two, country number three, and so on.

This is what is going to happen when they get to country number ten.

"Mr. McNugget, is it true that you approached the King of country number ten and asked him for fifty million dollars?"

"I didn't approach him. I got on my hands and knees and licked his slippers. I know a little something about protocol."

"What did you tell him you wanted the money for?"

"I said we wished to build an Arabian Film Studio in Nicaragua."

"What did he say to that?"

"He said he wasn't interested unless the money went for arms to the Contras. I replied the President wouldn't hear of funds going to the freedom fighters without Congressional approval."

"How did the King react to that?"

"He was very disappointed and said he didn't understand how a friend like the United States could reject a gift from one of its most loyal allies."

"Mr. McNugget, did you get the impression that the King of country number ten was expecting quid pro quo in exchange for the fifty million?"

"He never mentioned quid pro quo, but he did say something about wanting to own Florida."

"He asked for Florida in exchange for the fifty million?"

"As I understand it, sir, Ollie North suggested he ask for it. I don't believe the King expected to get it. I told him Florida was out of the question but I could see the White House letting him have one of the smaller states."

"Mr. McNugget, did you promise the King of country number ten two dozen AWACs in exchange for the Contra donation?"

"Yes, sir. I felt the King deserved something tangible for his donation. After all, he was sticking his neck out for us."

"What did the President think of all this?"

"He didn't know we had solicited country number ten for money."

"Then why did the President publicly thank the King for his contribution in the Oval Office?"

"I wasn't at that meeting. But if he did I will take full responsibility for it as I have for everything the President has done for the last six years."

"Besides Florida, was there anything else the King demanded?"

"Not that I recall. His majesty said the fifty million dollars was a gift and he was pleased it was going for a worthy cause. He told me his country considers Nicaragua the biggest danger there is in the Middle East."

"By the way, Mr. McNugget, whatever happened to the fifty million?"

"The King put it in a numbered bank account in Switzerland."

"And then what?"

"It was lost because Ollie North gave His Majesty the wrong number."

"What was Colonel North's reaction when he found out?"

"He felt very bad about it."

The Last Japanese

THE last Japanese soldier from World War II was holed up in a cave on Okinawa. A team of Americans and Japanese with loudspeakers was trying to persuade him to come out.

"Corporal Nakajinko, it's all right to surrender. The war is over."

"How do I know that you are not lying to me?" asked a plaintive voice from the cave.

"I can assure you, Nakajinko," a Japanese official yelled back, "all hostilities have ceased."

There was a silence of about three minutes, and then the voice said, "Who won?"

The official shouted, "The Americans. The Japanese laid down their arms forty years ago."

"This could be a trick. Prove to me that the United States won."

"The Americans now have a trade deficit with Japan of thirty-seven billion dollars," the officer said.

"How can the Americans have a thirty-seven-billion-dollar trade deficit if Japan lost?"

"Because the Japanese rethought their strategy in 1945 and it made more sense to invade the United States with automobiles than with soldiers. The Americans are buying everything Japan produces, but the Japanese are not buying much of what the U.S. makes. It's all here in *Fortune* magazine if you want to read about it."

"Leave it at the entrance to the cave," the voice said.

A half hour later, the rescue team was getting impatient. "Nakajinko, are you now persuaded that Japan lost the war?"

"I am puzzled," the corporal said. "If we lost, how can we export twenty-five percent more cars to the U.S. than we did last year?"

"Because we had a voluntary quota, and once it was lifted, we decided that this was the best time to flood the American market."

Corporal Nakajinko asked, "Didn't Premier Nakasone realize that this would anger the Americans?"

"He's trying to make up for it now by asking all the Japanese to buy U.S. goods."

Nakajinko yelled back, "I'm not coming out if I have to buy American products. I still remember Pearl Harbor."

"As a Japanese veteran you will be exempt from buying their goods. We want you to come out of the cave so we can declare World War II officially over."

"American goods aren't made as well as Japanese," he shouted. "Every time I stole something from the U.S. Army Quartermaster depot, I had to take it back."

"Nakajinko. This is no time to discuss the merits of U.S. and Japanese manufactured items. We have a trade mission in Washington trying to iron things out right now."

"Does that mean there is going to be another war?"

"Of course there isn't going to be another war. Countries don't go to war over trade differences."

"That's what the Japanese cabinet said on December 6th, 1941," Nakajinko cried.

The American liaison officer called out through his bullhorn,

"Look, if you don't come out in the next thirty minutes, we're going to have to shoot you."

"Why? Because my country won't order any telecommunications equipment from you?"

"It has nothing to do with telecommunications equipment," the American yelled. "It's because of your people's refusal to buy Alka-Seltzer."

"I think I'll stay here until the Americans and Japanese resolve their differences."

"Why, Nakajinko? Why?"

"Because if they don't, I'll just have to find myself another cave."

The President's Image

"GENTLEMEN, I have been recruited by the President to find out what has gone wrong with his well-oiled public relations machine. Let's start with Nicaragua. Can anyone explain the foulup with the Nicaraguan refugee kid who gave the President a bunch of flowers at the dinner in Washington?"

"We couldn't find a Nicaraguan kid, so we dug up an American one. The chairman of the dinner is hard of hearing, so he introduced the kid to the President as a Nicaraguan refugee. How did we know the Prez would kiss her, and that the press would find out she was born in the U.S.?"

"You'll admit the photo opportunity couldn't have come at a worse time. It was made to appear that the White House staff doesn't do its homework. Which brings me to my next question. Who told the President the Pope supported United States policy in Nicaragua?"

"You can't lay that one on us. The President received a personal cable from the Vatican wishing him a Happy Easter, and he interpreted it as a signal that His Holiness would join our covert operations in Central America."

"Even if the President thought it, how did you allow it to appear on his cue cards?"

"The President ad-libbed that one. He does it every once in a while just to keep in practice. If the Pope hadn't denied it, no one would ever have known."

"I'll take your word that the President dropped the ball on the Pope issue. Let's get to the little old lady from the Navajo tribe who the President honored at a White House Rose Garden ceremony."

"That was a darn good photo opportunity."

"It was until the woman told the President she couldn't live on her Social Security income."

"How did we know she would say that? No one in the White House speaks Navajo."

"Correct me if I'm wrong. But didn't the lady bring some Indian gifts for the President?"

"Yeah. She brought a woven blanket and a sand-painting."

"According to the newspaper reports, after she made her remarks about Social Security, a White House aide came up to her and bawled her out publicly for not following the script. They also said that the aide told her to take her gifts and beat it."

"You would have done the same thing if a Navajo Indian screwed up your photo opportunity."

"Do you believe that such a scene helped the President's image?"

"Well, it did send a strong message to anyone who was thinking of giving the President trouble on our budget cuts in Social Security."

"All right. Can we now get to Bitburg? Who was the brain who thought it would be a good idea for the President to visit a German cemetery in April?"

"That wasn't our baby. Chancellor Kohl's PR people felt that it would make a good photo opportunity."

"You can't blame the Germans for suggesting it. But who in the White House agreed to go along with it?"

"The Prez. He didn't tell any of us. We were in the dark as much as anybody. Kohl and the President cooked up the cemetery stop in the White House when the Chancellor started to cry and the President didn't know how to stop him. By the time the trip hit the fan, the President had his feet in cement and we couldn't budge him from Bitburg. We were lucky to talk him into visiting a concentration camp."

"Well, what do you propose to do now?"

"We have to come up with a photo opportunity which will make everyone forget Bitburg."

"Such as?"

"We're building a ramp and we're going to get Mike Deaver to drive his BMW over the Berlin Wall."

"I Did It"

THE White House has changed its strategy in regard to what the President knew about the Contra connection and when he knew it. Originally the President didn't know anything. He didn't even know where Nicaragua is.

But now he insists he not only knew what was going on, but he thought up all the ideas in the first place. Happily, the President prefers taking the credit to having to say he lost his memory.

"Well, boys, are we going to overthrow any governments today?"

"We can't do it, Mr. President, without the approval of Congress."

"Congress has no right to tell me what to do. Where is my attorney general who is so well versed in the Constitution?"

"He's being investigated by a special prosecutor for a conflict of interest case in the Bronx."

"I'll take full responsibility for that."

"Mr. President, you don't have to take the blame for everything that goes on during your administration."

"I insist on it. I'm the Commander in Chief and anything that happened was my idea. You know, I was the one who encouraged Mike Deaver to go into the public relations business."

"Please, Mr. President. You're taking enough flak by sticking your neck out on the Iranian-Contra business."

"I'm not going to turn my back on Colonel North, no matter what he's done. He is like a son to me."

"We don't expect you to deep-six Colonel North."

"If he did anything illegal, which he couldn't have if he was working for me, he's still a hero. I'll make him Commandant of the Marine Corps. That will fix those wimps in Congress. I have the urge to make a speech defending my policy in Central America and then give a pardon to everyone involved in the mess."

"I'm not sure that's legal sir."

"If it's not legal I'll say I knew it was illegal and that's why I did it. Is there anything else I can be blamed for?"

"President Botha of South Africa is arresting thousands of blacks every day."

"That's my fault. Our foreign policy in South Africa is a mess."

"Mr. President. Are you sure you want to say that?"

"Everything that happens has to be placed on my doorstep. Besides, I like to be held accountable for things when they go wrong."

"Do you want to say you're responsible for the attempted overthrow of the government in Fiji?"

"It took place on my watch. Fiji is in our backyard. This is so much more fun than saying I can't remember. Are there any CIA covert operations I can say I bollixed up?"

"Mr. President, we prefer to keep you out of covert stuff as sometimes it's better when the White House doesn't know what's going on."

"Not this President. I want to go down in history as a man who knew *everything* that went on during his term, including where Fawn Hall hid her notebooks."

"You really are a hands-on executive, sir."

"That's how they taught us at Warner Brothers. What else can I answer for?"

"Not much, Mr. President, unless you want to take the blame for the garbage barge off Islip, Long Island."

"Why not? Call Colonel North and tell him to raise some money from the conservatives to liberate the scow."

National Reconciliation Week

S INCE this is a period of reconciliation and the President is in a forgiving mood, I called one of his close associates and asked him, "Now that President Reagan has forgiven the Germans for what they did in World War II, do you think he might forgive the American air-traffic controllers who went out on strike?"

"The President would never go *that* far. You have to remember what the air controllers did. When they walked out on their jobs they committed an atrocity against every man, woman, and child in the United States."

"I know it was a despicable thing to do," I said. "But I thought that after Bitburg, it would be the perfect time for the President to heal the wounds here at home."

"The President is the first person to let bygones be bygones, but to my knowledge he has never forgiven anyone who has gone out on an unauthorized strike."

"Okay. Forget the air controllers. Do you think in his present mood of reconciliation Mr. Reagan might forgive the mother in Chicago who chiseled on her welfare?''

"How could he forgive her?''

"Maybe the President could fly to Chicago and lay a wreath in front of the liquor store where he claims she bought a bottle of vodka with her food stamps.''

"Too many people in this country have suffered because of that welfare mother in Chicago. It's one thing to forgive people you fought against during a war—it's another to turn the other cheek to those who cheat on their food stamps.''

"I guess there is no way for the President to reconcile with the American farmers who went bankrupt due to bad management.''

"By reconciling with the farmers at this time the President would be sending the wrong signal to the agricultural community. The Germans may have made some mistakes in World War II, but you could never accuse them of looking for a bailout from Washington when they couldn't sell their crops.''

"I don't imagine that the President would be willing to make a gesture of reconciliation towards the Congressmen who voted down aid for the Contras fighting in Nicaragua.''

"How can you compare what the people buried in the Bitburg cemetery did to left-wing, spiteful legislators who exterminated Mr. Reagan's foreign policy in Central America?''

"My mistake. Since this is National Reconciliation Week I thought the President might want to forgive those who voted against him on Nicaragua, just so he could get his budget package through.''

"Nicaragua is a moral issue, and Mr. Reagan will never compromise on a moral issue for political gain. That was the message of Bitburg.''

"Is there any possibility that the President would want to

make peace with the big spenders in the Senate, who for the past forty years have driven this country into debt with their wild socialist schemes?''

"It's much too early to offer an olive branch to them. Although everyone who fought on the German side in World War II is no longer alive, there are many big spenders walking around scot-free who have never answered for their economic crimes. Someday they will have to face a higher judge than the President of the United States.''

I asked, ''Do you think it's too soon for the Reagan administration to bury the hatchet with those people in the media who have blown the Nazi thing way out of proportion to what it really is?''

"If you're asking the President to pardon them for what they have written about Bitburg, the answer is no. Mr. Reagan still believes in collective guilt where the journalists of this country are concerned.''

Rewriting History

THERE is a great deal of rewriting of history in the United States these days. One of the most oustanding scholars in the field is Professor Heinrich Applebaum, who chairs the President's Commission for Historical Revisionism.

I found Applebaum in a tiny government office off Lafayette Park, tapping away on his word processor. He seemed to be grateful for the interruption.

"What are you working on?" I asked him.

He replied, "*I was a Teenage SS Colonel*. It is the diary of a child who serves for fourteen years as a storm trooper, only to become one of the millions of victims of World War II."

"Where did you find the diary?"

"I was tipped off to it by one of President Reagan's speechwriters."

"How do you explain the sudden interest in historical revisionism?"

Applebaum said, "You can't learn from history unless you rewrite it. The job of the revisionist is to make people forget the past. The neo-historian looks at what has been printed so far and then asks himself, 'Will this hurt or help our present alliances?' If it hurts, then he must reconcile the facts with what is in the nation's best interest."

"Can you give me an example?"

"When the revisionists saw that the fortieth anniversary of the end of World War II was coming up, we realized that the German people would be very sensitive if they were shown in a bad light. So we assigned a crack team of neo-historians to make their role in the unpleasantness more palatable. This book was the result." He handed me a volume titled *We Were All Guilty*.

As I leafed through it, he told me, "It proves that Adolf Hitler started World War II against the express wishes of the German people. As a matter of fact, we discovered the entire population rose up to stop him from invading Czechoslovakia, Poland, and France."

"That's quite a scoop," I said. "You must have done a lot of research."

"We interviewed hundreds of people who lived through those days and we couldn't find one who admitted to supporting Hitler's mad ambition to take over the world. This confirmed our earlier suspicions that Hitler worked alone."

"It sounds like you've got a Pulitzer Prize–winner here," I said. "What's this other manuscript?"

"That's my revisionist history of the war in the Pacific. It sheds a whole new light on how we got involved."

"In what way?"

"I discovered that the Russians bombed Pearl Harbor."

"That's one I hadn't heard before."

"They wanted us to think the Japanese had done it so we would declare war on the Axis powers. Roosevelt fell for it hook, line, and sinker."

"I always thought there was more to Pearl Harbor than any of us had been led to believe. But if the Russians sank our fleet, why did the Japanese capture the Philippines?"

"Who says the Japanese captured the Philippines? They were Cubans dressed as Japanese."

I looked over the manuscript and was impressed with what

I read. "If the United States had known who really bombed Pearl Harbor, I'll bet we would never have dropped the atom bomb on Hiroshima."

"Who said the United States dropped the bomb on Hiroshima?"

"Don't tell me. If we didn't do it, who did?"

Applebaum said tersely, "The Nicaraguans."

We'll Get Back to You

ONE of the serious charges made against White House aide Pat Buchanan was that he didn't return people's phone calls.

Buchanan wasn't the only one. The telephone is the main form of communication in Washington (except for sending a message to Moscow by putting a trade embargo on Nicaragua), and media people are particularly sensitive as to when (and if) their calls will be acknowledged.

The no-return call in the nation's capital is the cruelest call of all.

This is how the system works. You place the call, but you have no illusions that you'll get through to your quarry the first time around. Government officials worry that if they are too easily available you'll assume they don't have enough to do. So secretaries are trained to automatically inform the caller that the boss is "in conference."

What constitutes a conference in Washington has never been defined. It could be a gathering of twenty people or just two. It could be taking place in the office or on another floor—and for really top-flight executives, it could be held "up on the Hill."

You know you're talking to power when a secretary informs the caller that her boss is "out of town traveling with the President."

Those of us who have been around for a while deal with brush-offs in different ways. I have a friend, Barry Sussman, who when informed that the person he is telephoning is in conference, always asks the secretary, "Who with?"

When the secretary says she doesn't understand, Sussman tells her, "They are probably discussing what I'm writing about. You better break it up and tell Michelle Wilson I'm on deadline and I would prefer to get her side of it before I go to press."

Bruce Henderson, on the other hand, never makes the call himself. He has the pool secretary do it because he has a horrible fear that the person on the other end of the line will make him spell his name.

One person I work with likes to keep track of how his personal stock is doing in Washington. So every once in a while Joe Gradisher calls someone in the administration. When he is given the standard "conference" alibi, Gradisher leaves his name and phone number with the secretary.

Then Joe sets the clock on his desk with the hours, days, and months and proceeds to time how long it takes for the official to get back to him.

If the call is returned, Joe will just say he was testing the system. If it isn't returned, he will put out the word that the appointee is not long for this world.

More and more administration officials and bureaucrats are refusing media calls on the assumption that if they don't talk to the press, they can't be misquoted. While this is not a bad strategy, it does have its drawbacks. It leaves the journalist free to write whatever he pleases, adding this line to cover himself, ''Godzilla did not answer this writer's calls.''

Which brings me back to Pat Buchanan, about whom I can write objectively since I never called him, and therefore hold no grudge because he failed to call me back.

It used to be said that Buchanan was second to Don Regan in influence in the White House. He was also the President's Communications Director. If you phoned Pat and he didn't respond within a reasonable period of time, it could be a terrible blow to your reputation. This is particularly true of the opinion-makers who do not agree with the administration's policies, but who put great store in how fast the President's men answer their calls.

In fairness to Pat, he was quite busy just feeding the journalists who support the administration line, and should not be faulted for putting so many unfriendly reporters on Hold. White House sources have told me that after returning one Evans and Novak call, Buchanan was wiped out for the rest of the day.

You Can Bank on It

January 2

D EAR Freddy,
I know you haven't heard from me for some time. But I'm writing to ask you if you would attend a dinner in which I'm going to be honored as the Good Citizen of the Year at the Grand Milkwood Hotel on June 3rd.

I guess you've been wondering what happened to me since I stopped selling encyclopedias door-to-door in Bethesda. Well, believe it or not, I'm a hotshot banker in Maryland. I know what you're thinking. What do I know about banking after selling encyclopedias for the last ten years?

It's a business just like any other business. People are always looking for bargains and if you can offer 'em a better deal than the guy down the street you've got a customer.

Banking is really a snap if you know anything about human nature. The trick is to have a solid-looking building with lots of marble, and a guard standing by the door with a gun on his hip, who looks real serious about protecting the customer's deposit.

Since I pay more interest than other banks in the area, the money just keeps pouring in. People are lining up in front of my window right now with paper bags full of currency, scared silly our safes will run out of space before they can open an account with us.

I don't have any problems attracting deposits. My difficulty is figuring out how to spread it around. Heh, heh, heh. What I mean, Freddy, is if I'm paying 7 percent to the depositors I have to loan it out at 15 percent to make any money. Well, fortunately there are a lot of people in America who are more than willing to pay above the going rate to borrow money. Most of them were turned down by the other banks for one silly reason or another.

These guys and dolls are salt of the earth. They're real estate developers, commodities speculators, oil drillers, take-over artists, and horse-racing enthusiasts.

Besides the money I make on loans, my bank also invests with go-go securities firms in Florida and New Jersey. They pay us interest rates you wouldn't believe.

So you can see I've got a foolproof thing going. The depositors are getting rich, businessmen are getting their loans, and the bank is earning a huge return on its money.

The reason I'm being made Citizen of the Year is I have just bought new uniforms for the high school football band and the people of Milkwood don't know how to say thank you. Hope you can make it.

Best regards,
George

* * * * *

Dear Freddy,   *May 10*
The dinner has been called off. I don't know if you saw it in the papers or on TV but my bank has been taken over by the state. What happened was this dipsy-doodle securities outfit in Florida walked away with our money.

We could have survived that, but the news of our losses got into the papers, and suddenly the depositors made a run on the bank. It was a small run until the TV stations showed the people with their beach chairs and paper bags waiting to take their dough out. Then all hell broke loose.

Obviously we couldn't give everybody their money back since it was all out on loans, or lost somewhere in the swamps of Florida and New Jersey. What with the unfortunate publicity, the bank examiners decided to come in with their crummy little hand calculators. They found some discrepancies on the books, which they claimed were fraudulent but which were really mistakes in bookkeeping. They also said I took out several million dollars for my own personal expenses, which they're going to have to damn well prove.

Anyway, the governor is blazing mad and the people who lost their savings are kinda upset, so we decided to postpone the Citizen of the Year dinner until I could work out some sort of plea bargain with the attorney general. Besides, I'm now living in the Bahamas and it's hard to pin me down for a date when I can pick up the award.

Keep the faith,
George

The TSF

I N a recent Senate budget vote, the Defense Department wound up with a zero growth figure for 1986, which was quite a comedown from the nine percent increase Secretary Weinberger had originally asked for. It came as no surprise to Harold Simon, who keeps track of Pentagon spending.

"The Secretary has nobody to blame but his toilet seats," Harold said.

I seemed puzzled, so he continued. "Weinberger lost the battle for more funds the day the story broke that the Defense Department was paying six hundred dollars a seat. I call it the Toilet Seat Factor or TSF. For several years Charley Taxpayer bought the whole Pentagon Disneyland package, MX missiles and all. Charley assumed our defense brass were handling his money as they would their own. The poor guy had no idea how much to pay for an F-16 fighter, M-1 tank, or Trident submarine, so he gave his proxy to Weinberger and his merry band of men. After all, when you start talking millions and billions of dollars you are no longer talking Charley's language.

"But then came the revelations about the six-hundred-dollar Lockheed commode cover and suddenly Charley said, 'Hey, wait a minute. What kind of a dummy do you think I am? I may not know the price of a B-1 bomber but I sure as hell know what a toilet seat costs—and it ain't six hundred dollars—no way.'

"For the want of a reasonably priced seat, the battle for the big toys was lost. Weinberger's people misread Charley's patriotism as a sign they could throw around his money, particularly at a time when the government was cutting student aid for his kids and freezing his mother's Social Security payments."

"I thought it was the news of the four-hundred-dollar hammer and seven-hundred-and-sixty-dollar screwdriver that got Charley mad."

"The price of the hammer and screwdriver made him more confused than angry. Then came the seven-thousand-nine-hundred-dollar coffeepot. Charley's a good guy and laughed it off. But it was the toilet-seat price that got to him. That's why I call it the Pentagon's Toilet Seat Factor rather than the screwdriver or monkey wrench factor. When Charley read about the commode he just opened his window and shouted, 'I'm mad as hell and I'm not going to take it anymore!' The moment I heard him I knew Weinberger had blown his budget request."

"Poor Weinberger," I said. "He probably didn't know any more than Charley what it was costing the American people for an airborne toilet seat."

"That's why the TSF is so important to the Pentagon. They can go to Charley and ask for a billion dollars for a Star Wars laser gun, and he'll write out a check without a whimper. But don't try to con him on an item that costs less than one thousand dollars."

"Does the TSF only apply to hammers, screwdrivers, and toilet seats?"

"No, it's become synonymous with hunting lodge weekends, lobbying, and public relations fees that the defense contractors have added onto their bills, plus private plane trips to the Super Bowl, and of course, kennel boarding charges for executives' dogs. The contractors were nickel and diming poor Charley Taxpayer to death, and he was getting sick of it.''

"Maybe when Weinberger counterattacks with announcements about all the new weapons the Soviets have built, Congress will relent and forget the TSF.''

"I doubt it.''

"How can you be so sure?''

"Charley has spoken and the voice of the taxpayer has been heard in the land. The memory of the commode cover is still too fresh in everyone's mind. The Defense Department has to clean up its act before Charley will give them a blank check again.''

"What can Weinberger learn from all this?''

"The lesson is, if you want to avoid a toilet seat factor in the Pentagon, don't ever overcharge the man in the street for something he can price in a hardware store.''

This Is a Test

PEOPLE are constantly asking me if the Reagan administration ever comes to me for personal advice. Until recently the answer was no. But, lo and behold, not long ago I received a letter in the form of a poll. It said that the President wanted to know where I stood on the controversial issues of the day. I was urged to answer the list of unbiased questions which were enclosed.

Some of them weren't easy, such as, "In the 1970s funds were cut off for development of the MX missile, causing our strategic defenses to become dangerously obsolete while the Soviets escalated their weapons buildup. Do you support continued U.S. efforts to modernize our strategic defenses by funding this weapons system?" I was instructed to check off one of three boxes: yes, no, or undecided.

I had no problem with that one. But the next one was a mind-bender. "Should the U.S. continue research and development of a space-based missile defense system to give the United States protection we do not now have against a Soviet nuclear attack?"

I took a gamble and said yes.

The question that followed also required tremendous concentration. "Do you agree with the Democrats who say the Soviet/Cuban efforts to topple pro-West governments in Central America pose no direct threat to U.S. security?"

I tried to figure out what answer the President would want to hear, and on a hunch said no.

By this time I was perspiring. Ideological tests always make me nervous.

"Should the United States continue providing support to people in Central America who are fighting for their independence from Soviet-backed Marxists?"

I put a big black *X* in the yes box so the President wouldn't miss it. Then came the question which made me think the President might be considering me for the job as Secretary of the Navy. "The Soviets have amassed the largest naval force in the world and have increased the number of submarines patrolling the U.S. coast. Should the U.S. Navy receive more funding to replace our aging sea force and build more Trident nuclear submarines?"

I called up a friend who works at the Pentagon for advice on how to answer the question.

"Oh," he said. "You got one of those Republican fund-raising letters too."

"What do you mean, fund-raising? It says the President wants to personally know where I stand on the issues of the day. He probably wants to make me the new U.S. ambassador to Ireland."

"If you read the letter closely you'll see it was sent out by the Republican party and you're supposed to enclose your check with the answers."

"Are you trying to tell me the President isn't interested in my opinion?"

"He probably doesn't even know you were sent the letter. And he may never know unless you send the Republicans a whopping check."

"I was hoping he was considering me for his new budget director," I admitted, "and the questions were just to see if I was a team player. Why did they write to me?"

"The Republicans probably bought your name for five cents from a credit card company."

"It's not fair to make someone answer a bunch of tough questions on national defense and then ask for money for the party."

He said, "It was either P.T. Barnum or Richard Viguerie who said, 'There's a sucker born every minute.' "

"Just in case you're wrong and the President wants me to be National Security Advisor, what should I answer to the question on our need to replace aging subs with Trident nuclear submarines?"

He said, "The answer is yes, but that's still a secret. So for heaven's sake don't tell anyone you spoke to me."

Is Anyone Listening?

IF people don't think Attorney General Ed Meese is all heart, they ought to take another look at the settlement of the Justice Department's case against the brokerage firm of E. F. Hutton.

The company pleaded guilty to two thousand felony counts of mail and wire fraud which involved kiting checks worth more than a billion dollars to four hundred American banks.

E. F. Hutton made a deal with the government and was

sentenced to pay a fine of two million dollars (which boils down to one thousand dollars for each count) and eight million dollars to the banks it defrauded.

When somebody asked the Attorney General why no individuals were prosecuted, Mr. Meese replied, "In this case it was more important to get recompense to victims (read banks) than to prosecute the individuals." Meese called the settling of the case a "comprehensive and open-ended restitution plan." He said the plea-bargaining agreement showed the Justice Department's concern for victims and "its desire to make whole those banks and other institutions who suffered any loss."

The Attorney General's decision to let E. F. Hutton buy its way out of trouble for a few million bucks made us reassess our opinion of Meese as a tough law-and-order man. When it comes to crooked brokers Ed Meese is a toasted marshmallow.

I called my man at Justice and asked why the big turnabout on crime by the Reagan administration.

"E. F. Hutton has suffered enough," he said. "Will justice be served if we send anyone to jail over a little billion-dollar check-writing scam?"

"You've sent people up the river for stealing a lot less," I pointed out. "I know a lady who embezzled ten thousand dollars from her credit union and she's doing seven years in a Federal penitentiary."

"That was a serious white-collar crime, and if we had let her plea-bargain we would be saying that we were soft on credit-union theft. The Hutton scheme, on the other hand, involved over a billion dollars, and the Attorney General decided he'd rather collect restitution for the banks than try to send a few misguided employees to jail."

"Why couldn't he have done both?" I asked.

"You mean you would want us to fine one of the leading brokerage houses in America and also put their people behind bars? What kind of animals do you think we are?"

"Nobody wants anyone to go to jail," I assured him. "But what kind of message are you sending white-collar criminals if people can get away with stealing eight million dollars and not have to worry about going to the pokey?"

"I suppose you'd want us to prevent E. F. Hutton from selling securities as well?"

"Why not, if it would make other people who deal with the public's money think twice about committing fraud. One crooked bond dealer in Florida almost brought down the entire banking system of Ohio. I say if you commit a felony you should get out of the investment business and go into making license plates where you belong."

He protested, "Even if we wanted to we couldn't prosecute anyone in the check-writing scheme."

"Why not?"

"Everybody turned state's evidence so we wouldn't send them to jail."

"Why did you agree to that?"

"Because we would have never had a case against them if they didn't tell us how they did it."

"I'll take your word for it that you were as tough on Hutton as you possibly could get. But what do I tell the lady who is doing seven years for stealing from the credit union?"

"Tell her she has to pay her debt to society like almost everybody else."

The House Sitters

THE best time for parents of teenagers is when they can get away and take a short vacation by themselves. The worst time is when they call home to find out if everything is going all right.

"Hello, Alfred, this is Mummy. Well, we just arrived at the beach. Where's Grandma? . . . Why did she go home? She said she would stay for the week. . . . What's that music in the background? . . . How many friends? . . . You're not sure? . . . How many did you invite? . . . You only asked ten but forty showed up? . . . Alfred, we told you you couldn't have parties while we were gone. . . . If it's not a party what is it? . . . A high school reunion? . . . but you don't graduate from high school until next year. . . . It's a reunion of the kids who have already graduated from the school? Where do you come off entertaining college freshmen? . . . They're not freshmen, they're rugby players from Detroit? . . . That does it. Put your sister Grace on. . . . How can she be out? She promised to stay home and guard the house while we were gone. . . . Alfred, you gave us your solemn word you would not fight with your sister. . . . What was that crashing noise? . . . Where are you talking from? . . . It does make a difference. If you're speaking from the kitchen it means someone has just broken my china— and if you're speaking from the upstairs bedroom it means someone just smashed my perfume bottles. I'm going to put your father on."

"Hello, son, how goes it? I hear you're throwing a little

party? . . . It sounds like everyone is having a lot of fun.
. . . Seems to me we had a deal. In exchange for your using
my car, when we went away you'd kinda keep people out
of the house. Isn't that what we agreed on? . . . I tell you
what, son. Why don't you just ask everyone to leave the
house quietly, and if they don't want to go tell them you'll
kick their butts in for them. . . . No, I must admit I have
never asked a Detroit rugby team to leave my house. At the
same time, since you let them in, you're going to have to
figure a way of getting them out. . . . Alfred, are those
sirens? . . . Out of curiosity, are they police sirens or fire
sirens? . . . Police sirens. Well, at least that means the house
isn't burning down. Any idea, Alfred, why the police are at
our house? . . . You'd prefer to put the sergeant on.

"Yes, Sergeant, this is Sam Savage. I know something is
wrong so we better get to it right away. . . . I see. There
have been complaints from the neighbors about screaming,
shouting of obscenities, breaking windows, beer cans on the
lawn, and some nudity in the bushes.

"Yes, there is a possibility that our son could be hosting
such a party. If his head comes to a point and if he strikes
you as a first-class idiot who can't say no when his parents
go out of town, then that has to be our Alfred. . . . Sergeant,
how much damage do you estimate has been done? . . .
Yes, include the bottle of red wine that was spilled on the
sofa. . . . Two or three thousand dollars? . . . Well, it seems
Mrs. Savage and I got off cheap. . . . What do I want you
to do? I'm not in a position to say. Are you people into
police brutality? I'll tell you what, Sarge, any way you could
clear out the house would be very much appreciated. I'll
see that your men get a commendation medal for each kid
they throw out in the street. Let me speak to my son again.

"Alfred, the sergeant has offered to persuade the Detroit

rugby team to leave the premises. Tell them not to take it personally. I've asked him to bounce everyone whether they're involved in sports or not. It has nothing to do with your friends. It's because of your mother's, and my, dream of spending a few more years in the house after we get home from vacation.

"Look, son, after the sergeant boots everyone out he could take you down to the station house and book you for disorderly conduct. If he does, he may give you the right to make one telephone call. If this happens don't waste your quarter on us, because we're going to try to get some sleep."

Sex and Tennis

A very revealing book about tennis has just crossed my desk. It's titled *Sex as a Sublimation for Tennis* (Workman Press, $4.95) and was written by Theodor Saretsky, a Freudian specialist at Adelphi University and full-time tennis fanatic.

Saretsky told me on the phone, "It was Freud who first wrote that 'all human beings are motivated by a primal lust which translates itself into the endless and fruitless search for an unused tennis court on the weekend.'"

Saretsky said he lucked into all of Freud's writings on the subject when he bought a trunk at a tennis memorabilia sale at Sotheby's in 1980. The trunk contained some of the master's greatest work, including *The Myth of the Sweet Spot, Interpretation of Tennis Dreams, The Primitive Taboo of the Foot Fault,* and *The Nightmare of the Canceled Tennis Game: A Study in Obesity, Perversion and Suicide.*

This year Saretsky decided to share this gold mine with the public.

The professor said one of his most fascinating discoveries was that Freud lost interest in the sex act when he discovered that a tennis game lasted much longer.

Saretsky has found Freud's theories invaluable because more and more patients are coming to him with tennis problems rather than sexual ones. Until recently experts in the psychoanalytical profession refused to accept tennis-court mental cases because they were too difficult to cure.

"The hardest thing for a patient with a tennis neurosis or psychosis is to find an analyst who will take the time to treat him," Saretsky said. "Freud discovered that the more a patient talked about his deep-seated tennis problems the more anxious the analyst was to go out on the court and hit a few balls himself. This attitude is diametrically opposed to how the analyst feels when he listens to a patient talk about sexual dysfunction."

Saretsky says, "Freud took one of the great steps in modern analysis by stating categorically, 'The only way to know one's patients is to play tennis with them.'"

I don't have the space here to reveal everything that Professor Saretsky says Freud said about tennis other than to print a few highlights.

One is, Freud observed that individuals who immerse themselves in work, who stress family obligations and engage in extensive sexual activity to the point where they are prevented from playing sufficient tennis, will suffer from severe tension, anxiety, and nosebleeds.

Another is that people who are constantly measuring the height of the net have a paranoidal delusion that the net is higher on their side of the court.

When a distinguished colleague, W. W. Wilner, after years of research, arrived at the conclusion that tennis spelled backwards was "sin-net" it confirmed Freud's scientific theory that there are murky, mysterious forces buried alive in the human psyche.

As soon as he checked it out, Freud rejected his own classical view of infant sexuality as the mainspring of the human condition, and replaced it with the dictum that "tennis truths lie everywhere; they are the essence of being."

This led him to devote the remaining years of his life to studying the lingering fantasy of the empty tennis-ball can.

Saretsky believes that Freud's tennis writings undermined all orthodox thought in the Western World. The Viennese doctor exposed the offensive lob for what it really was, a sadistic underhanded shot of which he wrote, "The lob must be given its chance, but this is a disgusting stroke to use in mixed company if its sexual and exhibitionist roots are not honestly acknowledged and properly analyzed."

In conclusion, if you buy only one book during the summer I would recommend *Sex as a Sublimation for Tennis*. If you don't play the game yourself you could save the life of someone who does.

Pray at Home

ALABASTER was furious as he came in the kitchen door.
"They've gone too far," he shouted, waving the newspaper in his hand. "The Supreme Court won't let my kids pray in school."

"I'm sorry to hear that," I said. "Why don't you let them pray before they leave home in the morning?"

"They don't have time," he said with fury. "They have to get dressed, eat breakfast, and do their homework. The first chance they have to pray is when they get to their classroom."

I scanned the article. "The court isn't taking away the voluntary minute allotted to meditation. It just struck down the words 'voluntary prayer' at the end of it."

"Why should we let your kids have a minute of silence just to meditate? If they can't use it for prayer then I say forget about it."

"Maybe that's why the Supreme Court ruled against you. It's really a question of separation of church and state. I believe the Court is saying that the government cannot force prayer on children in a public place."

"That isn't what they were saying at all," he retorted. "They are telling us that God can't be in our classrooms, the secular humanists have taken over our schools, and communism has won again, and that this ruling is just what the Soviets ordered."

"You read all of that into the decision?"

"That and a lot more."

"Why don't you admit it, Alabaster? You don't want voluntary *silent* prayer in the schools. You want voluntary *spoken* prayer, with a strong tilt towards the church of your choice."

"That's because we know the truth," he retorted.

"Religious truth lies in the church and the home. The minute you bring it into the classroom all hell breaks loose."

"How can you prevent tiny little kids from asking God's divine guidance every morning before class begins?"

"Why can't they do it on the way to class? It wouldn't hurt to pause one minute for a prayer. They wouldn't even have to keep it to a minute. They could pray as long as they liked provided they are not late for classes."

"God doesn't listen unless they pray in their school," Alabaster shouted.

"Calm down. The ruling doesn't say that the minute allotted can't be used for prayer. It just says the state or government cannot specify it be used for that purpose."

"That's what we are yelling about. By not specifying what the minute is to be used for it bans prayer in the school."

"Alabaster, your problem is that you think every religion calls for prayer whilst standing up. This is not true. Some require that you kneel and bow your head forward. Others insist you sit straight up, and there are some that instruct you to prostrate yourself in a certain direction. Once you bring prayer into the schools you must allow those participating to do it their own way. And as soon as you permit that, you split the children into religious factions until the classroom turns into Beirut."

I could tell Alabaster wasn't convinced. "The only way now to get God into the schools is through a constitutional amendment," he said. "He'll never get there as long as a bunch of atheistic old men sit on the bench."

"God is in the schools already. It may not be God according to you, and it isn't God according to me, and it isn't God according to Ronald Reagan. But it is God, and for the good of the country that's the way it should always be."

"You should be burned at the stake," Alabaster said.

I knew he was upset so I didn't get angry. "I'm sorry you lost this one, Alabaster. The only thing left to do is for your kids to get up a little earlier so they can pray at home. It will be good for the entire family."

Magnificent Obsession

SHERLOCK Holmes was studying the newspaper. "No matter where one goes to track down the secret of the Marcos fortune, the trail always leads back to the shoes."

"Why is that?" I asked him.

"I'm not sure, Watson. Let's see what we know already. Imelda had three thousand two hundred pairs of size-eight shoes in her closet, most of which had never been worn. Why, Watson, why?"

"Suppose Ferdinand Marcos had a foot fetish. Many men with power do."

"It's too easy, Watson. Even someone with an extreme foot fixation could never go through three thousand two hundred pairs."

"I've known people with fetishes who went through a pair of new shoes every day. Perhaps Ferdinand was one of them."

"I checked around at the palace. No one ever saw Marcos playing with Imelda's shoes."

"Well then, Holmes, maybe Imelda was the one who had a foot fetish."

Holmes smiled as he usually does when he's caught me. "Wrong, Watson. Not a foot fetish. If anything, Imelda had a shoe fetish."

"What is a shoe fetish?"

"It's a compulsion to hold and caress a piece of footwear to assuage one's guilt."

"And what causes this kind of fetish?"

"We're not sure. All we know is that many people who have a shoe fetish also have a numbered bank account in Switzerland."

"It's all starting to come together, Holmes. Mrs. Marcos bought shoes on her trips abroad to disguise the fact she was opening numbered bank accounts."

"Just the opposite, my dear Watson. Imelda opened numbered bank accounts abroad to disguise the fact she was buying shoes."

"Of course," I said. "But why?"

"Imelda had a very deprived childhood. The money she sent out of the country was to assure her that no matter what happened to the Philippine government, she would always have something to wear to the ball."

"But, Holmes, we're talking about three billion dollars. Are you trying to tell me that all this money was set aside for footwear?"

"Have you priced women's shoes lately, Watson?"

"That's all well and good. But suppose Imelda had stocked

up on the shoes so that when she was booted out of Manila she could open her own store in Honolulu?''

"Take a look at this photo. Does Imelda look like somebody who would work in a shoe store?''

"Probably not. But she could own it and not work there.''

"Except for one thing, Watson. All the shoes are size eight. You can't open a store where all the footwear is the same size.''

"Hmmmn. Well, tell me, Holmes—does solving the shoe enigma help you discover the whereabouts of the Philippine treasury?''

"Not necessarily. A lot of it is hidden in real estate, gold, jewelry, banks, and legitimate companies that Marcos bought when he was riding high. But all that's surfaced are the shoes.''

"Quite. Say what you will, Holmes, the Marcoses always covered their tracks.''

"Watson, I would like to go back and take one more look at Imelda's closet.''

"Why, Holmes?''

"The Marcoses had a dog guarding their clothes. On the night they sneaked out of the palace the dog did not bark. Why not, Watson?''

"Why, Holmes?''

"Elementary. The dog had a shoe in his mouth.''

#E3VLPBUT+X: $2.52

I came into the office and found my assistant, Cathy, crying. "What's wrong?"

"I've been trying to get the phone company for two days to move the telephone two and a half blocks to our new offices."

"So what's the big deal?"

"I finally succeeded. Do you want to hear the rest of it? AT & T will come in to disconnect the phones and reconnect them for $90 for the first hour and $1 for each MINUTE after."

"You're kidding me. Not even lawyers have the nerve to charge by the minute."

She said, "That's not all of it. AT & T is no longer involved with installing the dial tone. The tone can only be created by the C & P Telephone Company. They charge $94 for a one-time connection fee, plus $33 for the FIRST FIFTEEN MINUTES and $11 for each additional quarter hour. There is also a $3 fee for the cost of the jack in the closet."

"Let me get this straight," I said. "AT & T is socking us for the connection and the C & P people are mugging us for the dial tone. Did you ask either company how we can be sure they don't waste a minute while they're doing all this?"

"They said we should trust them."

"Okay, so they are behaving like the Mafia. Is that any reason to cry?"

"I'm not finished. If we want to keep our same number we have to pay extra for that too. They want $9.55 per line per month, which they call a 'mileage' charge. In case you're interested, they charge $8.20 for the first quarter mile and 45 cents for each additional quarter mile.''

"That's more than a New York taxi charges," I said. "Where do they find people to come up with these numbers?''

"I just got our phone bills for the month. We used to get one bill, now we get two—one from AT & T for our equipment and one from C & P for their service. Here, look at this. Everything is in computer code. Do you know what product E3VLPBUT+X, description: BUT-SIGNAL, unit price $1.22, total amount $26.36 is?''

"Not right off hand," I admitted.

"It's our button signal," Cathy said. "AT & T charges us to let our phone ring and the button light up. They've made a price increase retroactive from July of 1984, but so many people have complained about it that if you holler loud enough they'll take it off your bill.''

"There, you see?" I said. "The phone company does have a heart.''

"Then there is the $2.62 monthly charge for an intercom line.''

"That sounds reasonable.''

"It is except we don't have an intercom line. They're also charging us $1.66 for the buzzer for the intercom line we don't have.''

"The phone company would never cheat us. Call them and tell them they made a mistake.''

Cathy turned red. "I'm not going to try to get through again. No one can get through to them because everybody is complaining about their telephone bills.''

"What's this charge of $7.56 for a PICKUP BUTTON?"

"As far as I know," she replied, "it's this plastic button on the phone. I'm not sure if they're charging us for the button itself or the connection when we push it in. But whatever it is, AT & T has made it retroactive."

"This is more serious than I thought," I said. "Take a letter to Judge Harold H. Greene, U.S. District Court for the District of Columbia, One John Marshall Place, Washington, DC 20001. Dear Judge Greene, since you were responsible for the breakup of the phone company, the greatest and cheapest system in the free world, I am writing to you for guidance. You have maintained that the divestiture would encourage competition and save the consumer money. Pray tell, dear Judge, what exactly did you have in mind? Since no sane jurist would be stupid enough to tear apart something that was working so well, I'm sure you have a secret plan. You at least owe it to the American people to let us know how we're benefiting from your historic decision. If you don't tell us before we get our next phone bill I'm going to print your home number in the paper. Respectfully yours, An Admirer."

Walker on the Right

WHEN I heard that John Walker, the Soviet spy, was a flaming conservative, I immediately called up Bubba Peterson, who speaks for the right when Pat Buchanan is sleeping.

"How come Walker turned out to be one of your guys and not one of ours?" I asked him.

"Where do you get that stuff?" Peterson retorted. "We can't take responsibility for every right-wing nut in the country."

"Well, he's definitely one of yours, and we don't like it when someone sells this country's most vital secrets. How could you have let it happen?"

"Why should we take the blame for what Walker did?"

"Because you laid it on all the liberals when the Rosenbergs and Alger Hiss were caught. We still get blamed for what they did."

"I don't blame you."

"Nixon does. The right has been painting us red for years. It's about time they got splattered with a brush of their own."

"The Walker family has no connection with the right-wing movement," Peterson protested.

"You can tell that to Robert Novak, but we neo-socialists aren't buying it. How many more spies do the right-wingers have hiding in safe houses around the country?"

I could tell I was getting to Peterson. "I ought to come over there and punch you in the nose."

"Sure, that's the way all you people behave when faced with treachery in the ranks. Why don't you admit you made a mistake by letting Walker into your club?"

"I never heard of John Walker or his family until the spy story broke."

"Then you're twice as guilty. Are you telling me that the conservatives don't check the backgrounds of their members?"

"We're a political faction. Why should we give anyone a security check?"

"Because they could turn out to be spies. Do you think we limousine liberals would have let Walker sign up without making sure he wasn't working for the Kremlin? Why don't you just come out and admit your people were duped? Your mistake is that you think because a guy denounces abortion and the Equal Rights Amendment that he's a hundred-percent loyal American. I hope the Walker case teaches you a lesson."

"What lesson?" Peterson wanted to know.

"That the guy who screams the loudest against gun control could be the one closest to Gorbachev."

"Why are you doing this to me?"

"Because, Peterson, every time we came out against the B-1 bomber, you said we were on the KGB payroll. You claimed anyone who was for the arms talks was a victim of Soviet disinformation. You have coupled people who don't want to go to war over Nicaragua with the Politburo. Why shouldn't we make you feel bad about John Walker?"

"How do we know Walker wasn't one of yours, pretending to be one of ours?"

"Because he did it for *money* instead of for Mother Russia. Don't you understand, Peterson, we can no longer depend on your people to keep us safe from communism? You've been infiltrated by the Russkies and until you clean house we can't let you have a monopoly on waving the American flag. How many more Walkers do you have on your rolls?''

There was a lot of sputtering on the other end of the line. ''I never believed you'd stoop this low. Don't you have any shame?''

''I'm not questioning *your* loyalty,'' I said. ''And I certainly don't blame you for what the Walker family did. But I do have something further to say to you.''

''What's that?''

''Don't let it happen again.''

A Born-Again Nonsmoker

WHEN someone gives up smoking he or she wants the whole world to hear about it. I know you weren't ready for this, dear reader, but I have given up cigars. I am a born-again nonsmoker—a confessed sinner who can now walk into any crowded room without stinking up the joint.

Don't go away. I want to tell you the story of my conversion. It doesn't do any good to stop smoking if no one will listen to how you did it.

First, I have to give credit where credit is due. I couldn't have done it alone. I got some help from that Big Nonsmoker in the sky.

It all began six months ago when, after lighting up one of the six or seven cigars I smoked every day, I suddenly heard loud coughing in the heavens. Then a thundering voice boomed, "PUT OUT THAT DAMNED CIGAR."

I didn't pay any attention because I was sure He wasn't talking to me. After all, I had been smoking for over forty years and He never raised any objections before. So I continued for another week. Then my chest started to feel lousy and I became hoarse.

I looked up and said, "What's going on?"

The voice came down and said, "I THOUGHT I MADE MYSELF CLEAR. WHAT KIND OF MESSAGE DO I HAVE TO SEND YOU?"

"Okay," I said. "I'm willing to deal. Let's just say I cut down to two or three a day?"

He would have none of it. "THE NUMBER IS NON-NEGOTIABLE."

"How about one petit corona after dinner?"

"DON'T YOU UNDERSTAND ENGLISH?" the voice said. To make His point He shoved a hot coal down my throat and I started to gasp for air.

Yes, He was responsible for my quitting, but He didn't give me *that* much help once I gave it up.

After I went cold turkey I had to face the prospect of earning a living. I could smoke a cigar without writing, but I couldn't write without smoking a cigar. In the beginning I just stared at the paper. To get going I tried typing exercises such as "Now is the time for all good men . . . for all good men . . . for all good men . . . for all good men to light up a Monte Cristo Havana No. 3."

My mind would work in curious ways. I would want to

write about the MX missile system, and the only thing that came out was "Puff the Magic Dragon." The song "Smoke Gets in Your Eyes" droned in my head, and the Marlboro Man kept riding across my computer screen.

Finally, in desperation, I looked up to the heavens and said, "How long do you expect me to keep this up?"

The voice came down, "TRY CHEWING GUM."

I was skeptical, but the first time I shoved a stick of gum in my mouth it worked. I found out if you have to keep moving your jaws all the time, you don't miss having a wet stogie between your lips.

Well, it's been all uphill since then. After my decompression period I discovered the beautiful world of nonsmoking. My lungs are now getting all the oxygen they so richly deserve, and my brain cells seem to be relieved they don't have to absorb soot from morning until night.

What is even better is I am now a member of that band of brothers and sisters who can walk into a restaurant or get on an airplane and say loudly to the hostess, "No Smoking section, please!"

I have to admit that like all born-again nonsmokers I look down on those who are still hooked. I don't get angry with them but I do something worse. I bore them. I tell them my story from beginning to end—how I was once a seven-a-day Dunhill man, but through the intervention of a higher spirit became a six-pack Doublemint gum fan. Then I warn them that we nonsmokers not only consider ourselves holier than they, but believe we have a mission to either convert all smokers, or persecute them until we drive the tobacco demons from their souls.

Up in Arms

IT seems like only yesterday that we signed a peace treaty with the Japanese aboard the battleship *Missouri*, and told them they would never be allowed to make arms again.

"What should we do instead?" a defeated Japanese admiral asked.

"Why don't you make automobiles?" one of General MacArthur's advisers suggested.

"Ah so. But Americans make automobiles. How can a poor defeated country like Japan hope to compete with your wonderful cars?"

"Well, of course you can't compete in the United States because Americans would never buy a Japanese automobile after what you did to Pearl Harbor. But perhaps you could make something which could be sold in Southeast Asia and other markets where people don't care about quality."

"Ah so. How do you build an automobile?"

"It sounds hard, but I'm sure you people can get the hang of it. Here's a book of instructions. You see, you put the engine up here and then the seats here, and wrap a body around them, paint it all a nice color, and you have yourself a car."

"Can I keep the book?"

"Why not? Now that you are a poor defeated country we have no secrets."

"You are kind, sir."

A year later, the first Japanese car came off a jerry-built

assembly line. The Japanese admiral, who was now in charge of Tojo Motors, showed it to the American aide.

The ex-admiral bowed. "Forgive us for this unworthy thing we call an automobile, but we do not have much to work with."

The aide slapped the ex-admiral on the back. "Don't apologize. You did right well with what was available. I'll tell you what I'll do; I'll bring some of our boys over from Detroit, and they'll give you a list of things you will need to build a decent vehicle. We'll also send some of your designers and engineers over to the United States so that they can pick up some American know-how."

"Ah so. You would do that for a poor little struggling Japanese automobile company?"

"Why not? It isn't as if you're ever going to be able to sell any of those rickshaws in the States."

Several years later, the MacArthur aide, who was now working for a large New York bank, bumped into the ex-admiral in the Waldorf-Astoria. "What brings you to New York?" he asked jovially.

"I am arranging dealerships all over America for our four-cylinder Kamikaze 3 × 2. It gets twenty-four miles to the gallon and has front-wheel drive, disc brakes, and a rear defrosting window. Here is a photo of it."

The American looked at it and shook his head. "You're wasting your time, Admiral. Americans will never buy a small car, particularly one with front-wheel drive."

"Ah so, but we only hope to take one percent of the market among the teenagers and college students."

"It won't work. We have a love affair in this country with gas guzzlers and big fenders. As a friend, I'm telling you to save your money, and try to sell your product to the Third

World. They will drive anything they can get their hands on.''

The ex-admiral bowed and said, ''Perhaps you are right. But as long as I am here maybe I will find someone who is interested.''

Then came 1981, and both the American ex-aide and the Japanese ex-admiral had aged considerably. When the American walked into the luxurious offices of the ex-admiral, the Japanese stood up slowly and bowed.

''Ah so. And what brings you to Tokyo, my good friend?''

''I've been sent by the President of the United States,'' the American said. ''He knows we go way back, and felt I should bring his message personally.''

''What message?''

''He wants you to stop making so many damn Japanese cars.''

''But if we can't make cars, what else can we make?''

''He wants you to start making arms.''

''But we don't know how to make arms.''

''The President told me to give you this.''

''What is it?''

''A book of instructions.''

The Real Thing

GARFINKEL called me up. "I would like you to become a member of the Sons of Ma Bell Telephone Users Association."

"What's your story?"

"After all the hype about launching a new improved drink, Coca-Cola was willing to salvage the original Coke. We hope to persuade the telephone company to bring back the old Ma Bell system. After all, telephone consumers have taste too. The reason Coca-Cola gave in to the public was because they couldn't take the flak from their customers about their 'new improved product.' If the Coke Company is unable to take the pressure, we figure the telephone company is vulnerable as well."

"Do you want everyone to go back to the old phone system?"

"No, we're following the Coke marketing philosophy. We don't want them to drop the new way of providing phone service. All we're asking is that everyone in the United States be given a choice between the old Ma Bell and those that they have inflicted on all of us since. We're not ones to tell a user what to choose. If you like the present telephone system with its fancy prices, hi-tech recorded voices, and unintelligible computer-coded itemized bills, then we say stick with the new. If you prefer constant breakdowns and service technicians who deny jurisdiction over your phone problem, you're probably satisfied with the improved product."

[118]

"But if you long for the days when your bills were low, a friendly human voice gave you information, and the repairman was at your house before you hung up, then you should have a right to opt for the old system. The Sons of Ma Bell believe in free choice.''

"I admire your goals, but it seems to me that it's easier to bring back a soft drink than it is to resurrect an entire communications system.''

"I don't agree with you,'' Garfinkel said. "The Coca-Cola company is the most powerful institution in the world. If they can admit they've made a mistake, surely a piddling telephone system can do the same thing. It's no big deal for the people who run our telephone companies to go on television and say, 'We've been listening to what you're saying. Maybe the breakup of Ma Bell wasn't such a good idea after all. So now we're giving you the choice of the new phone system or the "Classic" one you were attached to in the past. Our only concern is satisfying our customers. Like Coca-Cola, we blew it, and want to make it up to you.' ''

"Telephone executives hate to admit they make mistakes,'' I said. "I doubt if you'll get them to go on the air.''

Garfinkel said, "If the old Coke lovers can bring Atlanta to its knees, the Sons of Ma Bell should be able to make the phone people cry 'uncle.' ''

"There is one thing wrong with your crusade,'' I told him. "Coca-Cola was able to bring back the old Coke because it still exists as a company. The telephone system has been broken up by the government, and even if the phone execs wanted to replicate the old system, the Justice Department wouldn't let them do it. Washington doesn't give a hoot about the consumers.''

"The Sons of Ma Bell intend to change all that. We're

asking each member of our organization to send every Congressman and Senator ten six-packs of empty Coca-Cola cans. Our message to Washington is that the telephone is almost as important as a soft drink, and if Coke drinkers now have a choice between the old and the new, the telephone consumer has a right to the same thing.''

Nearly All

''IT says here in *The Wall Street Journal* that *nearly all* the nation's top defense contractors are under criminal investigation by the Pentagon.''

My wife was aghast. "*Nearly all* of them?"

"Yup, according to the Inspector General *nearly all* of them are being checked out for making false claims on costs and labor, kickbacks, and bribing government officials. Of course we have to use caution here. Just because they're accused of wrongdoing doesn't necessarily mean they did it.''

"I could see one company, possibly two, but nearly all of them? That's a lot of companies.''

"Not really. When it comes to the big boys we're only talking about possibly two dozen or so contractors that were involved.''

"Why did it take so long to catch them?"

"They haven't caught them yet," I told her. "And with any luck they never will. But in answer to your question, the Pentagon has gone soft on whistle-blowers. There was a time when, if anyone blew the whistle on a defense contractor, the country would hang him from the flagpole in front of the Secretary of Defense's office. Now we coddle them, play up to them, and even let them talk to Congressmen. Is it any wonder there is a scandal in the military establishment when they can't even keep a lid on their accountants?"

"I don't understand. You sound as though you don't mind if they overcharged us and engaged in kickbacks, bribes, and wrongdoing."

"Most of the companies are guilty of nothing more than sloppy bookkeeping. When you're building billion-dollar weapons some money has to fall through the cracks."

"*Which* cracks?"

"The ones caused by using cheap cement," I said. "It's easy for the two of us to sit in this comfortable living room criticizing people who make submarines. It's another thing to actually build them."

"I don't see what building a submarine has to do with whether someone is honest or not. If those people can't make money the old-fashioned way like Smith Barney, they shouldn't be in business."

"They *were* making it the old-fashioned way. That's why they're being investigated. It was par in the old days to pile on extra costs for defense work, and everyone accepted kickbacks and bribes as part of doing business. The reason it's a big deal now is a few guys overdid it and Weinberger is boiling mad because he can't get the money he asked for. We're making far too much of illegitimate overruns. Whatever the gumshoes come up with will be peanuts compared to what the weapons cost us. Besides, there's always one bad apple in every barrel.''

''Suppose nearly all the apples are bad?''

''Would you rather have lots of weapons and a little hanky-panky—or no weapons and honest bookkeeping?''

''Are those my only choices?''

''If the top defense contractors can't have a little fun while they're building weapons systems, they just might go out of the business.''

''I think you're putting me in an impossible position. You're saying just because they make things that kill people they should get away with murder.''

''I'm not saying anything until all the facts are in. It wouldn't surprise me if when the Inspector General gets finished *nearly all* of them will have a very good reason for doing what they did.''

''*Nearly all* of them?''

A Seat in the Royal Box

CHARLTON Heston once told the *London Daily Mail* that he would not sit in the Royal Box at Wimbledon because he was afraid John McEnroe might embarrass him. "I do not want to sit . . . and risk embarrassment, as an American, of watching an American disgrace his country."

I know exactly what Chuck is talking about. I've turned down invitations to sit in the Royal Box for several years because I was afraid McEnroe might do something to make me terribly ashamed.

It was a great sacrifice for me because that's the only place where I enjoy watching the matches on center court.

I recall the last time I sat there a few years back. I was squeezed between Queen Elizabeth and Prince Philip. Seated in front of me were Princess Di and Prince Charles and Princess Anne. Behind me were the Duke and Duchess of Kent.

We were laughing and joking as one always does in the Royal Box, when John McEnroe came on the court. I stiffened measurably as McEnroe gave the drinking fountain a good kick. It was going to be a long afternoon.

No sooner had play commenced when John complained that the ball boys were not retrieving his tennis balls fast enough.

The Queen turned to me and said, "A fellow countryman?"

I smiled weakly. "Not really, your Majesty. He's from Long Island."

A few points later McEnroe grabbed a photographer's hat and poured Schweppes tonic all over it.

It was either the Duke of Kent or Prince Philip who said, "The chap has a lot of spunk."

I wanted to crawl under my chair.

With the set six all and a key point at stake, McEnroe launched into a vicious verbal assault on a lady linesman at our end of the court. He used words never uttered at Buckingham Palace.

Red-faced, I turned to Queen Elizabeth and said, "Do you want me to leave?" She smiled and patted my hand gently. "You can't be responsible for what another American player does. I recall when you played Wimbledon. Your manners were impeccable."

"I was representing my country. In those days we left the line calls to the officials."

We were into the second set when McEnroe approached the umpire's chair and started what could charitably be described at Wimbledon as a "heated discussion." He was not only questioning the umpire's call, but also the parentage of the gentleman himself.

Princess Di put her hands over her ears as Prince Charles tried to console her. "It's going to be all right, my dear. The man is just trying to psych himself up."

Then Prince Charles turned to me and said apologetically, "I don't know why women insist on coming to Wimbledon when they know tennis, as played by Americans, is a very bloody sport."

Having lost his argument, McEnroe went over to a bench, picked up an equipment bag, and started to slam it against the umpire's chair.

The Queen said to me, "Would you care for some tea?"

I was dying inside. "Lemon and one lump of sugar, please."

The Duke of Kent squeezed my shoulder. "I once knew a

Yank who destroyed his metal locker with his racket. Except for that he was quite a relaxed player.''

It was toward the end of the match that McEnroe, having double-faulted three times in a row, started to deliberately smash balls at our box.

This was too much for me, and as the Royal Family ducked under their seats, I left the box in shame and disgust—never to return again.

Chuck, you can take it from somebody who has been there. Even if you now have a lousy seat at Wimbledon, you did the right thing.

RSVP

EVERYONE in Washington is talking about the visit of Prince Charles and Princess Di to the U.S. Most people are behaving like idiots trying to wangle an invitation to one of the glittery affairs. I'm happy to report my wife and I couldn't care less.

"I never was big for royalty," I said to her as we roasted potatoes in the fireplace.

"Me neither. If you've seen one Prince of Wales you've seen them all."

"The thing to do is not answer the phone for the next

two weeks. Then if Buckingham Palace calls we can always say we were out.''

''Suppose they deliver the invitation by hand. I saw a wigged footman in the neighborhood yesterday. He was only two blocks away.''

''Don't open the door. Once royalty serves you with an invitation you have to go.''

''I don't know why the girls who patronize my beauty parlor are making such a fuss,'' my wife said. ''After all the Prince and Princess are just like any young married couple having marital trouble.''

''How do you know they're having marital problems?''

''I read in *People* magazine that Charles and Di aren't getting along. She keeps going out until four in the morning and he keeps falling off his horse. They say that Di has fired all of Charles' servants as well as his private secretary.''

''That's what you call tough love,'' I said.

''What makes it even worse is Di has cut off the Prince's contact with all his friends from his bachelor days, and will not allow him to see any of his old girlfriends.''

''Why would a wife do that?''

''She's very headstrong. She's not the shy virgin we saw being married on TV by Barbara Walters.''

''You never know what is going on behind closed doors.''

''It wasn't behind closed doors. It was in *Vanity Fair*.''

''What did they say about the Prince besides the fact he keeps falling off his horse?''

''He's lonely and bored. The reason is that they say his mother won't give him anything to do. Queen Elizabeth is keeping a tight rein on the throne. The Prince has no duties, and seems to be out of it.''

''I'm glad we're not going to any of the parties, because we wouldn't have anything to discuss with him,'' I said.

"You're not supposed to talk to royalty unless they talk to you first," she told me.

"Where did you hear that?"

"I read it in *Miss Manners*."

"Well, if you can't talk to them, what's the big deal about getting invited to a party?"

"The *National Enquirer* said that although you can't talk, you can stare at them," my wife said.

"Why do people kill to go to that kind of bash?"

"I guess it's just to say they've been there."

"Are you sorry you weren't invited?" I asked her.

"Of course not. What woman wants to go to the trouble of buying a brand-new evening gown and silver shoes just to meet the next King of England, when she can stay home in her bathrobe and watch *Dynasty* on TV?"

"That is exactly the way I feel. Let other people fight for two chairs at J. C. Penney's. I'd rather have two seats to a Redskins game. Did the mail come today?" I asked.

"Yes, it's over there."

"Anything in it?"

"Not really."

I peeked out the window. "Maybe the British Embassy doesn't know where we live."

Mik Deavervitch

E VERY TV network is feverishly competing to get an interview with Mikhail Gorbachev.

The person who will make the final decision is the incomparable Soviet image maker, Mik Deavervitch. It was Deavervitch who sold the Russian people on the fact that style was more important than substance. As Gorbachev's press chief during the recent Soviet elections, Deavervitch came up with the catchy slogan "Vote for somebody who is red, but not dead."

So effective was Deavervitch's political strategy that when Konstantin Chernenko died, Gorbachev was elected less than five hours later—in a landslide. Since then Deavervitch has been consulted on everything Gorbachev does. He was responsible for advancing the Secretary's trips to London and Paris as well as setting up photo opportunities with Margaret Thatcher, François Mitterrand, and Tip O'Neill.

Deavervitch has posed Gorbachev talking to nurses in a Lenin hospital, listening to hard hats in a Lenin auto works, and shaking hands at a university with Lenin grads.

Not only does Deavervitch serve Gorbachev, but he also works for the Soviet leader's wife. Moscow watchers say that Raisa Gorbachev, who is the real power in the Kremlin, does not make a move without first checking it out with Deavervitch.

This being the case I decided to pick up the phone and speak to the man. It was much easier than I thought.

The Soviet operator put me right through, after saying "Thank you for using ST & T."

"Mr. Deavervitch, I'm calling about the selection you have to make concerning the Secretary's first American television appearance."

"We are noodling it. Goodbye."

"Wait a minute. How will you arrive at your decision?"

"I just received the overnight ratings from our KGB man in New York. Daniel Rather defeated Peter Jennings and Thomas Brokaw. What kind of a man is this Rather?"

"He's a very decent sort, but then again so are Jennings and Brokaw. The three are only a point apart."

"Our mole at ABC says a point means a million viewers. I cannot allow the Secretary to appear in a vast wasteland."

"So you're putting your boy on the *Evening News?*"

"Not necessarily. We are also considering one of the morning shows. The Secretary likes Phyllis George very much."

"Phyllis is a fine interviewer, but unfortunately she no longer works on the CBS morning show. What about late-night? Ted Koppel is hot right now."

"The Secretary doesn't want to go head-to-head with Johnny Carson. Since our leader is making only one TV appearance, we're hoping to make the top ten."

"Would Mr. Gorbachev consider a walk-on part in *Dallas?*"

"No, our Bulgarian agent in Hollywood reports it is full of filthy double-crossing capitalists. What other shows would you suggest?"

"There is *Entertainment Tonight, Miami Vice, The Phil Donahue Show,* and then my favorite, *Wheel of Fortune.* The best thing about *Wheel of Fortune* is that Gorbachev will not only have a large audience, but he can also win some very valuable prizes."

[129]

"It's not dignified. Tell me, Comrade, what is this Howard Cosell like?"

"He tells it like it is," I said.

"How do you mean, 'like it is'?"

"Remember when Khrushchev took off his shoe and banged it on the table? Well, if Howard doesn't agree with the person he is talking to he does the same thing."

No Dumping Place

Aᴛᴏᴍɪᴄ waste is not the only thing you can't dispose of in America.

"I would like to purchase a twenty-five-inch TV set."

"You came to the right place. Simple Simon has the best video bargains in the city."

"What do I do with my used one?"

"Anything you like. We never tell a customer what to do with his old TV set."

"Will you give me a trade-in?"

"You're kidding. Do you know how many TV sets in the U.S. are thrown out every day?"

"Would you haul it away if I buy the new one?"

"I may be simple, but I'm not crazy. Thousands and thousands of people are stuck with aging TV sets. They can't sell them, they can't give them away, and they can't throw them out. Garbage men don't even want them.''

"So what does one do with the old set?''

"The same thing you do with nuclear waste. Find a deep hole in South Carolina and bury it.''

"I can't even lift my TV.''

"Then soak it with gasoline and set a match to it.''

"In the living room?''

"If it will make you feel better do it in the kitchen. Look, mister, there is something you have to understand. The greatest thing about America is that you can buy the newest appliances known to man. The worst thing about it is that you can't get rid of the old ones. Once you own a fridge, a washing machine, or a TV set, you're stuck with it for the rest of your life. That's why you see so many of them on people's back porches.''

"I have a mind to keep my old TV and have it fixed. How much would it cost?''

"Five hundred and fifty dollars.''

"You haven't even seen it yet.''

"Every TV set costs five hundred and fifty dollars to fix.''

"For that kind of money I could buy a new one.''

"I know. That's why we charge five hundred and fifty dollars to repair the old one.''

"Perhaps I could donate my TV set to a senior citizens' home or an orphanage.''

"I wouldn't try it. They've been stung with too many second-hand sets. Why don't you just put yours in the attic and forget about it like everybody else does?''

"We don't have any room. Our old stove is in the attic and, come to think of it, so is the sink that came with the house.''

"Listen, I'm busy. Do you want the TV or not?"

"Yes, I do—if you could just give me some idea how we can move the other one out."

"If I could tell you that, I'd be able to sell twice as many new TV sets."

"What if I told you I'd be willing to pay to get rid of the old set. How much would you charge?"

"Where do you live?"

"Wesley Heights, off New Mexico and Cathedral."

"It will cost exactly five hundred and fifty dollars."

"But that's as much as you'll charge me to fix it!"

"Mister, we don't make any money hauling away sets. We just do it to beautify America."

Overkill

I T is only fair at this time that we pay tribute to the world's great stockpiles of atomic weapons. Without them, there is a good chance that the U.S. and the Soviet Union might not be holding arms-control talks.

A recent survey revealed that being blown up by a nuclear weapon is not the biggest fear in the world today. It's the fact that people can be snuffed out more than once that has most citizens slightly nervous.

According to a report by Ruth Sivard, a former official of the U.S. Arms Control and Disarmament Agency, there are now enough weapons on earth to kill fifty-eight billion human beings. The catch is that there aren't fifty-eight billion people in the world.

Professor Sowa Bratten, who specializes in nuclear snuff statistics, says that there is an answer to this. "Since we're short on the living and long on the weapons, the scientific community no longer counts how many people we can kill, but rather how many *times* we can kill them."

"How many times is that?"

He took out his pocket calculator. "We can knock off everyone in the world 12 times—with favorable wind conditions, of course."

"That's a big improvement," I said. "I recall that only a few years ago the superpowers were lucky if they could kill each person five times. To what do you credit the breakthrough?"

"Better quality control. In the old days building atomic weapons was little more than a mom-and-pop business. Mom stuffed the bombs with uranium, and Pop screwed on the fuses. This was okay for Hiroshima and Nagasaki, but it just wasn't good enough for a global arms race. No one was thinking big."

"How did number one and number two move the arms buildup into the twentieth century?"

"Their military advisers warned them that the low, post–World War Two kill ratio would no longer keep the pace. Without extra fallout they could not guarantee the safety of their citizens."

"Thank God for the military," I said.

He continued, "Crash programs were started, and larger

bangs were developed, with the help of giant cost overruns. It was obvious, as the demand increased for third-generation hardware, that the nuclear powers would spend more and more of their gross national product on weapons. Edward Teller, the father of the H-bomb, said, 'The building up of larger and more powerful atomic weapons is the only way to stop the arms race.' ''

''He didn't say that,'' I said.

''Maybe not,'' Bratten admitted, ''but it sounds like something he would say. In any case, we all know that if you're going to make a nuclear omelette you first have to crack the plutonium.''

''This still doesn't explain how the superpowers managed to increase their stockpiles.''

''The powers didn't intend to make so many deadly weapons. They just got lucky. But it wasn't the size of the bombs that made everyone happy. Any fool can make a nuclear bomb. The trick is to deliver it where you want it to go. That's where the real progress has been made. The breakthrough in present delivery systems has given man new hope.''

''Do you think we have now reached a plateau in overkill?''

He laughed. ''You ain't seen nothing yet.''

The Stately Homes of Queens

Years ago when Jackie Onassis was the first lady of our land, she conducted a TV tour of the White House. My sister was so inspired by the event that she gave me a tour of her three-room apartment in Queens, New York.

I was under the impression she had retired from the stately home business until I received a call from her the other day. "The British swells have sent their greatest art treasures to the National Gallery in Washington this month," she said. "What are we sending them in return?"

"Nothing special that I know of," I said.

"That's what I thought. My girlfriends and I have a great idea. In exchange for the English lending us their heirlooms we would like to ship them treasures from the homes of Flushing, New York."

"You told me the people of Flushing would never let their heirlooms out of their houses."

"We're now willing to do it provided they are insured by Lloyd's of London."

"Who is 'we'?"

"A few homeowners in my neighborhood. We call ourselves the Magnificent Six. We would have been the Magnificent Seven except Martha Bordinsky's slipcovers won't be ready for months. The thought we had is that if the British are willing to display what they have in their stately homes, we should give them some idea of what we have in ours."

"What art treasures are you prepared to send to them?"

"I'm willing to lend *The Blue Boy*—the one I bought in a garage sale in Astoria last year."

"Did you ever find out if it's the original *Blue Boy* or not?"

"The man who sold it to me said if it wasn't the original it came awfully close. I'm not the only one willing to part with treasures. Doris Dembow wants to send a needlepoint sampler which she made herself, titled 'God Bless Our Home.' "

"That's classy. The only place I've ever seen anything like it was in a Hallmark greeting card shop."

"Barbara Lupin has offered to part with a color photo of her grandchild. She says it has never been shown in public before. But she won't lend it unless a guard is stationed in front of it day and night."

"The Tate Gallery has plenty of guards. What other treasures would you like to send to London?"

"Laura Brown has a pair of Ron and Nancy toby mugs which she purchased in Atlantic City. They were crafted by skilled artisans in Hong Kong, and the shopkeeper told Laura that they were already collectors' items."

"I may be wrong, but I don't believe the British have ever seen a Hong Kong toby mug before."

"What we're trying to do is organize our treasures so that it gives the English some idea of how the bluebloods live in Flushing. We have Myra Stieglitz nearly talked into parting with her queen-size sleep-sofa. It's an heirloom because it has been used by three generations in her family."

"What is so special about it?"

"In the daytime it can seat three people, and at night all you have to do is remove the cushions and it turns into a bed."

"Why is Myra hesitating?"

"She is afraid if the Tate Gallery borrows it, her kids' friends won't have anyplace to sleep when they come home on school vacation."

"You seem to have everything under control. Why did you call me?"

"The girls wondered if you would contact Prince Charles and Princess Di and ask them to stop by to preview our art treasures on their way to Kennedy airport."

"I would be happy to. One more thing. I'm curious about how you selected the masterpieces for the exhibit."

"We all closed our eyes and thought of England."

The Big Lie

THE Great Lie Detector Test Flap has come to an end. When President Reagan signed a directive ordering thousands of government officials to hook up to a polygraph machine, Secretary of State George Shultz balked, and announced he would resign.

The President then backed down and said the lie detector would be used only in special cases.

What nobody knows is that it wasn't George Shultz who was responsible for getting Mr. Reagan to rethink his security plan. It was Nancy Reagan.

Three days after the President signed the directive, two men came into Mrs. Reagan's sitting room and attempted to place electrodes on her head.

Mrs. Reagan said, "What are you doing?"

One of the men replied, "The President has ordered everyone to take a polygraph test. We wanted to get the White House people out of the way first."

"Leave immediately. I will never submit to a polygraph test."

"Gee, Mrs. Reagan. It isn't a big deal to take one if you have nothing to hide. But it's going to make everyone wonder about you if you refuse."

"I'm going to speak to the President about this."

"Nancy, why are you getting your hair done so early?"

"These are not hair curlers, Ronnie. They are electrodes for a polygraph test. Will you please tell me why I have to submit to one?"

"I can't very well ask George Shultz to take the test if I won't ask my own wife."

"Ronnie, have I ever lied to you?"

"Of course not. That's why I wasn't afraid to okay the polygraph for you. I knew you would pass with flying colors. Can't you see the headlines—'Nancy Reagan Tells Truth Again.'"

"There is no reason for me to take a test. I don't know any state secrets."

"That's the point, Nancy. If you did know any secrets, the threat of a lie detector test would make you think twice before you passed them on."

"Ronnie, why are you making everyone do this?"

"Bill Webster and Cap Weinberger think it's a dandy idea.

They believe the tests will have a chilling effect on would-be traitors.''

"Am I considered a would-be traitor?"

"Of course not. I know it, and you know it, but how can I prove it to everyone else if I can't produce the results of your polygraph tests?"

"Everyone says lie detector tests are no good. They can't even be used in court as evidence. And they violate people's civil rights."

"I have done more for civil rights than any President in the past fifty years. Let me read you a letter I received from a little girl in Iowa."

"Ronnie, I want those men out of the boudoir in two minutes."

"Nancy, you are the crown jewel in my administration's polygraph program. We'll make the questions very simple, such as, why did you exile our dog Lucky to the ranch in California?"

"I've never hesitated to cooperate with you before, Ronnie. But this time the answer is NO."

"Since you feel that way about it, I'll cancel the lie detector program. But when the next commie spy surfaces in the government, you'll have nobody to blame but George Shultz and yourself."

Peace Shield

I was over at Barry Israel's the other night when his eight-year-old daughter, Alison, came into the living room.

"Have you done your homework?" her father asked.

Alison handed him a sheet of paper with a drawing on it. "What is it?"

"It's Star Wars," Alison said. "This is the sun and this is the house, and this is the mommy and this is the daddy, and this is the little child, and this is the cat and this is a tree."

"That's fine, but how do you get Star Wars out of all this?"

"The blue circle over everyone is Star Wars. The rockets can't get through to kill the mommy, the daddy, the child, and the cat."

"I don't see how that blue arc can stop missiles from hitting your family," Barry said.

Alison pointed to three red missiles bouncing off the arc. "You see. The bombs are stopped and can't hurt anyone."

"Where did you get the idea that a blue crayon can stop a red one?"

"I saw it on television. It said that if everyone supports Star Wars we will be safe from getting killed."

"Don't lie to me," Alison's father said.

"She's not lying," I told him. "I saw the same TV commercial. It's put out by some outfit called Peace Shield to convince people that the President's Strategic Defense Initiative works.

They're hoping that if they make it simple enough, Americans will buy it.''

Barry said, ''What a crock. They're using a kid's drawing to sell a pie-in-the-sky idea.''

I said, ''Don't jump to conclusions that a child was the artist. I know several scientists who could easily have drawn it.''

''The picture doesn't convince me that we should spend zillions on Star Wars.''

''It's not intended to convince you—it's supposed to convince Alison. After all, it's her generation that's going to have to live with laser beams and enhanced deterrence. If kids believe a blue crayon can stop a red one then they won't be afraid.''

Alison was standing there quietly. Finally she said, ''Is my drawing all right?''

Her father replied, ''As far as it goes, it is. Hand me a red crayon and a black one. Okay, now watch carefully, Alison. The red crayon can't get through the arc, and the house and family are perfectly safe. Right?''

''Uh-huh,'' Alison said, not knowing where her father was going.

''Now I take the black crayon, and it slices right through the shield and knocks out the sun, the house, and the family of three.''

''Why?''

''Because black crayons can always go through blue ones. Even a nuclear umbrella won't stop them. That's why a blue crayon is not going to save us.''

Alison looked to me for some help.

''I have to agree with your father,'' I told her. ''There are too many different colored crayons for one blue arc to stop. Even if only one color got through, it would wipe out your mommy, daddy, and cat.''

Barry said, "Did you hear what your Uncle Art just said? Listen to him. He knows *everything*.''

Alison's lower lip was quivering. "You ruined my drawing.''

Her father replied, "I just wanted to teach you a lesson. Don't believe everything you see on television.''

Winnebago

"MAY I help you, sir?''

"My name is George Shultz and I'm Secretary of State. I would like a Winnebago, or something like it.''

"Were you planning a long trip?''

"No, I want to park it outside the American Embassy in Moscow so I won't be bugged when I'm having a meeting. With all the listening devices planted in our buildings, I feel a mobile home is the only safe place to conduct America's diplomacy.''

"Good thinking, sir. How big do you want the trailer to be?''

"I would like something practical—a place where I could meet the Soviet Foreign Minister in the daytime, and sack out at night so I could save on my per diem.''

"If you'll forgive me for saying so, you need something grander. The Kremlin will not take you seriously if you park outside the embassy in a mobile hutch. As the representative of a superpower you should have this luxurious Winnebago which will not only handle a full-blown disarmament conference, but comes complete with airbags for both sides."

"It doesn't look like it holds many people."

"The roof comes out and the back goes down. Believe me, if I had to negotiate the future of the Western World, this is the only vehicle I would use."

"What else do you have?"

"We have had a lot of success with this mini–motor home. It's been used several times to work out a durable peace in the Middle East. What makes this one so special is that it self-destructs when the participants fail to come to an agreement."

"I was really hoping for something I can tool around in with Mrs. Shultz to Russian trailer parks."

The salesman said, "I just thought of an RV that you might like. It's called the Tara Motor Home and comes air conditioned with a CB radio. You can talk to anyone in Washington without leaving your bunk."

"Suppose somebody in Moscow overhears me?"

"They can't. Anyone who listens in on you would be violating Soviet law."

"I have to be sure my van is completely bugproof."

"I guarantee a quiet ride from Omsk to Murmansk."

"Is your Winnebago large enough to have a summit meeting?"

"It's bigger than a summit. You can sleep the Reagans in the front and the Gorbachevs in the back and still have room to invite sixty people for a state dinner. With this Winnebago we're talking top-of-the-line summitry."

"You make a very convincing case. I think I'll take it. What's the warranty on it?"

"We give the State Department the same warranty on our vehicles that it gives the public on its treaties."

"I warn you, if it's not safe I'm going to bring it back."

"If you're not happy with the Winnebago I have a wonderful alternative for you. It's a Good Humor truck. All you have to do is wear a white hat, white shirt, a black bow tie, and you'll have the Russians eating out of your hand."

A Message to Moscow

[WASHINGTON - President Reagan upped the ante just two weeks before his summit with Soviet leader Mikhail Gorbachev by suggesting that the time had come to "stop futzing around."
—From the front page of *USA Today,* 7 November 1985.]

W HEN Soviet leader Gorbachev read the quote, he called in his Kremlin advisers.

"What does 'futzing' mean?" he asked them.

"I don't know," his foreign minister said. "We've asked the White House to clarify it. Here is their reply: 'Don't play dumb. You do it all the time.' "

Gorbachev was furious. "The President knows we don't know. Why would he send us a message we don't understand? Can't anyone in our embassy in Washington find out what it means?"

"Our ambassador advises us that 'futzing' relates to our putting medium-range missiles along the Czech border."

A Soviet marshal said, "He's mistaken. It refers to the buildup of conventional forces in Poland. The Americans are saying they want us to pull them out or they will 'futz' us."

"You're both wrong," the KGB director said. " 'Futzing' is another word for defecting. Reagan couldn't believe it when our man, after defecting, turned around and redefected to us. We 'futzed' the CIA and the President didn't like it."

Gorbachev said, "You all have theories but you don't have facts. How can I face Reagan in Geneva when I have no idea what he is talking about?"

The General Secretary's scientific adviser said, "My people have studied the message and concluded that it's about Star Wars. Reagan was talking about the shield the U.S. plans to build to prevent our missiles from hitting them."

Gorbachev declared, "What is my response if he tells me in Geneva to stop 'futzing' around?"

"You tell him that you'll be glad to when he stops 'futzing' around with Star Wars, and not a minute sooner."

"He won't go for it," Gorbachev said. "Why don't I offer to cut back on 'futzing' by fifty percent, provided Reagan does the same?"

The Soviet marshal said, "They will cheat."

"Then we'll cheat too. We will match them 'futz' for 'futz,' " Gorbachev told them. "But I still have the feeling the President was talking about something else."

The Foreign Minister said, "Did you do any 'futzing' in your private life that Reagan may have found out about?"

Gorbachev shouted, "They're lies, all lies!"

The KGB director added, "I can attest to that."

The press chief said, "Perhaps the President misspoke and

didn't mean to use the word 'futzing' at all. He's been known to say something and then take it back three hours later.''

Gorbachev was getting impatient, ''We can't speculate. We have to find out exactly what his message meant or cancel the summit.''

A secretary came into the room and handed a cable to the KGB director, whose eyes almost popped out of his head.

''Our language experts have tracked down the word. ''It's Yiddish and means 'fooling around, or not being serious.' ''

''You're crazy. What is Ronald Reagan doing speaking Yiddish?'' the Foreign Minister asked.

''It makes you wonder,'' Gorbachev mused. ''Find out what his name was before he changed it to Reagan.''

''Yes, sir,'' the KGB director said.

''And,'' Gorbachev continued, ''also get me a Yiddish dictionary so I can answer him in kind.''

''We can't, sir. They've all been burned.''

The Joy of Sex?

THE Supreme Court has upheld a Georgia law making sodomy a crime. It is a landmark decision, and as with all landmark decisions, many citizens are very nervous. Not only homosexuals are worried by the Court's ruling, but it has scared the pants off heterosexuals as well.

I know this because some of my best friends are heterosexuals and they confide in me a lot. Matingly said, "If homosexuals are not safe in the privacy of their homes, who will be next?"

"I believe you are unduly pessimistic," I said. "The Court would never do to heterosexuals what it has done to homosexuals. Many of the justices are heterosexuals themselves."

"Nevertheless, their decision is a dagger aimed at the heart of anyone who believes in a private sex life. If the state can go into the bedroom and arrest two people performing an act which has been declared illegal, what is to prevent it from going into a room next door and rousting out a couple doing something that is considered twice as weird?"

"Why would the state want to do something like that?"

"Because the very people who write laws dictating which sex acts are legal and which are illegal would like to rule out everything but the missionary position. They want to tell us how to do it."

"No, they don't. No one has ever told me what to do in the bedroom."

"Then let me ask you how you feel about the pillow game?"

"I don't know the pillow game."

"You beat each other with pillows until there are no feathers left in the cases. They're talking about forbidding that in Virginia."

"You heterosexuals are so hysterical. The next thing you're going to tell me is that body painting your mate will be declared a crime in South Dakota."

"It will be if tickling is involved. Don't you understand that once the Supreme Court has gone through the bedroom door, there is no way of getting them out. Eight men and one woman are no substitute for one Dr. Ruth Westheimer."

"This is no time for panic. What you practice in your own home, whether it be the Jewel in the Lotus, the Gift to the Ceiling, or the Corkscrew Motion, will not be forbidden provided it meets the community standards of at least five of the nine judges. It is only homosexuals who can't practice these things behind closed doors. You heterosexuals should be happy that what you revel in is not against the law, and that you live in a country where anything goes. In some societies, achieving the Great Delight of Enlightenment with the large toe can get you twenty years in jail."

"But the Supreme Court has everyone cringing. If Georgia can pass a law against one type of lovemaking, why can't Arkansas enact one against another? Pretty soon there will be no positions left."

"Even if they do pass a law," I said, "your home is still your castle, and it would have to be very unusual circumstances that would allow the police to crash in."

"Possibly, but heterosexuals are very nervous people, and just the knowledge that there may be someone on the other side of the bedroom door will inhibit us from engaging in the Yab-Yum positions."

"Why blame the Supreme Court for that?"

"Because when you start taking away the Yab-Yum position from one person then you start taking it away from all."

To Catch a Spy

THE toughest thing about catching a spy is seeing that he gets the punishment he deserves. As soon as one is arrested, his attorney starts bargaining for a lighter sentence in exchange for the fink's revealing how much information he turned over to the other side.

"Hello, Justice Department? This is Mat O'Hara representing Collard Cosmos, the weasel who sold the plans for the Stealth bomber to the Bulgarians. What kind of deal are you offering us?"

"We don't plea bargain over spies, O'Hara. Your guy sold out his country and the government intends to hang him by the neck until he is dead."

"You better think it over. Except for the Stealth bomber, you have no idea what secrets Collard walked away with, and we don't have any intention of telling you if you keep demanding your pound of flesh."

"We're not talking about some two-bit code clerk, O'Hara. Cosmos is the biggest fish we've caught in years. We intend to put him in the freezer for life."

"What if I were to tell you that my client is willing to name over one hundred twenty people in the U.S. government who are still on the KGB payroll?"

"O'Hara, did it ever occur to you that we may not want to know who they are? The more spies the government uncovers, the worse we look. Every time we arrest somebody, Congress wants to know why it took us so long to flush him out. We reject your offer of the list of KGB agents, and we're still holding the position that Cosmos has to serve a minimum of twenty years."

"Would it whet your appetite if I told you my client smuggled blueprints of Star Wars in Nancy Reagan's cosmetic case when she went to Geneva?"

"That's impossible."

"I have films of Gorbachev switching cosmetic cases with Nancy at the airport. My client will tell you how he did it for a reduced sentence."

"The law is the law. Every person in this country must be punished according to his or her crime. In this case, Cosmos must do at least seven years for compromising the security of the nation."

"Apparently you don't realize what a predicament you're in. You people have spies coming out of your ears and spies coming out of your socks. If you don't show mercy to Cosmos, I'll advise him to remain mum about the nuclear submarine codes that he has stashed away in a pumpkin in the northeastern part of the United States."

"What sub codes?"

"I can't say because we might have to sell them to another country for legal expenses if you make us go to trial."

"O'Hara, we have an open and shut case on your client committing treason. No matter what information you say he can turn over to us, he will still have to rot for thirty days in the county jail.''

"I can't believe my ears. Collard made one lousy mistake of selling his country down the river, and when he says he's sorry and offers to make amends, your response is that he spend a month behind bars.''

"What do *you* think Cosmos should get for cooperating with us?''

"It wouldn't bother me if you charged him with one count of failing to curb his dog.''

"The government can live with that. We were afraid you were going to hold out for the Congressional Medal of Honor.''

Two Lawyers With a Case

Two lawyers were talking to each other at the next table. One was wearing a fire chief's hat, so I assumed he worked for Texaco. The other was putting Pennzoil on his salad.

The Pennzoil man said, "I feel like eleven billion dollars.''

The Texaco man took a swig of wine and replied, "You don't have to rub it in. You know you'll never see the money. We've gone into bankruptcy.''

"Great,'' said the Pennzoil man. "That means we're going to have to sue you for it. I was wondering how we were going to get some additional fees after the original suit was settled.''

"We're *counting* on Pennzoil suing us. With that suit and our fees for bankruptcy every partner in my law firm will be able to send his kid to college.''

The Pennzoil man admonished, "Lawyers shouldn't become rich on litigation. Their job is to serve the client at the least possible cost.''

"I'll drink to that,'' the Texaco man chuckled as he drank directly from the wine bottle.

"I wouldn't be *too* happy about the way things are going. My Pennzoil clients are talking about settling out of court. If that happens we can both sell our houses in East Hampton.''

The Texaco man looked shocked. "You can't let them settle out of court. That would make Pennzoil look chicken throughout the free oil world.''

"If they want to settle I have no choice.''

"If you don't sue us then we are going to sue you,'' asserted the Texaco man. "We have a lifetime of legal work staring us in the face and we're not letting it go down the drain because you people will settle for less than eleven billion to cover the pain and anguish Texaco caused you.''

"On behalf of everyone in my firm I welcome your lawsuit and will set aside the next five years to take depositions.''

"Good. We'll hire twenty more lawyers to work on the appeal just in case we lose in court,'' the Texaco man said. "Boy, it's great to be on the losing side of a multibillion-dollar lawsuit.''

The Pennzoil man retorted, "It's great to be on *any* side of a billion-dollar suit. What I would like to do is take this one to the Supreme Court. Then I could buy a new boat I've got my eye on.''

"If we can take it to the Court of Appeals I'll be able to purchase that chalet in Aspen."

The Pennzoil man asked, "Suppose the judge throws the suit out of court because it has no merit? Where does that leave us?"

"We'll sue him."

"We can't sue a judge. But we can do the next best thing—fight the thousands of unhappy stockholders who are lined up ready to sue Texaco and Pennzoil for screwing up. We'll be in court until the year 2001," the Pennzoil man declared.

"You make it sound so good I think I'll buy a private airplane."

"There is an old saying in our profession: 'When you have a sick rich client, a private plane pays for itself,' " the Pennzoil man commented.

"When this case started several years ago I was so sure we would settle out of court I figured I would only make enough on it to buy a home in Great Neck," said the Texaco lawyer. "Little did I dream I could buy the Trump Tower."

"I felt the same way. Winning isn't everything in this case. The big money is coming in now that Texaco won't pay the eleven billion."

The Texaco man inquired, "What are you going to do with your fees?"

"The same thing any struggling corporation lawyer would do. I'm going to buy a sunflower painting by Vincent Van Gogh."

Don't Laugh at Oil Barons

THERE are some people who are laughing because the oil barons have to sell their oil at seventeen dollars a barrel. I don't happen to be one of them.

It's true that OPEC had every intention of sticking it to the non-oil-producing countries, but that doesn't mean we should be celebrating like America's Cup fans.

Many of the oil producers have been humbled by the glut.

Just the other day Prince El Glami, a polo-playing friend of mine, stopped me on Fourteenth Street and asked me if I wanted to buy a "genuine" Rolex watch. When he recognized me he seemed embarrassed.

"Your Highness," I said. "What are you doing selling Rolex watches on Fourteenth Street?"

"Where would you sell them if crude was going for seventeen dollars a barrel?"

"But surely you still make more money selling oil than watches."

"I might, except everybody has a lien on my crude. I can't ship a barrel without some credit union seizing it at a foreign port. Fortunately they don't know about my watch business."

"What watches?"

"When oil was thirty-six dollars a barrel, I bought ten thousand watches to hand out as tips to the hotel help during my travel abroad. Now the watches are worth more than my oil. Don't you need a timepiece that will tell you the phase of the moon?"

"I can't believe you're that broke. What about the military equipment you bought? That has to be worth something."

"Mastercharge took it all back when I missed two payments."

"I never thought I'd see a Middle East prince so down on his luck."

"Neither did I. The last time I was in Washington I stayed at the White House. Now I'm sleeping a block away."

"In a hotel?"

"No, in Lafayette Park. Do you know what's driving the price of the oil down? It's greed."

"I thought that's what drove the price of oil *up*. As I recall it, OPEC's greed almost bankrupted the world."

"That wasn't greed. That was supply and demand. There wasn't enough oil to go around, so the prices rose, as they should in a free market."

"But isn't the reason they tumbled also because of supply and demand?"

"No, that was greed. Everyone who was pledged to drill only so much crude cheated and caused a glut. Then, because of the glut, they had to produce more crude which caused a bigger glut, and then it was glut, glut, glut."

I said to the Prince, "How can you expect the OPEC oil barons to honor their quotas when they're in hock for so many of the good things in life? I'd think you would keep drilling even if you only got five dollars a barrel."

"I would, except for the fact that I don't own the oil anymore. The insurance companies own it."

"How can the insurance companies own your oil?"

"I borrowed one hundred million dollars to build a new airport, a fleet of airplanes, and an air-conditioned polo field."

"Why would you do that?"

"To attract tourists so my country wouldn't have to depend on cheap oil."

Seeing Halley's Comet

THE country seems to be divided between those who saw Halley's Comet and those who *say* they did. It isn't like 1910 when everyone saw it. This time, if you blinked your eyes you could easily have missed it.

After Halley's Comet faded behind the sun, more and more Americans began pretending that they had sighted it. These citizens say things like, "I saw Halley's Comet with my opera glasses."

There is no reason to doubt them until you remember that it was so foggy on that particular night that they had to shut down the airport.

Why do otherwise honest people, the pillars of our communities, lie about what they saw in the heavens?

The answer is that since Halley's Comet was so hard to spot, status seekers were forced to resort to perjury in order to impress their friends.

If claiming that you saw the Comet when you didn't is just another way of keeping up with the Joneses, then I say more power to the fibber. But what makes this practice so dastardly is that it does an injustice to the people who actually have spotted it.

Those who stood outside all night in the freezing cold, stabbing their fingers at the skies, deserve a lot more respect than the ones who stayed under the blankets looking at photos of Halley's in *People* magazine.

The reason why I am incensed about all this is that I happened to see Halley's Comet. I refused to mention it to anyone because it's the sighting and not the bragging that counts with me.

Then Novak came down the hall and claimed that he had seen it.

I have been suspicious of Novak's comet sightings ever since he announced in 1973 that he viewed Kohoutek and told everyone it was on a crash course with Earth.

The people in the office were quite impressed that Novak had seen Halley's Comet, but no one thought to find out if he was telling the truth.

"What did it look like?" I wanted to know.

He replied, "A dirty snowball."

He could easily have read that in *Penthouse* magazine, so I asked him, "How long was it?"

"As long as the dirtiest snowball I've ever seen," Novak replied.

"That long?" I said. "Did you see the tail on it?"

I thought I had him. Novak said, "It was too dirty to see the tail. I was lucky to get a glimpse of its mouth."

I was leading him right into a trap. "And what did the mouth look like?"

"A big dirty snowball streaking across the sky."

"Did it fly past the moon?"

"Of course it flew past the moon. What kind of comet do you think it is?"

"Not so fast, Novak," I said. "I saw Halley's Comet and it was nowhere near the moon."

"Well, it was so dirty I couldn't tell what it was passing. All I know is that the sky is falling."

"People have been lying about Halley's Comet for 2,225 years."

Novak was adamant. "I know what I saw. It was a snowball, and it whizzed right past the moon."

"Where was it going?"

"It was on a crash course with Earth."

Computer Madness

THE envelopes with the little cellophane windows have been pouring into the house for three weeks. They're the computer bills from our Christmas binge.

Before computer billing I never doubted the charges. But now I feel different—computers lie. I'm not saying all computers lie, just as I'm not saying all credit managers tell the truth.

Take this bill from the Donation Department Store: "Six golf club mittens—$50.00."

Do you see anything wrong with that statement? Well, what would you say if I told you I have never bought golf club mittens in my life?

I called the Donation Department Store and was turned over to the credit division.

"I'm phoning about a set of golf mittens I didn't buy."

"You forgot you bought them. Most people do."

I wasn't going to let him bully me. "I didn't buy them and no one in our family bought them, because we don't play golf."

"What did your family buy in the sports department?"

"As far as I know, a tennis sweatband for my wife."

"Your wife plays tennis?"

"No, but it helps her to see better when she's working around the house."

"It's your word against the computer's. Who do you think I believe?"

"You have to take my word. I'm a customer."

"All you people who threw your money away like drunken sailors over Christmas would love to blame a computer. Ours never makes a mistake, but let's say for argument's sake it did. Our hands are tied. You can't expect us to go back into the system and rectify the error."

"Give me an alternative."

"We might let you have the mittens for twenty-five dollars."

"I *never* received any golf mittens. Why should I pay for them?"

"Because our computer says otherwise."

"Why don't you find the person who bought the golf club mittens and charge him?"

"We would if we could find him. But our computers are not programmed to separate the golfers from the tennis players."

"Do you admit this is the Donation Store's problem?"

"It is now yours. If you fail to pay, our computer will notify every computer in the world what a slimy credit-card holder you really are. My advice is send in the fifty dollars and be grateful you're not the victim of a serious mistake."

"Why can't you just pull my name and transaction out of the memory?"

"Our computer can't spend all its time tracking what a customer bought for Christmas."

"What's the solution?"

"We've found that when a computer makes a mistake by charging for an item you didn't buy, it forgets to bill you for something you purchased. So it all evens out at the end of the year."

"For me?"

"No, for the computer. The only thing I can suggest is that you bring the golf mittens back and we'll give you a fifty-dollar credit."

"I don't have the mittens."

"No problem. I'll transfer you to the sports department and you can order them over the phone."

Music Appreciation

THERE was a time when, if you wanted to hear good music, you put on a record or attended a concert. Now all you have to do is pick up the telephone and dial an institution. As soon as they put you on Hold you can enjoy the great masterpieces of all time.

A big fan of this type of music is Stuart Brotman. He maintains the only way you can really appreciate the classics is to be left hanging on the line waiting for a live person to talk to you.

"Once you've heard Mozart on the phone you never want to hear him live again," Stuart said.

"I didn't know you could get Mozart on the telephone," I said.

"You'd be surprised what you can get," he said. "The other day I called to make an airline reservation to Atlanta and was plugged into Handel's *Messiah*."

"Is *The Messiah* a favorite of yours?"

"It wasn't. But I had to wait so long that now I know the lyrics by heart."

"What has been the most memorable music ever played for you on the phone?" I asked Stuart.

"I once dialed Sears Roebuck about a lawnmower sale and they immediately switched me to *Aida*. At the finish I lost my head and started shouting 'Encore! Encore!' and the clerk hung up on me."

"I've called Sears many times and I've never heard Verdi."

"They only play him during Columbus Day sales," Stuart said.

"How do you feel about Stravinsky?"

"I can take him or leave him. My problem with Stravinsky is that when you have the telephone up to your ear, he can blow you right out of the booth. When I'm waiting to speak to someone on the phone I prefer a Chopin sonata."

"If I wanted to hear some good music, what company would you suggest I dial?"

"American Express has excellent taste. If you call their credit card complaint department they will pipe in the 'Blue Danube.'"

"That's no big deal. My gas company plays the 'Blue Danube' every time they put me on Hold."

"The difference is American Express pipes theirs in *live* from Vienna."

He then explained to me what was going on. "In the beginning most firms didn't pay much attention to the music they played, but as they kept cutting personnel, there were fewer employees to answer the phone. So with a smaller staff the companies had to play longer pieces. The days of piping in 'Begin the Beguine' are over. The average wait for a car-rental agency to take your call now is at least a Beethoven symphony."

"I didn't realize so much thinking went into institutional answering services."

"I'll prove it to you," Stuart said. "I'm going to dial the IRS. They *always* put you on Hold."

He handed the receiver to me. I listened and then said, "I don't believe it. The IRS is playing Wagner's *Götterdämmerung*."

"Why are you surprised?"

"It's a funeral march."
"What did you expect—'Happy Days Are Here Again?' "

Gramm Rudman—Where's Hollings?

Repeat after me. Gramm-Rudman! Gramm-Rudman! It doesn't ring a bell? Don't worry, I've anticipated all your questions.

What is a Gramm-Rudman?

Gramm-Rudman is not a what, but a who—actually three whos—Senator Gramm of Texas, Senator Rudman of New Hampshire, and Senator Hollings of South Carolina. They spearheaded the Gramm-Rudman-Hollings Act. Hollings is usually dropped from the credit because most newspapers do not have the space to include all three names in the story.

Is Gramm-Rudman-Hollings for real?

No, it's a dream decreeing that by 1991 the government must balance the Federal budget by not spending any more money than it takes in. This has been man's fantasy since he learned to fly.

It sounds like a musical comedy.

Some people consider it a tragedy. The military hate Gramm-

Rudman because they fear their appropriations will be severely cut. The Democrats are afraid Gramm-Rudman will knock out all the progressive legislation achieved over the past fifty years. And the President fears Gramm-Rudman will wipe out his authority to dictate a budget he can live with. You will hear a lot about Gramm-Rudman, but don't expect it to get a standing ovation.

What kind of money are we talking about?

The first cut is twelve billion dollars, followed by another of fifty billion dollars for fiscal 1987.

Isn't that a drop in the bucket for Washington?

It's peanuts, especially when we're spending a trillion a year. But Gramm-Rudman's goal is to eventually chop off two hundred billion dollars.

Now you're getting into street theater.

It could develop into a good fight, because President Reagan has no intention of cutting Star Wars. At the same time, Reagan has no problem using Gramm-Rudman as an excuse to shut down the Small Business Administration, the Job Corps, the Student Loan Program and the Department of Education.

Why did Congress vote for Gramm-Rudman?

Some voted for it because 1986 was an election year. Others voted for it because they believed the bill would embarrass the President. Still others thought Gramm-Rudman would help the President. But the majority voted for it because they didn't understand it.

Didn't Congress realize that there would be a day of reckoning if they threw in with Gramm-Rudman?

Most of those who say they are for it are hoping the law will be declared unconstitutional. They even put a clause in the bill saying it had to be brought to the courts as soon as possible.

Where does the President stand on Gramm-Rudman?

Nobody knows. When he signed the bill, he said he would be happy to see it tested in the courts. But now he wants the Justice Department to keep it from getting to the courts. The thinking is the President loves the *idea* of Gramm-Rudman but not the bill itself. Reagan's biggest worry is that in order to meet the requirements of the act Congress will demand that he raise taxes.

If the President won't raise taxes, what can he do to meet the Gramm-Rudman conditions?

Ask for revenue enhancers, which are not taxes although they look like taxes, feel like taxes, and taste like taxes.

Why are they called enhancers?

Because if the President called them taxes the Democrats would accuse him of going back on his pledge to lower them.

What else does the Gramm-Rudman act promise besides burlesque, tragedy, melodrama, and musical comedy?

Try soap opera.

Working for the Government

ACCORDING to the Tax Foundation, a typical American will have to work 123 days for the government to pay his taxes in 1987. Yes, for 123 days we will all be slaving for Uncle Sam before any money trickles down to us. Unlike many, I consider it an honor and a pleasure to labor for my country. I'm ready to devote my 123 days to any department in the government that will have me.

There are so many to choose from. The first thought is to put in my time with the IRS. As a taxpayer I could teach them a lot. I would like to revise the 1040 Form so people can understand it. Even if I just simplified the first three paragraphs I could become a national hero and run for President. My only fear is if I do a good job the IRS will get mad and keep me there as a hostage while they audit the last five years of my returns.

I wouldn't mind serving 123 days in the State Department. I understand you meet some very interesting people in State and you go to a lot of nice parties behind the Iron Curtain with beautiful girls named Natasha and Olga. You can't become an ambassador in 123 days, but there is nothing to prevent you from rising to Assistant Secretary of State. Give me a bucket of acid rain and a school of whales and I'll negotiate any treaty the President wants.

One of the departments I would seriously consider is Defense. What I like about the DOD is you get to spend unbelievable sums of money in a span of 123 days, and half the hardware doesn't work. Besides spending money I would be a spoiler. My dream would be to wait until the disarmament people drew up a complete arms-reduction plan and then sabotage it just as it was about to be signed.

I've never told this to anyone before, but I've always wanted to do a 123-day stint for the Justice Department. Justice lawyers have all the fun. They fight affirmative action, have oddball ideas about what the Constitution means, support prayer in school, and launch attacks against the Supreme Court.

One of the reasons I want to be part of Justice is it would give me a chance to sit next to Attorney General Ed Meese and devise a defense for him when he is asked why he covered up evidence during the Irangate investigation. Ed has had problems with his Irangate alibis and he needs somebody for 123 days to make his tales jibe with the facts.

Although I'm big on the Justice Department, I doubt if I want to work for the CIA. They're always giving you lie detector tests and truth serum, and I am in deathly fear they're going to find out what I did with the money which was supposed to have been turned over to all the sleazeball arms dealers in the Middle East with the CIA's blessing. If I worked for the CIA I know it would take less than 123 days to wring me dry.

The one spot left where I could serve my government for 123 days is the White House. It would be interesting and at the same time restful. Everybody has a different opinion as to what it's like to be on the inside. Don Regan says toiling at the White House is nothing to write home about. Yet Ollie North and Admiral John Poindexter both say it's a great place because you can do anything you want to and they leave you alone.

The Gadhafi Fantasy

EVERY New Year I change fantasies. Last year's was about football commissioner Pete Rozelle coming to me and saying, "We'd like you to sing the 'Star-Spangled Banner' at the opening of the Super Bowl." To which I reply, "I can't sing." And he responds, "Then hum it."

I've replaced last year's model with a new one and it concerns Libyan leader Moammar Gadhafi. Make no mistake, I wish only good for the Colonel, but I have to dream.

My fantasy starts as I am taking my morning jog in the Libyan desert. I pass a tent and hear moaning from inside.

"What's up?" I ask one of the guards.

"Colonel Gadhafi has a toothache," he replies.

"That's terrible. Gadhafi shouldn't suffer like this after what he has done for the world. I have an Uncle Herman in New York who is the foremost specialist in tooth pain."

Gadhafi comes out of the tent. "How soon can he get here?"

"Twelve hours if you don't hijack his plane."

The Colonel says, "All right. But if he hurts me I'm going to blow up twelve department stores."

"Don't worry about Uncle Herm. He did all of the Ayatollah's root-canal work."

"Well, hurry and call him."

"Here he comes now," I say. My uncle steps out of a plane with his black bag. After being introduced to Gadhafi, Uncle Herm says, "It's a great honor to be working on your mouth, Colonel. I've seen it on television many times, and I've said to my wife, 'Boy would I like to get a crack at his teeth.' So sit over here on this anthill in the blazing hot sun and let me take a look. Oh, is this bad; oh, is this bad.'' Uncle Herm stuffs all the cotton he possibly can down Gadhafi's throat and starts to drill. It doesn't take long for Herm to hit a nerve, and for the Colonel to shriek. When Herm wearies of drilling one tooth he goes to the next one. Then he pulls a few to break up the monotony.

Every time Gadhafi complains, Uncle Herm tells him to "spit."

Two hours later Uncle Herman says, "Okay, we got all the preliminaries out of the way; we better break your jaw now and rewire it."

"Why wire?" Gadhafi mumbles.

"Because if we don't wire, every tooth will fall out of your head. I hate to say this, Colonel, but you've been so busy training terrorists to blow up innocent women and children that you're not brushing your teeth twice a day. I have to break your jaw to do the job you should have done with your toothbrush."

Uncle Herm breaks Gadhafi's jaw and then rewires it. Unfortunately the wire Herm uses is rusty and the Colonel develops lockjaw.

"Don't worry, Colonel," Uncle Herm says. "I know the greatest specialist for lockjaw in the world."

Herm suggests he fly to London and see him. When the Colonel gets to the clinic, the lockjaw specialist turns out to be Uncle Herm.

"This is a terrible mouth," he says to Gadhafi. "Who broke it?"

"Youfffdid," Gadhafi says through clenched teeth.

"The work does look familiar. I think I'll have to break it again."

Gadhafi dashes out of the clinic and takes the next plane back to Tripoli. As he is being escorted out of the airport the whole place blows up. Unbeknownst to the Colonel, the bomb was planted by terrorists who had been trained and financed by Libya.

As Gadhafi lies on the floor, full of glass shards, Uncle Herm shows up. "You look terrible. I guess we're going to have to operate right here. I hope it's all right if I don't use anesthesia."

"Why no anesthesia?" gasps Gadhafi.

Uncle Herm responds, "The guy whose fantasy this is asked me not to."

Death in the Afternoon

ACCORDING to my contract, I am entitled to write one column a year about taxi drivers. I don't always do it.

And speaking of taxis, what has happened in the United States is that more and more cabdrivers are being recruited from overseas. Our hack companies have their agents out on every road from Vietnam to the Vale of Kashmir, scouting out Persians, Ethiopians, Sudanese, Syrians, and Cossacks. In his own way, each driver is a freedom fighter, determined not only to risk his life for his country, but his passenger's as well.

"Why so many foreign cabdrivers in the U.S.?" I asked Fleetstreet, a Washington taxi-company owner.

"American taxi drivers have lost their courage. They stop for red lights, slow down in school zones, and pull over to the curb to let an ambulance go by. My foreign drivers have never seen a red light. They barrel through intersections at sixty miles an hour, jump lanes, honk their horns, and don't know what the word 'yield' means."

"How do you find them?"

"We have people all over the world looking. I just received this cable from our man in New Delhi. He found a 6'7" Sikh who has slam-dunked four cabs in less than thirty days."

"He sounds like an excellent prospect."

"When it comes to driving taxis, the Sikhs are known as the 'warrior class.' I have one problem. New York is after him also. It's hard to compete with New York because we have nothing here to compare with their Queensboro Bridge gridlock."

"How do you persuade them to come?"

"I assure them that as soon as they clear immigration, they can work the airport. We promise our people that they can drive as fast and as recklessly as they did in the old country. This prevents them from getting homesick."

"Don't you lose a lot of cabs that way?"

"Not as many as you would think. They may be crazy drivers, but they're all insured."

"I've been driven by Iranians and Iraqis, Indians and Pakistanis, and Ethiopians and Somalis. Since these nationalities are always at each other's throats, do you find any dissension amongst the cabbies in Washington?"

"No, on the contrary, they get along fine. If they are going to attack each other, it won't be because of politics. It will be over their place in line or because they're bored with waiting too long for a fare at National Airport."

"When you recruit a driver from overseas, do you teach him how to find Washington streets and addresses?"

"We never force a cabdriver to learn anything about the city unless he wants to. Our position is if the passenger doesn't know where he's going, why should he expect a Peruvian to have any idea?"

"What's the life span of a foreign cabdriver?"

"It depends. I've known some who lasted two years. And I've known others who have bought the store in six weeks."

"Have you ever hired foreign drivers who become unhappy here and then leave Washington?"

"All the time. They might hear from one of their countrymen that it's much more fun to drive in a snowstorm in Boston, or if they really want to slide down mountains, they should move to San Francisco, or someone tells them they haven't lived until they have driven on the ice-filled Kennedy Expressway in Chicago. If they want to go I won't keep them. I've never stopped a cabdriver from improving himself. The great thing about foreign cabdrivers is that no matter how long they're here they never lose the killer instinct."

No Apologies

AT the end of each year a pundit must examine his work and confess to any mistakes he or she committed either by accident or through malice. Having searched through my scrapbook for 1985, I was amazed to discover I had made none. Every prediction was right on the money and every story not only checked out for authenticity but read better than the original. It was indeed a banner year, not only for myself, but also the readers.

The first major prediction which got me off to a good start was that Reagan and Gorbachev would never attend a summit conference in Geneva because both men were afraid to fly.

This was followed by another scoop when I wrote last February, "Teddy Kennedy will throw his presidential hat into the ring before '86, causing all the other Democratic candidates to withdraw." I bet my life on this story because I got it while bowling with Tip O'Neill.

Not all the columns dealt with politics. Early in April I wrote an open letter to Coach Mike Ditka of the Chicago Bears, warning him that he would become the laughingstock of football if he ever sent in a lineman called "The Refrigerator."

Probably the one most people laughed at was my prediction that once the British royal yacht neared U.S. shores, Princess

Diana would jump overboard and seek political asylum. Well, people aren't laughing anymore, particularly since U.S. Immigration turned her down.

You didn't have to be a genius to foresee what would happen in the Justice Department. I said early on that the first time Attorney General Ed Meese misinterpreted the intentions of the founding fathers, as written in the Constitution, Reagan would force him to resign and become the U.S. ambassador to Ireland.

I guess there are not many pundits who take as much interest in the economy as I do. Therefore I can point with pride to a tip I gave my readers in March. "Sell all your stocks because the Dow Jones will plunge below 500 points by the end of the year." I still get letters from grateful investors who got out of the market in time.

I don't take credit for everything written about Jerry Falwell in 1985. But I can't help reminding people that it was I who foretold that the Rev. Falwell would go to South Africa and hug Bishop Tutu to dramatize Falwell's anti-apartheid stand. I also predicted that when Falwell returned to the States he would urge all his followers to dump their gold Krugerrands down the toilet until Premier Botha came to his senses.

It wasn't a crystal ball, but just plain shoe leather that made me write that Defense Secretary Cap Weinberger would turn down any increase in the defense budget so domestic spending would not suffer.

People think I'm some sort of seer because a few months ago I predicted that National Security Advisor Bud McFarlane would be safe in the White House as long as Don Regan was Chief of Staff. An unnamed inside source in the administration confirmed this and confided to me the President told him if he had to choose, Regan would be the one to go.

How many of you were aware of this one before I wrote it?

''The Bhagwan Shree Rajneesh will sell all his Rolls-Royces so that he can buy CBS and fire Dan Rather.''

I'm sorry to say that many of my colleagues prefer to sit in their ivory towers rather than go out and scramble for the facts. Does being 100 percent right in 1985 make a person perfect? I don't believe that it's my place to say. Let the record speak for itself.

The Marcos "Landslide"

ONE of the most miraculous political victories in modern times took place in San Nicolas, the hometown of Philippine President Ferdinand Marcos.

Marcos received 13,643 votes, and his opponent, Mrs. Corazon Aquino, got 0. There has never been an election consensus like it in the free world.

I called Manila and congratulated one of Marcos' campaign managers for the outstanding job his people did in San Nicolas.

"We were hoping to have a larger turnout to add to our plurality."

"How can you be sure that if you'd had a larger turnout, the voters would have gone for Marcos?"

"No one can be sure of anything in a Filipino election; you just hope for the best."

"Weren't you surprised that not one voter in San Nicolas cast a ballot for Mrs. Aquino?"

"We had a gut feeling it might happen. Marcos ran an awfully good campaign promising the people rice and housing, jobs, and a discount on office space in any building Mrs. Marcos owns in New York City."

"There are some people in the United States, and I'm not one of them, who insist that there must have been at least token opposition to the President. They can't believe the shut-out for Aquino."

"There was opposition to the President. You can't have a democracy without opposition. Many people in San Nicolas wanted to vote for Mrs. Aquino."

"Why didn't they?"

"They couldn't get out of their homes."

"Why not?"

"Because the Army had surrounded them to protect them from the supporters of Marcos. Our main objective in the election was to save lives. I will tell you about one man in San Nicolas. His name is Juan and he was mad at Marcos because someone had put his father and mother in jail. So he said he was going to go to the polls and cast a ballot for Aquino."

"We said very politely, 'Juan, don't be a troublemaker. Mrs. Aquino has no experience. Only Marcos can get your mother and father out of jail.'

"But he said he would still vote for Aquino. So when he dropped his ballot in the box, we fished it out and tore it up and made him eat it. Then when Juan tried to vote again, we arrested him for voting twice in a presidential election. Now Juan is with his mother and father in jail. President Marcos believes in keeping the family together."

"It's fortunate you stopped Juan. Otherwise Mrs. Aquino would have received *one* vote in San Nicolas."

"He would never have slipped by us. Our poll watchers are too good. San Nicolas is very dear to President Marcos' heart and it would be terrible for him if the outside world saw that there were people in his hometown who did not want him to serve again."

"Did you use force to prevent many people from voting?"

"Not many. It was easier to buy their votes. We have a hospital and orphans' fund just for the elections. It's the First Lady's pet charity."

"Then I assume that you are satisfied with the results in San Nicolas?"

"One is never satisfied in an election. We know we could have done better."

"If you could sum it up, what made Marcos win so handily in San Nicolas?"

"Charisma."

Christa's Legacy

Awhile back I wrote a piece about schoolteachers going up in space. I speculated about what kinds of candidates my own teachers at PS 35 would have made if they had applied for the trip. It was a light piece because, like most Americans, I never dreamed that anything could happen to the flight of the shuttle Challenger.

While watching all the replays of the Challenger disaster, I got to thinking about teachers. Although Mrs. Christa McAuliffe wasn't a professional astronaut, she did leave behind a wonderful legacy.

Consider this:

For the past fifteen or twenty years, America's teachers could not have been held in lower esteem. They were underpaid, underrated, and blamed for anything that went wrong in our schools.

It seemed as if the only time we saw teachers on TV was when they were on strike, or being arrested for child abuse. The perception was that teachers were people who taught because they couldn't make it in the *real* world.

Except for covering vandalism and crime in the schools, the media ignored what was going on in the classroom. And with reason; if teachers were teaching, and students were learning, it wasn't news—that is, until the destruction of Challenger.

Suddenly our schools received more attention than they have ever been given before. Seven brave people died that morning, but it was the death of a schoolteacher that made our children cry.

When the TV cameras entered the nation's classrooms to record their grief, we saw principals and teachers fighting back their own tears as they tried to comfort the students.

The cameras not only focused on teachers, but also panned to the agonized faces of the students. They showed teacher to pupil and pupil to teacher—and in that moment of sadness we witnessed the educational process at its best.

When these pictures came into our homes we were reminded of something we tend to take for granted: the role teachers quietly play in the lives of children.

The lesson was not just for grown-ups. You got the feeling that the students had gained a new respect for teachers as well.

It went something like this: "Christa was a teacher, and Christa died in space, but it could have been anybody's teacher—including mine."

So what was Christa McAuliffe's legacy?

When Sputnik went up and we knew that the Russians were ahead in the space race, there was a great clamor to educate American children and make our schools second to none. Then, after the successes of our own space program, the clamor died down. Education was dropped as our number-one priority.

At least it was until recently. After that one horrifying moment in Florida, things changed again. The parent-teacher-pupil bond that had been fraying for a generation seemed to be whole again.

Christa McAuliffe's gift to us is not in the skies but here on Earth. From everything you can read, she was a teacher before she went up and she intended to be a teacher when she returned. In death her legacy gives her fellow professionals new dignity and honor. Thanks to Christa each one of them can say with pride, "I'm a teacher too."

Ask the Pothole Man

THE Pothole Man is happy to report that the mailbox has been overflowing with letters. Thanks to a cold and wet winter, potholes are now flowering in neighborhoods that have never seen them before.

Unfortunately there is still a lot of ignorance about the care and feeding of potholes—and that's where the Pothole Man comes in.

Our first letter is from Laurie Kramer, who writes:

I have a beautiful pothole in front of my house measuring two feet by two feet, and one and a half feet deep. What would you advise me to plant in it?

Dear Laurie,

What you plant in your pothole depends on whether you want to use it for show or eat from it. Since I assume it will be run over at least two hundred times a day, I would plant something low to the ground, such as petunias for show, or dwarf pear trees for food. Make sure you have a good drainage system in your pothole, or it will fill with water and become a breeding ground for malaria mosquitoes.

The second letter, from Connie Coopersmith, asks us to discuss pothole ownership:

We bought a home last month with an art deco pothole that the previous owner insisted was at least fifty years old. Actually, we bought the house for the hole. Now it turns out we do not own the pothole—the city does. Can we still fertilize it and treat it as our own?

Dear Connie,

It is interesting that the city would claim ownership of a pothole on your street. Municipal authorities, when called, not only deny they own the pothole, but attempt to prove your street is not even within the city limits. Consider the street hole your own.

A letter from Joey Fontana deals with fixing up potholes:

My hobby is finding rundown potholes in the neighborhood and improving them so they look almost brand new. I drive a cement truck so I think I do as good a job as anyone. The other day at Cathedral and 44th Street, I made a beaut—I mean a Greyhound bus could disappear in it and never be heard from again.

Well, this guy, Charlie Guggenheim, who owns a house right there, said I was getting too close to *his* pothole. He told me to fill it in or take it somewhere else. I'm not taking it anywhere. Am I right?

Dear Joey,

You certainly are. Guggenheim should be pleased with having your pothole in front of his house. If he had any class he'd fill it up with humus and plant some tulips. Recently the courts have ruled that a pothole belongs to all the people. Our founding fathers wanted America's potholes to be shared by everyone—from sea to shining sea. By enlarging and widening the pothole in front of Guggenheim's house you enhanced all the real estate values in the area.

Dana Williams wrote one of the most interesting letters:

There was this pothole at the end of the block and it kept getting larger and larger. Every time a car went "kerplunk," an axle broke. Then one day a neighbor planted a bush in it so people could see it. The following Friday, for no reason at all, the bush caught on fire and burned. The next morning a city repair truck came by and filled in the hole. My question: Was the burning bush a miracle?

Dear Dana,

I'm not sure about the burning bush, but the city truck showing up to repair the pothole sure as heck was.

Bush Leans Right

No matter how hard Vice President George Bush works to convince people that in his heart he is really right, there are still some Republicans who aren't buying it.

I thought Niblock would be convinced of Bush's conservative credentials after the Vice President addressed a dinner for the late William Loeb in New Hampshire, the New York State Conservative Party, and Jerry Falwell's Liberty Federation (the old Moral Majority) in Washington, DC. But I was wrong.

"I don't care what right-wing groups he addresses—the man's a closet middle-of-the-roader," Niblock said.

"That's not fair," I retorted. "George Bush is as much a conservative as I am, possibly even more. He believes in prayer in school, overthrowing the government in Angola, and the sanctity of Jesse Helms' political fund-raising campaigns."

"Bush only says that to get votes," Niblock said. "What he really wants to do is hijack the conservatives pledged to Jack Kemp."

"Perhaps he started out with that goal. But now George is convinced the conservative way is the true one. Have you seen where he stands on pornography?"

Niblock sneered, "He's coming out against pornography awfully late."

"As vice president he couldn't afford to get the pro-pornographers mad. But now that Reagan is a lame duck, Bush is his own man."

"I still don't think he is far enough to the right."

"George has hugged Jerry Falwell. Falwell has embraced ex-President Marcos. By any stretch of the imagination, the person who embraces the man who embraced Marcos cannot be considered a man of the center."

"It all sounds like left-wing opportunism," Niblock said. "What I think is that Bush's presidential election team decided the only way to beat Kemp was to have the Vice President show up at more conservative dinners and prayer breakfasts than Jack does. They keep feeding Bush speeches about Nicaragua, abortion, and the family, hoping that people will forget what he said about Reagan's voodoo economics."

"When will you be convinced that Vice President Bush is truly a man of the right?"

"When he attacks the gays. I don't trust any politician who doesn't harangue homosexuals."

"It's too early in the campaign to attack gays. You have to save them for the last week of the primaries."

Then I asked Niblock, "Will you grant that even if Bush isn't a hundred-percent right-wing activist at the moment, he's off to a good start?"

He replied, "Maybe, but I'd prefer he wrap himself in the flag a little more."

"He is doing the best he can. In attacking Governor Cuomo the Vice President said, '. . . He (Cuomo) is telling us to be ashamed to stand up and say we're proud of this great land and the freedom and opportunity it has made possible for generation after generation.' If that isn't wrapping yourself in the American flag I don't know what is."

"All right, let's say for argument's sake that Bush is as far to the right as Attila the Hun. Why should I give him any money when I'm already supporting another Attila the Hun?"

"Because George has a chance of being elected President of the United States and your Hun doesn't."

"Three conservative appearances don't make an ultra-right-wing candidate," Niblock said. "I'll believe he's one of us only after I see him dancing with Phyllis Schlafly to the 'Darktown Strutters' Ball.' "

The Reds Are Here, The Reds Are Here

I want you to pay close attention. Unlike Pat Buchanan, I don't consider you all Communists just because you refuse to support President Reagan's request to send money to the Contras in Nicaragua. It's quite possible that you're either a dupe of Daniel Ortega, or you're a registered Democrat. In any case, they love you in the Kremlin.

I know I told you the last time out that twenty-seven million dollars would be sufficient to support the freedom fighters in their battle to win their homeland. Well, now it's no longer a fight over one country, but rather a life-or-death struggle for Western Civilization. Are you going to let the western hemisphere go down the drain for a lousy one hundred million? If your answer is yes, then go back to Russia where you belong.

What, you ask, am I going to get for my money? You're going to get a first-class fighting force with guns, ships, tanks, helicopters, and a light at the end of the tunnel.

The answer is yes, they can buy all that for one hundred million dollars—though supplemental funds may have to be added at a future date to protect the stuff when it arrives.

Now I want to talk to you about San Diego. You all have an approximate idea where San Diego is. It's located on America's doorstep to Central America. A nice clean city, it has friendly people and a sun that shines 365 days a year. Suppose I told you that if we don't give the one hundred million dollars to the Contras, Nicaraguans will march barefoot right through downtown San Diego, and continue along the coast until they reach Disneyland and turn it into a Marxist training camp.

I'm not making it up. I read it in an article by Pat Buchanan, and he worked in the White House, where they know these things. It is the administration's position that only those Americans who support Ronald Reagan's Central American requests give a damn about what happens to San Diego. The rest of you are in bed with Gorbachev whether you know it or not.

Don't shout at me. I know what's coming next. You're going to ask, if we give one hundred million dollars to the Contras does that mean we will have to send American boys to eventually fight there? The answer is an unequivocal NO— although we have to keep our options open in case the freedom fighters have trouble against the overwhelming superiority of the Sandinista Army, which is secretly supported by most of our Democratic members of the House and Senate.

I want to assure every father and mother that no one wants to see our boys in Central America, and we won't have to send them if each and every one of you goes along with sending the money instead.

You are going to have to dig deep into your pockets to make up for Leninist idiots, Marxist clergy, congressional fellow travelers, and pinko do-gooders, who would rather give the hundred million to Castro.

I believe I've made my case. The people who love this country are for Reagan's policy of involvement in Nicaragua. Those who are against it, for whatever reason, are hereby ordered to report next Monday morning to their nearest passport office to take a lie detector test.

The time for debating Reagan's adventures in foreign lands is over. Stand up now and be counted. Which side are you on? If you have forgotten ''Remember the Maine'' . . . RE-MEMBER THE MAINE!

The Vending Smashers

I N Concord, California, a customer became enraged at an automated teller and kept punching it because the machine refused to dispense eighty dollars from the man's account.

The customer was arrested and charged with malicious mischief.

This is not an isolated incident. According to police reports, so many people are beating up on automated machines that it has become this nation's most serious crime problem.

Johnny Hawke, who runs a home for battered machines, told me that more than fifty percent of all aggravated assaults are committed against coin machines.

"Upright, law-abiding citizens now think nothing of kicking a Coke machine in the groin or shoving an index finger down the throat of a coin-return slot. Priests have been known to punch out the glass panel of a cigarette machine over a two-bit misunderstanding. Vending-machine hospitals are filled with broken candy-bar racks and fractured Kleenex dispensers, while the perpetrators of these dastardly crimes are walking around scot-free."

I tried to defend the man in the street. "It's true that people shouldn't assault coin-operated machines, but you have to blame some of the violence on the public's frustration when they don't get the product they paid for."

"What kind of country would this be if everyone kicked a vending machine that didn't work?" he cried.

"What are you suggesting people do?"

"If you can't get your money back, write a letter to the company," he replied.

"I tried that once," I protested. "I couldn't spring a Sprite out of the machine and it wouldn't give me my money back. So I wrote a letter on the spot to the soft-drink people. Then I went to buy a stamp and damned if *that* machine didn't work either. So I drove a stake right through the heart of the word 'Sprite.' "

"Why did you stab the Sprite sign?"

"So there wouldn't be any witnesses to what I did to the stamp machine."

Hawke said the assaults are getting so serious that many machines are refusing to work unless they have guards. This defeats the whole idea of mechanical devices replacing people.

"Why are there so many attacks on automated tellers?"

He told me, "The automated teller muggings are acts of pure spite. People used to rob banks, now they would prefer to beat up their teller machines. Things have gotten so bad that people kick an ATM whether it makes a mistake or not."

"How do you stop the violence?"

"We want tougher criminal penalties for any premeditated attack on an automated teller, and we are insisting that anyone who hits the bulletproof glass with an umbrella be charged with assault with a deadly weapon."

"Will you catch them?"

"People are starting to wake up to the vending-machine crime wave in this country. They are furious at the bleeding heart judges who will not hand out tough sentences to abusers. Just the other day a man was accused of putting a bullet through a Laundromat machine because it missed the rinse cycle. He was sentenced to twenty years for involuntary manslaughter. The man will be out in fourteen years to shoot another washer. When he does we will all ask, 'Why did it happen again?' "

"Do you find people beat up machines more in the daytime or at night?" I asked Hawke.

"It doesn't seem to matter. They beat up the machines in the daytime to get their money back. And they beat them up at night to hear them scream."

Citizen's Watch Committee

THE best thing about the report of Attorney General Meese's Commission on Pornography is its call for "Citizen's Watch" groups to monitor what types of publications are sold in the stores. If, in the view of the group, the material is pornographic, the citizens' groups will organize a boycott, and God knows what else, to rid the store of the rot.

I don't know how the people are going to be selected for this type of work, but I would like to volunteer my services. One of my greatest fantasies has been to censor magazines and send those who sell them to jail.

What, you may ask, are my qualifications for being part of a Citizen's Watch group? For one thing, I've read many of the magazines that the Pornography Commission finds objectionable. Secondly, I know exactly where in the store such reading materials are kept. I have done a lot of dry runs since the report was published. I know how to distinguish between literature with no redeeming value whatsoever and magazines which are just trying to give me a cheap thrill.

If you elect me, I promise to go through every store in your neighborhood and dump out anything that I feel might offend the community. You can trust me that no page will be left unturned without my stamp of approval. I'm not only talking about nudity, depravity, and sexually obnoxious material, but also other stuff that might not look offensive on the cover, but when you read between the lines, could lead to crime too horrendous to mention.

Many of you may be asking, "How will the Citizen's Watch Committees perform?" The guidelines haven't been laid down yet, but I would like them to work something like this: Every member of the committee will be issued a CW armband, which will give him or her permission to go into any store suspected of selling pornographic material. If such material is found, the CW Committeeperson will throw it on the floor, pour cigarette lighter fluid on it, and start a fire in the aisle. If there happens to be a lot of pornographic material, other members of the CW Committee will stand outside and break all the windows in the store.

If the owner protests this type of treatment, the CW Committee will then organize a boycott. During the boycott the CW will take down the names of customers entering the store. These will be sent on to Ed Meese, who will put them into the Attorney General's computer so that Washington will have some idea about who is pro-pornography. Each Citizen's Watch Committee will be able to plug in to the computer in case they have suspicions about a stranger hanging around a magazine stand.

I don't want anybody to get the idea that this is some sort of vigilante committee the Attorney General's Commission is recommending. We can not prevent you from buying anything you want. But as Americans it is our right to make you damn sorry you did. The Citizen's Watch Committees are your guarantee that you won't be poisoned by filthy pictures again.

The question will come up as to what qualifies the CW Committees to decide the reading tastes of others. Their main strength is that they care about what is on sale and they're willing to do something about it. Once appointed as a CW deputy, each committee member will study at night to become

[193]

an expert in pornography. The CW's primary role is to do the job which the Justice Department, because of the Constitution, can't do on its own.

So I need your vote. Without wanting to brag, I think I'm the best man for the job. I've hung around newsstands all my life. I can spot a *Playboy* or *Penthouse* reader a mile away, and I know how to read any magazine sealed together with cellophane.

As soon as they start electing Citizen's Watch Committees in your community, please think of me—the anti-pornographer everyone can trust.

Malpractice

I⊤ had to happen sooner or later. Lawyer Dobbins was brought into the emergency room on a stretcher, rolling his head in agony. Dr. Green came over to see him.

"Dobbins," he said. "What an honor. The last time I saw you was in court when you accused me of malpractice."

"Doc, doc. My side is on fire. The pain is right here. What could it be?"

"How would I know? You told the jury I wasn't fit to be a doctor."

"I was only kidding, doc. When you represent a client you don't know what you're saying. Could I be passing a kidney stone?"

"Your diagnosis is as good as mine."

"What are you talking about?"

"When you questioned me on the stand you indicated that you knew everything there was to know about the practice of medicine."

"Doc, I'm climbing the wall. Give me something."

"Let's say I give you something for a kidney stone and it turns out to be a gallstone. Who is going to pay for my court costs?"

"I'll sign a paper that I won't sue."

"Can I read to you from the transcript of the trial? 'Lawyer Dobbins: Why were you so sure my client had tennis elbow? Dr. Green: I've treated hundreds of people with tennis elbow, and I know it when I see it. Dobbins: It never occurred to you that my client could have an Excedrin headache? Green: No, sir. There were no signs of an Excedrin headache. Dobbins: You and your ilk make me sick.' "

"Why are you reading that to me?"

"Because, Dobbins, since the trial I've lost confidence in making a diagnosis. A lady came in the other day limping . . ."

"Please, doc, I don't want to hear it now. Give me some Demerol."

"You said during the suit that I dispensed drugs like a drunken sailor. I've changed my ways, Dobbins, I don't prescribe drugs anymore."

"Then get me another doctor."

"There are no other doctors on duty. The reason I'm here

is that after the malpractice suit the sheriff seized everything in my office. This is the only place I can practice.''

"If you give me something to relieve the pain, I'll personally appeal your case to a higher court.''

"You know, Dobbins, I was sure that someday you would be wheeled in here.''

"How did you know that?''

"At the trial I made a mental note that you were a prime candidate for a kidney stone.''

"You can't tell if a man is a candidate for a kidney stone by just looking at him.''

"That's what you think, Dobbins. You had so much acid in you when you addressed the jury that I knew some of it eventually had to crystallize into stones. Remember on the third day when you called me the Butcher of Operating Room 6? That afternoon I said to my wife, 'That man is going to be in a lot of pain.' ''

"Okay, doc, you've had your ounce of flesh. Can I now have my ounce of Demerol?''

"I better check you out first.''

"Don't check me out, just give the dope.''

"But in court the first question you asked me was if I had examined the patient completely. It would be negligent of me if I didn't do it now. Do you mind getting on the scale?''

"What for?''

"To find out your weight. I have to be prepared in case I get sued again and the lawyer asks me if I knew how heavy you were.''

"I'm not going to sue you.''

"You say that now. But how can I be sure you won't file a writ after you pass the kidney stone?''

"Author, Author"

I T was Monday afternoon and everyone in the White House was bent over his desk hard at work—on his book. David Stockman had inspired the entire administration to pursue writing careers.

Fiedler looked up from his typewriter. "What's the Vice President's first name?" he yelled above the din.

"I think it's Harry—no, it's George," Stretcher said. "I envy you. I'm not even up to how we took Grenada."

"My publisher said to start with Libya and work backwards. Did you have any luck with the paperback rights yet?"

Stretcher shook his head. "No, but CBS wants to see a typed manuscript. They're thinking of doing *Behind Closed Doors II*."

"Will you guys shut up?" Beerbaum said. "I'm writing the definitive chapter on Mike Deaver."

Fiedler was flabbergasted. "What right do you have to write about Deaver? You hardly knew the guy."

"I knew him well enough to buy a BMW from him."

Fiedler was red in the face. "Deaver belongs to me. I taught him everything he knows about acid rain."

"Okay, I'll give you Deaver for your book if you give me Meese for mine," Beerbaum said.

Fiedler thought it over and then said, "It's a deal. But from now on I'm going to write about anybody in the White House I want to."

The phone rang and Stretcher picked it up. "Aw gee, Mr.

Regan, I'd love to do it but I'm working on my book, *Why Reagan's Roses Failed*. Is it really important? . . . It's for the President to read to a joint session of Congress before we go into Nicaragua. . . . Wow, this is a moment in history. Can you tell me exactly who was in the Oval Office when the President decided? . . . Don't yell, don't yell. I'll write the damn speech.''

Stretcher hung up. ''Wait until I do my observations on Regan. He'll be sorry he talked to me like that.''

Dumbarton, who had been correcting galleys, looked up and said, ''Was Bud McFarlane National Security Advisor before Al Haig or after him?''

''Haig was never Security Advisor. McFarlane took over from Clark, who replaced Richard Allen. Haig was Secretary of State and he was succeeded by George Shultz.''

''You're making a mistake including facts,'' Stretcher said. ''The publishers don't want history. They want reputations wrecked, character assassinations, and cutthroating of the first order. That's why they're offering us such huge sums of money.''

Fiedler said, ''Have you been offered a large sum of money?''

''Not yet, but my agent tells me that when they see my chapter on Pat Buchanan's tantrums, I'm a certain Book-of-the-Month-Club selection.''

The phone rang again. This time Beerbaum answered. ''Yes, Mr. President. You would like to redo your entire fiscal budget? . . . Yes, sir, it can be done, but could it wait until tomorrow? You see, I'm researching the upstairs-downstairs part of my book, and I've set up an interview this afternoon with the chef. While I've got you on the line, Mr. President, what do you eat for breakfast? . . .

Yessir, Mr. President, I'll get on the new fiscal policy right away.''

Beerbaum said, ''Was he burned up! I thought he was going to jump into the receiver with both feet.''

Fiedler said, ''You lucky dog. You can now write an entire chapter on how you were personally chewed out by Ronald Reagan.''

''I wish he had fired me,'' Beerbaum said. ''When you get canned by the President you sell a lot more books.''

Where Time Flies

You've seen them in the morning and you've seen them at night—the wild commuter drivers hurtling their cars through traffic at rush hour on the way to and from work. They'll cut in front of you, honk behind you, and force you up onto the curb. What motivates these modern-day barbarians to risk not only their own necks, but yours as well?

The answer is TIME. The people you see driving hell-bent on the streets and highways are not only saving minutes but seconds from their trips. But no one has ever asked them what they do with the time they save.

I was curious so I decided to follow several of them home.

The first one I took after was a Mercedes-Benz convertible.

It wasn't easy to follow him to his destination, but I managed to do it. As I pulled up, the driver was on the stoop, kissing his little daughter.

"Sir," I said, "I noticed you were driving pretty fast. How much time do you save by scaring everyone off the road?"

"In a twenty-mile trip I usually save two to three minutes, unless some stupid moron stalls his car at a stop sign. Tonight that dumb school bus almost made me late."

"It's hard to believe after the way you drive that you only save three minutes on a trip," I said.

"No sweat. I've been the first husband on the block to get home before anyone else for over two years. No one takes that away from me."

"What do you do with the time?"

"I beg your pardon?"

"You save two to three minutes every night, and heaven knows you take your life in your hands. Surely you must do something with the precious time."

He thought about this. "I get to kiss my daughter."

"Couldn't you kiss her three minutes later?"

"Some nights she wants to go to bed early, and the three minutes is the difference between seeing her and not seeing her at all. I'm a good father. I always make sure that I'm pulling into the driveway as my daughter runs out of the house, even if I have to hit a school bus to do it."

I left him relating to his child how he almost hit a cement truck so he could be home in time to tell her a story.

The next car I followed was a speeding Oldsmobile filled with car-poolers.

I stopped them at the first turnoff. "I notice you're going pretty fast, gentlemen. Could you please tell me what you plan to do with the few minutes you saved?"

"I'm going to write a book," said one.

"I'm going to wash my dog," the second one told me.

"I'm going to reshingle the roof," the third said.

The driver said, "I'm going to watch tapes of the last three Redskins games."

"Okay, tell me honestly, why the reckless speed?"

"There are four of us," the man behind the wheel said. "If I didn't jump over Volkswagens, I'd get my last two passengers home late and then they would ask someone else to be the driver."

The final car I followed was a Japanese sportscar. I don't think I would have ever been able to catch up with him if he hadn't crashed into an eight-wheeler refrigerator truck.

"Well," I said, "you didn't save any time getting home tonight."

"I wasn't trying to save any time going home," he told me as he picked up the door and threw it in the back seat.

"Don't kid me. Are you denying that you were going at seventy-five miles per hour?"

"I don't deny that. I'm denying the part about me going home. I was leaving the house to go to work."

"What difference does a few minutes make?"

"The difference of me or Manny getting the number-one parking place in the TV station garage."

Hangar Sale

SINCE the Reagan administration has put parts of the United States up for sale, everyone is bidding on our more valuable properties. A British company has tendered an offer through the N. M. Rothschild Bank to buy Dulles and National airports. The Brits are willing to pay one billion dollars. This seems like a lot of money if you're thinking landing strips. But it's a spit in the bucket if you're talking real estate.

Jeff Doranz, America's leading developer, hopes to outbid the British for the two airports. He believes that air terminals have a great untapped potential for mass housing.

"If you bought Dulles and National airports would you tear down the present terminals?" I asked him.

"On the contrary, the terminals are very decorative and fit in with our housing and shopping architecture."

"Will you still permit planes to take off and land?"

"We will not only permit it, but encourage it. What we'll be selling with our condominiums is *access* to the airports. We're aiming our sales at the person who is always on an airplane. As a matter of fact, we want to put flashing signs at the ends of the runways which will say, 'If you lived here you'd be home now.'"

"Where do you plan to construct your housing developments?"

He took out his blueprints. "Right here, along both sides of the runway. We want to make this place a family community. On warm nights we hope people will sit in their backyards, drink beer, and wave at the passengers as they whiz by."

"The houses don't leave much room for the pilots to land," I pointed out.

"The pilots don't need much room as long as the townhouse gaslights act as beacons for them."

"Will the frightful noise be a negative factor for your home-owners?"

Doranz said, "Why should it be? Residents will have pride of ownership in what the airports do. When they hear a roar overhead they'll sleep better knowing Texas Air is bringing another payload safely home."

I studied Doranz's blueprints. "What's this circle located in the middle of the runway at National Airport?"

"That's the golf course."

"You are building a golf course on the National runway?"

"Where would *you* build one if you owned an airport? As the primary developers we don't have much space to work with. We have the Potomac on one side and this highway on the other. The only place for golf links is here, unless the government wants to sell us I-95."

"How do you play golf with the planes taxiing up and down all day long?"

"Golfers who buy into the development will have priority over the planes. Our flight tower will be instructed to hold up all landings and takeoffs until the members play through."

"Where are you going to put the shopping center?"

"Here on the first three floors of our forty-story hotel and office tower. We have to build up because we can't spread out."

"Does that mean you will raze all these giant repair hangars?"

"Of course not. We're just going to move the planes out and the cars in. Airplane hangars make marvelous parking garages. When you buy a terminal you have to use every inch of the ground for revenue. The reason airports are losing money these days is they spend too much on servicing planes.''

''Tell me the truth, Doranz. If you buy National and Dulles airports from the government, will you still allow air traffic to use them?''

''We will for the time being. But all bets are off if we need another golf course.''

This I Believe

THE rumor in Washington is that President Reagan has made up his mind he's going to take all of us with him when he goes. This decision was made after Mr. Reagan saw *Rambo* for the twenty-sixth time. The information came from one of my many White House sources.

''The President is tired of being Mr. Nice Guy,'' he told me. ''He has decided to show some muscle so people will sit down reasonably together and cry 'uncle.' ''

''I'm all for that,'' I said. ''What can I do to help him?''

''You can believe him,'' my White House source said.

''Believe him about what?''

''About everything. Do you believe that the Sandinistas can walk to Harlingen, Texas, in two days?''

''I'll believe less if you want me to.''

"Exactly two days—no more, no less."

"I believe it," I said.

"Do you believe that the Nicaraguans invaded Honduras with fifteen hundred soldiers as their first step to a takeover of Mexico?"

"If I didn't believe that there would be nothing to believe."

"Then do you believe that the only thing capable of driving them back to Managua is one hundred million dollars?"

"You mean you want to give the Sandinistas one hundred million dollars to get out of Honduras?"

"No, we want to give the Contras a hundred million to boot the Sandinistas out and overthrow their government at the same time."

"That's easy to believe."

"Okay, you've passed the first part of the test. Now let's see how you do on the budget. Do you believe the Defense Department needs every nickel it can get?"

"If Mr. Reagan says it, I believe it."

"Plus a lot more money for Star Wars, Stealth bombers, and other sophisticated weapons too secret to even discuss?"

"I have never doubted our needing them."

"Then you have to believe that the President needs a supplemental donation for naval actions such as the one we saw in Libya."

"I have no problem supporting the President on everything he did in Libya."

"Then you're not against the underground atomic tests in Nevada which the President has to have if he's going to get anywhere with Gorbachev?"

"Can I make a blanket deal with you and say I support the President on the whole kit and caboodle?"

"We have to do these one at a time, otherwise the press

will say the President doesn't have the support of the American people.''

''I believe that too.''

''How do you feel about the President's arms negotiations?''

''How should I feel about them?''

''Mr. Reagan is doing everything in his power to bring about an agreement.''

''I believe it.''

''Do you believe that in a nuclear war, which neither side can hope to win, we could still come out on top?''

''I haven't believed that up until now.''

''Think about it. Doesn't it make sense?''

''If it makes sense to the President, it makes sense to me.''

The White House man seemed very pleased with our session. ''How do you feel about prayer in school?''

''I don't believe in it.''

''I thought you supported the President.''

''I do on killing Sandinistas. Do I have to support him on prayer in schools?''

''In our administration you can't have one without the other.''

The Happy Freshman

THE following scene, or something like it, is being played out all over this country.

"Hi, Dad. The reason I came home is that I just had a great idea."

"What's that, son?"

"I want to go to college this fall. I'll make a wonderful student."

"But you're thirty-five years old. Why didn't you go to school when I begged you to seventeen years ago?"

"I was trying to find myself."

"All those years?"

"It took me longer than I thought it would. Aw c'mon, Dad. What can it cost you—a lousy five grand a year."

"Colleges don't cost five grand a year anymore. They cost fifteen grand. While you were out searching hither and yon for yourself, the admissions people were multiplying everybody's tuition by three."

"I always suspected you didn't want me to have an education."

"It's nothing personal, son, but after you left to work as a bartender, I decided to invest the money we had set aside in something more meaningful, like my retirement. The truth is, both your mother and I had decided you were on your way when you became night grillman at the Burger King."

"Boy, that is something—that is really something. I never

thought you'd take my education money and squander it on your old age."

"I know it's selfish, but how could we know after all these years that you would have the urge to learn? The offer I made to you when you were eighteen years old was not open-ended."

"Look, if I go now I'll graduate when I'm thirty-nine."

"You'll be the oldest student to matriculate."

"No, I won't. I know a lot of guys who will be older. You remember Henry Landwirth, the guy who played in the band I managed after I gave up Burger King? He's only a sophomore and he's forty-five."

"Did he find himself?"

"He says he was never lost. He claims he just needed a break after high school before he started college."

"Why is he going to school now?"

"He decided that without a college diploma you are nobody. With a sheepskin he feels he can charge twice as much to play gigs on New Year's Eve."

"What do you want to study?"

"I don't know, Dad. I figure I'll go to college and something will turn me on."

"You're telling me you want to go back to school and you don't know what you want to be?"

"I'm not one to go to college just to get a good job. It must be a meaningful experience to cherish forever."

"Good point. But you'd be so far ahead of the game if, at age thirty-five, you knew what you wanted to do."

"If you won't give me the money, I'll work my way through college."

"What a wonderful idea. It will give you moral fiber."

"But if I have to work I'll be cheated out of what everyone says should be the happiest days of my life."

"If you could just give me some hint about your goals, I might reconsider your request."

"Give me a break, Dad. Just because I found myself doesn't mean I have any idea about what I want to do."

House With a View

Thanks to the uncertainty abroad, many Americans have put their overseas travel plans on hold. Instead they are desperately trying to rent houses in the U.S. at the seashore and in the mountains. Newspapers are chock full of classifieds for summer rentals. The problem is that the properties are not necessarily what they are cracked up to be. Because people rarely get to see the summer homes they rent in advance, they have to take the description in the advertisement on faith. Sometimes this is a mistake.

It took me seven months to break the code for summer rentals, but it was worth it.

For example, when you read, "Charming two-bedroom, one-bath ranch house in forested area. Sleeps twelve, 20-minute drive to town," they're really talking about a matchbox in the woods that sleeps twelve if everybody takes turns sleeping throughout the day and night. The house is indeed twenty minutes from town—if you drive one hundred miles an hour.

Here's one: "Magic cottage overlooking the sea. Always a cool breeze blowing. Five thousand dollars for season. A steal due to minor work going on this summer." The minor work is an addition to the breakfast room and a new kitchen. The breeze is blowing through a hole in the side of the house.

This is one of my favorites: "House for rent by owner. Completely redone. Five bedrooms and playroom in basement. Color TV in family room. Swings, wading pool and sandbox on lawn. Fenced-in backyard. No children of any kind."

When advertising homes, people use the word "dramatic" quite a bit. "Dramatic four-bedroom house in town, a few minutes from beach." What makes this house dramatic is that in order to get to the beach, you have to run by a Hell's Angels clubhouse on the corner.

Beware of an advertisement which claims the house is "on the water," because that's very likely where it is.

A property that has the word "secluded" in the ad means no one will be able to find it.

I am not sure what a "sparkling" home means, but the word is usually used when an owner has little else to brag about.

"Spectacular" is the same as "sparkling." The only difference is "spectacular" has one and a half baths instead of one.

A "new contemporary" is a house that was built in the early sixties. An "old contemporary" could mean anything, and usually does.

If you see an advertisement which reads, "Unusual house built by owner," it means the dining room is in the basement and the washer and dryer are located in the bedroom.

Some people prefer the word "quaint." Now "quaint" could mean having to stoop to get into the front door or a climb up to a two-room apartment over the garage.

Here's one to look out for: "nestled," as in "Nestled in the forest by a stream." Houses like these always have plumbing problems, and because they are "nestled" no one will come out from town to fix them.

Even if you're not renting a summer place it's worth reading the real estate ads, because that's where some of the best fiction in the country is being printed.

Hell No, We Won't Go

THIS is the best year we've had for not going to Europe in a long, long time.

It's even better for those who weren't going there in the first place. Simply stated, the reason is that it has become very chic to say that you're staying home. Last Sunday I overheard the following comments at a party:

"Gloria and I have canceled our plans to go to Venice because of terrorism," Sherman said.

Davidov said, "We canceled all of Scandinavia because of the Soviet fallout. Too bad, because we could have met up with each other."

"I think terrorism is a better excuse not to go to Europe," Clinton piped up. "You never know where it's going to strike next."

Lincoln told us, "We have a better reason than either terrorism or fallout. We're not going because of the French. When they would not let our fighter planes fly over France I said to Myra, 'That does it. Scratch Paris and the Riviera too.' "

Arch Trinkle said, "We're not going because our children begged us not to go. They said they wouldn't be able to enjoy their summer if they knew we were touring abroad. Ordinarily, we don't let our children tell us what to do, but we made an exception for this trip to Europe."

Sumteem was holding a hot dog in his hand. "I wasn't going this year because everyone else was. Now that no one's going I'm telling everybody I canceled because I didn't want to be over there alone."

I tried to bring some sense to the discussion. "If you don't go, the other side will feel they have won the battle."

"You mean the Russians who let their nuclear plant melt down outside Kiev?"

"No, I mean the terrorists who have been trying to drive all the Americans out of Europe. Your job is to show them you are not afraid."

"Why do you say *your* job instead of *our* job?"

"Since I wasn't planning to go in the first place, I have no reason to cancel. The way I see it, the American tourist who was planning to go to Europe should still go, if for no other reason than to show the flag—like in the song, 'Over there, over there, send the word, send the word we'll be there.' ''

"It's easy for you to say *we* should go because we're the ones who have to take the fallout. You know why I'm not going to Europe?'' White said. ''Not because of terrorists or nuclear accidents, but because the dollar has lost a third of its value and you can't get bargains anymore. I can handle a nuke accident and terrorism, but I fall apart when I can't get a decent rate for my traveler's checks.''

John Haskell, who has always been a travel namedropper said, ''Let me tell you the places we're not going to this year: the Villa D'Este in Italy, the Palace in St. Moritz, the Grand Hôtel du Cap on the Riviera, the Ritz in Madrid, and Claridge's in London. Now let me tell you the restaurants we canceled.''

"Enough, Haskell. You don't have the money to stay at any of those hotels. You don't even have the money to cancel them. There is nothing worse than a tourist who says he's not going somewhere he never intended to go to in the first place.''

He replied, ''It's the truth—so help me. I could never live with myself if I lied about canceling the Ritz Hotel in Madrid. I have to look at myself in the mirror every morning.''

"There is too much defeatist talk at this party,'' I said. ''The Russians are laughing in Kiev at our panic. The terrorists are gloating in Libya, and taxi drivers from Dublin to Budapest are slashing their wrists because Americans are canceling their trips. Are we going to spend the entire summer sitting around in wicker chairs telling each other where we didn't go this summer?''

"I am,'' said Sumteem. ''But it won't be dull because I

have the slides from my previous trip to show everybody.''

''You can buy anything from Europe at Bloomingdale's,'' Mrs. Haskell said.

''Besides,'' Trinkle added, ''all the European art work worth seeing winds up at the National Gallery anyway.''

The Reason Why

THE reason I have a perfect marriage is that my wife believes I have a remedy for every piece of bad luck that befalls us.

Her faith in me is particularly strong when we're on a trip. We will be sitting on the plane waiting to take off when the pilot says, ''Ladies and gentlemen, we're sorry to inform you that we will be delayed on the runway for forty-five minutes.''

My wife immediately turns to me and says, ''What's wrong?''

Now a dumb person would reply, ''I don't know.'' But my wife would never accept that, so I reply, ''We can't take off until the Goodyear Blimp passes over the Sugar Bowl.''

We're finally in the air and are served our meal.

My wife looks at her platter. ''Why don't they put the sauce on the side instead of on top of the chicken?''

I am prepared for this question since she's posed it many

times before. I tell her, "FAA regulations require that the sauce is always to be served over the entire chicken so the passengers won't see the bird."

The plane lands, and, inevitably, it is *her* suitcase rather than mine that is lost.

She turns to me with fire in her eyes. "What happened to my bag?"

I tell her, "They must have thrown it off the plane as we passed over Kansas City."

The next question is, "What are you going to do about it?"

A wimp husband would say, "Let's report it to the airline agent so we can get it back." But that solution only arouses contempt in a woman who wants instant revenge.

I tell her, "Why don't I just wrestle those three six-foot pilots to the ground, and perhaps one of them will fess up who has your bag."

The fact that I am willing to die for my wife's suitcase is one reason she trusts me with all her questions.

We are now outside the Los Angeles terminal. "Why are there no taxis here?" she wants to know.

You have to admit that that's a reasonable question to ask me, especially since I just flew in from Washington with her a few minutes earlier.

I say, "It's 'Taxi Night' at the Los Angeles Dodger Stadium, and every woman gets in free if she has a cabdriver on her fender."

"You're just making that up."

"Probably," I say, "but it's as good a reason as I can come up with at short notice."

An hour later we're in the hotel where, as you may have already guessed, our room is not ready.

Let me set the scene for you. The three of us are in the lobby in a circle: my wife, the manager, and myself.

Ignoring the manager, my wife turns to me and says, "Why isn't our room ready?"

I pass this question on to the manager because it's obvious my wife can't talk to him since he is standing one foot away.

The manager replies, "The previous couple has yet to check out."

I feel like a translator at the Geneva peace talks. "The previous couple has yet to check out." The conversation continues in this way until our room is ready.

At last we get our room and I assume that I do not have to answer any queries for two hours.

I'm wrong. Just when I get stretched out on the bed my wife yells, "Why don't the windows open?"

"I DON'T KNOW."

"What do you mean, you don't know?"

I say, "Remember the rules. I'm entitled to one 'I don't know' per trip."

Sexual Harassment

THE Supreme Court has ruled that it is now possible to sue for sexual harassment in the office. It was a sweeping decision for the Supremes and I thought it would take care of sexual harassment once and for all.

Larry the lawyer thinks the decision was wanting. "They didn't say anything about sexual harassment in the home.

"There is a lot more of that than at the office," Larry said. "A recent survey showed that there was five times as much harassment where people dwell than where they work."

"How can you sexually harass someone in your own home?"

Larry said, "I represented a man last week in a very interesting case. One day he came home bushed and sank into a chair. Then his wife began to sexually harass him."

"How?"

"Well, first she undid his tie, and then started to rip off his shirt. My client begged her to desist. So she got mean and told him that if he wasn't going to be a good sport, he wouldn't get any dinner."

"That's a big club to hold over a guy's head."

"While the wife was trying to take off the husband's shoes, he pushed her away and told her that whatever she thought, she had the wrong idea."

"Then what did she do?"

"She refused to cook him dinner. It was too much for the husband. Having used this threat so often, he decided to sue the wife for sexual harassment in the home."

"How did it go?" I asked him.

"It was a pretty unusual trial. The wife claimed that the husband encouraged her to make passes—and on occasion even played Mantovani music in the bedroom. She testified that over the years, he had harassed her as much as she had harassed him. As a matter of fact, on the very night when the crime took place, she said her husband had pinched her, which was their sign to each other."

"That's a tough defense," I said. "What did you do?"

"I had no choice but to hold up the ripped shirt. It was the key evidence that my client did not cooperate willingly in the sexual harassment. I then called a string of witnesses to testify that the husband was too weak and exhausted to start anything. Then I called my client to the stand. He said that he never knew when he came home whether he would be harassed or not. He told of many instances when his wife ruffled his hair and tugged on his waist, and put her hands over his eyes so he couldn't see who it was."

"Was the husband emotional?" I asked.

"Yes. His chin quivered all the time he gave testimony. I finally asked him the crushing question. Why, if he thought he was being harassed, did he keep returning home? To which he replied that he didn't know where else to go for dinner."

"That must have won everyone over."

"The jury ruled against my client and in favor of the wife."

"How could they do that?" I said. "Your case was airtight."

Larry the lawyer said, "The jury told me later that I had failed to prove intent. The wife could have been sexually harassing my client, or, by taking off his tie and tearing his shirt, she could just have been preparing him for a great meal."

"Surely you're going to appeal?"

"To the highest court in the land. Only a conservative court will appreciate the significance of a ripped shirt."

The Test for Adultery

WASHINGTON has gone absolutely daft by insisting that everybody take tests to find out if we are fit to serve the country.

I was walking down Pennsylvania Avenue when a man with a clipboard stopped me and said, "Have you ever committed adultery?"

"Of course not. That would make a mockery of my marriage vows."

"Don't be a wise guy," he said. "This is a test to see if you are worthy of running for President of the United States."

"Are you saying if I haven't committed adultery I can be a candidate?"

"No, but if you have been unfaithful the public has a right to know the names of those involved. How do you feel about wife-swapping?"

"You mean wives swapping recipes and needlework designs? I have no objection as long as my meal is on the table when I get home at night." I started to walk away.

"Not so fast," a second man said as he got out of a van. "I have to give you a lie detector test to find out if what you told this gentleman is true."

"I don't want to take a lie detector test."

"If you refuse you'll never work for the Department of Agriculture as long as you live."

"I don't want to work for Agriculture. I'm happy doing what I'm doing."

"Then you have to be tested for AIDS."

"What the hell for?"

"You could have gotten infected being happy doing what you're doing."

"Beat it or I'm calling that cop over there who is having his eyes examined."

The policeman came over. "Officer," I said, "these guys are bothering me. Tell them to bug off."

The cop said, "Okay, but first I have to give you a literacy test to make sure you're not one of the aliens that should be kicked out of the country."

"I am not an alien."

The lie detector man said to the cop, "Don't let him go. My machine shows he could be a heterosexual."

"So what does that mean?" I asked.

"You have to be tested for heterosexuality," the man answered. "And if the results are affirmative your file will go to the *Miami Herald*."

The cop objected. "He can't be tested for that until I test him for dope."

"I don't know anything about cocaine," I protested. "All I'm trying to do is go to lunch."

The man who was doing the survey on adultery said, "You can't eat unless you've been tested for cholesterol."

He started taking blood out of my arm.

"I resent this!" I yelled.

"You have to have a high cholesterol count before Congress will grant you immunity."

"I don't want immunity."

"Is that because you are afraid they're going to find out about the adultery?"

"Can they do that by testing my cholesterol?"

"This government can do *anything* by testing. That's why they are so morally fit."

"Testing is wrong," I said.

Another man stepped up and started wrapping wires around my arms.

"Who are you?" I demanded.

"I'm the psychological tester for this block. Whenever someone refuses to tell if he has been an adulterer I find out what else he's trying to hide."

Quiet Diplomacy

"WHAT is our policy in South Africa?" I asked Nattily, a top-ranking source at the State Department.

"We deplore what is going on there and will take tough measures to see that the South African government changes its ways."

"What kind of measures?" I asked.

"We will threaten them with the only thing the Botha government understands—quiet diplomacy."

"What *kind* of quiet diplomacy?"

"It wouldn't be quiet if I told you, would it? I can only reveal that in our experience, the more you raise your voice, the less influence you have. But if we can go in through the back door there is always a chance that we can make a deal with Botha."

"And what if you can't?"

"Then we continue our quiet diplomacy, hoping that the South African leaders will see the light."

"Does quiet diplomacy really work?" I asked.

"All the time. We've used it in every Fascist country in the world and it's never failed."

"You mean governments have stopped beating up people in the streets after you've come in with q.d.?"

"You have to take my word for it. The quieter you are about human rights violations, the better behaved the foreign government is about putting its citizens in prison."

"What's wrong with instituting economic sanctions against South Africa?"

"They don't work."

"Then why do we have them against Cuba?"

"With Communists, they work," Nattily said. "But sanctions against a friendly Fascist power would hurt the very people we are trying to help."

"That means your chance of using sanctions could hurt our relations with South Africa?"

"Correct. I think Secretary of State George Shultz summed it up best when asked if the U.S. would levy sanctions, and he replied, 'No.' "

"What do you say to Bishop Tutu when he calls on the U.S. to invoke sanctions?"

"We don't say anything to Bishop Tutu if we can help it. Our policy is to remain neutral in South Africa."

I then asked Nattily, "Does it bother you that Botha has instituted a state of emergency and that anyone can be locked up for no reason?"

"Of course it bothers us, and we intend to bring it up at the next quiet diplomacy meeting in Pretoria. Surely you are aware that President Reagan sent Botha a very tough note about the South African martial-law edict?"

"Did it have any effect?"

"No, but that's the advantage of quiet diplomacy. Very few people know that Botha told Reagan to stuff it."

"That's our foreign policy?"

Nattily said, "Do you have a better one?"

"I might go for the sanctions if I was bankrupt for ideas."

"Forget it. We're on top of this thing. We've war-gamed it from one end of Foggy Bottom to the other. In foreign affairs there is a time to shout and a time to whisper."

"And?"

"Well, you don't hear anyone in the administration shouting about South Africa."

"So can we relax knowing that we're up to our necks in quiet diplomacy?"

"To quote the Secretary of State when asked on one of the morning news shows if we had the situation under control, his answer was, 'Yes.' "

See America First

IT happened on 3 July. The See America First Campaign had been a smashing success. Without exception, everybody turned their backs on Europe and decided to visit the U.S.A. instead. They all chose to leave on the same day.

As Conway drove down to the Beltway with his family of three children and his trunk loaded with gear, he noticed that the traffic was unusually heavy—so much so that he was stuck on a Beltway ramp and could move neither forward nor backward.

He said to his crying children, "You can't see America first without some hardship. Now either sing along with Bruce Springsteen or shut up."

After an hour, Conway rolled down his window and asked the driver in the next car what the holdup was.

The man replied, "I don't know. It says on the radio that every highway between here and Nebraska is gridlocked. The whole country started up its cars at the same moment."

"Where are they trying to get to?" Conway asked.

"Yellowstone National Park—I think."

"That's where we're going," Conway's wife said.

"We'll fool 'em," Conway told her. "Everyone thinks we're heading for Yellowstone, but we'll turn off at the next exit and go to Disney World instead."

"I wouldn't go to Disney World," the man in the next car yelled. "The fire department has just closed down Orlando, Florida, for overcrowding."

"The whole city?"

"All the way to Sarasota."

Conway's thirteen-year old daughter burst into tears, "You promised to show us America and we've been sitting here for four hours and we haven't seen anything yet."

"That's where you're wrong," said Conway. "This *is* America—cars bumper to bumper as far as the eye can see. You don't see this in the Soviet Union."

His wife said, "In the Soviet Union, we could have driven from Moscow to Leningrad by now."

"Wait. Once we get out of here we'll head straight for the Statue of Liberty. No one will be there on the Fourth of July."

A motorcycle policeman walked by.

"Officer, I would like to know what is the fastest way to get to the Statue of Liberty?"

"I wouldn't try it if I were you," the cop replied. "Manhattan is ringed with the National Guard."

"What for?"

"To put down the tourist riots. Apparently every family in America had the same reservations for the same rooms, and the only way to get people out of the lobbies was to tear-gas them."

"Has it quieted down?" Conway asked.

"It has now that the mounted police rounded up the tourists with cattle prods and put them all in Yankee Stadium."

"How long do you think it will take us to get to the Chevy Chase exit from this approach?"

"Three to four days at the most."

"But we can't survive for four days waiting to get onto the Beltway."

"You should have thought of that before you started heading west. Come to think of it, you're stuck—you can't move forward and you can't move back—so you're parking, correct?"

"I'm parking against my will."

"I don't care what the reason is. You're still illegally parked. Here's a ticket. If I find you in the same spot in a couple of hours, you'll get another one."

"This is unfair."

"I would like you to take a breathalizer test, too," the cop replied.

"What for?"

"Anybody who takes his family on an auto trip on July 3rd in the U.S. must have been drinking."

Odds on Marriage

According to an article in *Newsweek* magazine, single, educated women over thirty-five will have only a five percent chance of getting married.

Since their careers took precedence over marriage, the working woman starts looking around for Mr. Right much later in life. Too late in many cases, because he has already been captured by Little Miss Muffet, who couldn't care less about a title on her door.

How do I know all this? I have been serving as a volunteer matchmaker for my friends over the years. The hours are long and the work isn't easy.

Some weeks back a lady friend said to me, "I'm looking for Mr. Right and I want you to handle my case."

"You'll have to take a number. I now represent seven women, all of whom have asked me to find them a man."

"I insist on priority. I'm turning forty next week," she said.

"All right, but first I need a profile on you. I would like to ask you a few questions. What kind of man are you looking for?"

"I'm not fussy," she said. "Any superachiever will do."

"How about something on the order of a vice president of a large insurance company?" I suggested.

"He doesn't have to have a title as long as he is financially independent. I don't want to get involved with someone who admires me only because of my income or position."

"That sounds reasonable."

"Find me a caring, loving man who understands my many moods and will adjust to them."

"I think that's fair," I said.

"And I don't want anyone who is still in therapy."

"Now you're making it harder."

"I have very good administrative talents. Three hundred people answer to me. They say that I'm firm but fair," she said.

"Yet the word on the street is that you carry the iron fist that you use all day, home with you at night."

"People are jealous because of my fast rise to the top which prevented me from competing for the man of my dreams. I'm confident that you can find Mr. Right now because he is probably unhappily married and at this very moment searching for someone like me."

"It's not as easy to find an eligible man over forty as one would think."

"Who says he has to be over forty? Anyone twenty-one years and up may apply."

"I don't have too many suitable twenty-one-year-olds on my Rolodex," I told her.

"All I ask is that he be emotionally secure."

"You just made my task impossible."

"I want to make it perfectly clear that I am not desperate. I'm very happy with my situation. I have a lovely apartment, a large office, an American Express Card, and a cat named Sophie."

"I'm glad to hear that," I replied, "because your case, while not the most difficult, is not the easiest either. Could you give me any idea of how determined you are to find Mr. Right?"

"I'd go out with my UPS truck driver if he asked me."

"One more question: What sports do you like?"

"I adore tennis. I can wipe up the court with almost any man I play with," she said.

"Would you consider letting Mr. Right win just a few games until you know each other better?"

"I'm not that desperate."

Goodbye to Jewels

IN July of 1986 Don Regan, the President's then Chief of Staff, gave the only sensible answer to the question of economic sanctions against South Africa.

When asked by reporters about using tough measures against Pretoria, Regan replied, "Are the women of America prepared to give up all their jewelry?"

Though not the key question about South Africa, it certainly ranks up there with the important one. I hadn't realized this until Regan raised the issue about how American women felt about their jewelry.

As soon as the news article appeared, I took it down to the beach and read it to some very attractive women. Then I asked, "Who amongst you is prepared to give up your jewelry to stop apartheid?"

"Are we talking about the jewelry we already have or the jewelry we're going to get?"

"It doesn't say," I replied. "But I would assume Regan was talking about jewelry futures. My understanding is that if we lay sanctions on the South Africans it means that we will not be able to buy diamonds and gold for a very long time. Women in this country will suffer as they have never suffered before."

You could smell the fear on the beach.

"Why is the White House picking on us?" the lady asked.

"They're not picking on you, but Regan is trying to say that you can't make an omelette without cracking some eggs."

"I don't care about omelettes. I worry about my gold bracelets. My arms will be naked without them. Why can't we go along with sanctions for South Africa except for diamonds, gold, and platinum?"

"It's all or nothing. This is not my idea but Donald Regan's. It's one that the women of America must decide."

A man who wasn't in our party said, "Does it include men's gold chains as well?"

"Regan said nothing about them as far as I could see. But I would suspect eventually it would include men's jewelry as well. How do you feel about South African sanctions?"

The man put his head in the sand and said, "I don't want to talk about it."

One of the women asked, "Would the embargo include emeralds and rubies and sapphires?"

"No, but what good are emeralds, rubies, and sapphires without diamonds to make them look good? I know this is a very hard choice for every woman in America to make. At the same time, who else is going to decide it? Politically the administration can't afford to cut off women's jewels just to show South Africa how tough we can be."

One of the women had a question. "Would there be a safety net for those of us who don't have too many jewels to start with?"

I referred to the newspaper story. "There is nothing about a safety net in Regan's statement. If you want the truth, I think the administration is against sanctions and Regan wants to use the American woman to get the White House off the hook. When the administration starts feeling all the pressure in Congress to do something about South Africa, Regan will say, I wanted to but the American woman wouldn't let me. She was afraid that with sanctions she'd have nothing to put around her neck.

"Go away," one of the women said.

"There is more," I told her. "If we have sanctions against South Africa we won't get any chrome for our bathroom fixtures."

For the first time everyone looked up in horror. "That does it," the lady said. "Tell Regan we'll support Ronnie's South Africa no-sanctions policy all the way."

The Test

IT all started when someone came up with the idea of testing horses for drugs.

Then somebody else said, "As long as we're doing it for horses, why don't we test football players?" It seemed like a good idea until baseball teams complained that if the authorities were screening football players, they should do the same for baseball players. The track stars said that they wanted to be in on it too, and before you knew it, they were testing basketball players, croquet teams, wrestlers, and bowlers.

A female volleyball team in Alaska went to the State Supreme Court complaining that men were being tested ten times as often as women. The court ruled that women were entitled to equal drug checks under the law.

Although the dope screening started in sports, it soon hit the civilian population.

Politicians urged that every schoolchild in America be tested. Corporations gave all employees little paper cups as they lined up for their paychecks.

Banks demanded drug checks on customers in exchange for mortgages. No one could use a credit card unless he had a favorable report from the lab.

The Army, Navy, Air Force, and the Marines declared mandatory testing for our boys in uniform. And the White House ordered everyone from the Secretary of State to the lowly Secretary of Agriculture to bring in samples before a cabinet meeting.

SPECIMEN
THATCHER

½

2

¾

©1987 St. Mandela

President Reagan declared that everybody in Nicaragua had to be tested by the Contras, who were already tested by the CIA.

There was some hell to pay when the White House leaked a story that all heads of state would have to take a drug test before they met with the President. Prime Minister Margaret Thatcher was particularly disturbed when they sent her a kit in the diplomatic pouch.

To show that there was nothing to it, President Reagan took the test. As everyone suspected, the President passed it with flying colors, and Nancy was shown giving him a kiss when the results were announced.

Drug screening became the most serious obstacle to foreign relations.

One of the big stumbling blocks to holding a summit concerned the question of whether or not Gorbachev would take a drug test. The Soviets insisted that Mr. Reagan had to take their word that Gorbachev was not on dope. The Americans held out for on-site inspection.

Not only the White House but other branches of government are now insisting on checks for drug use. Congressional candidates are filming commercials holding up the results of their tests on television and demanding their opponents to do the same.

A suggestion to have the nine members of the Supreme Court take a test before deciding a case was greeted with stony silence by the Court. That is because the Supreme Court will have to decide sooner or later whether mandatory screening is constitutional or not. And if they take the test and fail, they could be held in contempt.

I don't wish to give the impression that everyone in Washington is being checked on a regular basis.

Many of us are just being subjected to random testing when we're in a public place.

I've been randomly tested only three times—once when I was drinking from a public water fountain outside Jesse Helms' office, once when I bought boxer shorts at Bloomingdale's, and once when I asked Attorney General Ed Meese at a press conference if he was having trouble understanding the Constitution of the United States.

The Killers

WHAT fascinates me about films depicting so much violence is not the shooting, knifing, and garroting of the good guys as well as the bad guys, but the damage done to innocent people who just happen to be on the scene.

When I watch Sly Stallone, Clint Eastwood, Arnold Schwarzenegger, and Charles Bronson blowing up buildings, smashing cars, and spraying lead with submachine guns, the first thing that comes to mind is how much hurt they inflict on everyone else in the film.

The other night I said out loud in the theater, "Is this type of picture worth it?"

"Of course it's worth it," the man in the next seat said. "It teaches the audience that violence must be met with violence."

"But look at what's up on the screen. The Super-American has wrecked six cars and an orphanage to get the bad guy. He's driving like a madman. Who is going to pay for the wrecked automobiles and the buildings that the Super-American is senselessly destroying?"

"The Super-American's liability insurance company," the man said.

"But the Super-American didn't even stop to see if the bystanders were hurt."

"What would you want him to do, hold up the movie? You have to have continuous action in this kind of film. And when you do that, a lot of innocents are going to get hurt."

"How about the Super-American's car going right through a fruit market and mowing down a Chinese laundry. Doesn't anyone in the theater care about the fruit dealer and the laundry-man?"

The man said, "That's nothing compared to the Super-American wiping out some of the country's worst villains. The only reason the Super-American is pursuing evil is because the police have failed in their job."

"Good enough, but why did he blow up the Senior Citizens' apartment building with dynamite? The bad guy still got away and now twenty families have no place to live."

"It's just a movie," the man said.

"Then why are all the kids in the theater cheering?"

The man said, "Because they identify with the Super-American—a lone warrior fighting the battle to rid the world of rot."

"If you believe in law and order, how do you feel about the Super-American hitting the bad guy over the head with a fire extinguisher?"

"The Super-American won't do it for long. As soon as he can grab the Uzi submachine gun, he'll fill the bad guy's stomach full of lead."

"Why doesn't the Super-American just turn him over for trial?"

"How can he after what they did to his brother?"

"I didn't know they did anything to the Super-American's brother."

"It was in the coming attractions. They cut it out in the final version so that they could spend more time showing the Super-American setting the villain on fire."

I said, "I can't believe what I'm seeing. The Super-American just pushed a crowded bus off the pier so that he could improve his line of fire to the hospital ship."

"You really pick up on every little thing, don't you?" the man said.

"What must our children think? They probably believe that what they see on the screen is the real thing."

"When you have every top-grossing male star in Hollywood fighting to do one of these pictures, then you realize that vigilantism is here to stay," he said.

"Even if the Super-American doesn't care a fig about constitutional rights?"

"If the audience doesn't care, why should he?"

"The Burning"

No matter how bad a military dictator you are, you can always find a friend in Senator Jesse Helms. General Augusto Pinochet, Chile's strongman, is devoted to the Senator and vice versa. Even when it comes to setting people on fire, the Senator is in the General's corner.

Not so very long ago in Santiago, a teenage boy and his girlfriend were doused with a flammable substance and set alight—the boy died.

The crime was so heinous that the Senator was one of the few people who could find anything good to say about the Pinochet government.

As a matter of fact, when Helms went to visit the good General in Santiago to pay his respects, he told reporters that he was incensed—not at what had happened, but at the way it had been reported. He said, "I am ashamed of the media in my country." When questioned about a five-hundred-million-dollar suit Pinochet was threatening against American newspapers, Helms said, "I assured President Pinochet that the major media in the United States have a tendency to be very unfair to anti-Communist governments."

What really boiled the Senator was that the U.S. Ambassador to Chile, Harry Barnes, attended the youth's funeral (which was tear-gassed by the government). This, Helms decided, was tantamount to going to a Communist rally. Helms wants the Ambassador sent home for "planting the American flag into the heart of a Communist activity."

Before you get upset at Jesse Helms, let's look at it from his standpoint. Chile is one of the few solid Fascist governments we've got in South America. You don't turn your back on a head of state just because he keeps tear-gassing his country's citizens.

Is Jesse Helms interfering with our South American policy by giving aid and comfort to Augusto Pinochet? Of course he isn't. But the Senator couldn't have dropped in at a more auspicious moment. The U.S. State Department has been trying to persuade the dictator-general to get his country to straighten up and fly right, and this was making Pinochet feel lousy. When your troops are accused of kidnapping, and jailing people, it's always good to talk to a senator who understands your problems.

You can fault Senator Helms for many things, but not for his foreign relations know-how. In complaining to the Chilean press about our ambassador, Senator Helms said that Ambassador Barnes had advised the State Department about the burnings of the two young people "in a manner calculated to produce criticism of the Chilean regime."

That says it all. Helms is going to do everything he can to get Barnes out of Chile. If he succeeds, there is only one person in the United States who is worthy of filling the post, and that is the Senator himself. Would Helms take it? That's the burning question they are asking in Santiago.

Long Live SALT II

A tall, official-looking man with a strong resemblance to George Shultz drove up to a dump site in New Jersey. He said to another man leaning on a shovel, "The President wants to bury this SALT Two treaty as quickly as possible."

"Why in New Jersey?" the man with the shovel asked.

"He didn't *say* where he wanted it dumped, but our understanding is that once it's buried here no one will ever find it again."

"Why do you want to dump a SALT treaty?"

The man who looked like George Shultz replied, "Because it's obsolete and has no relevance. It's never been signed and there is no sense abiding by its weapon limits when the Russians are constantly cheating. Now start digging."

"Are you sure you want it buried?"

"Of course I'm sure. Every part of it is dead and we must make certain that it never haunts us again."

The man with the shovel measured the treaty and began digging a hole. Then he stopped. "I just thought of something. If their side cheated on SALT Two, why are you now negotiating with them on another weapons treaty? Won't they cheat on that one too?"

"They probably will. And when they do, we'll bury that treaty as well."

The man said, "We only have so much dump space for nuclear treaties. How deep do you want me to go for SALT Two?"

The man who was the spitting image of George Shultz said, "Since it has ceased to be an effective vehicle for averting a U.S.-Soviet nuclear confrontation, I would say at least six feet."

"You want to save some of the treaty just in case you need it for later?"

"I don't want any of it," the man who looked like George Shultz said angrily. "Now hurry up—I have to get back to the office."

A car drove up and a man who looked exactly like Donald Regan jumped out and ran to the edge of the grave.

"Hold it," he said. "The President has changed his mind."

The George Shultz look-alike said, "He can't change his mind about SALT Two. He said it was dead."

"Well," said Don Regan's double. "He's announced to the world that SALT is still alive and breathing. The press wants to see the SALT Two treaty because you made such a deal about it being gone."

The man with the shovel said, "Are you guys in Washington crazy? You tell me to bury SALT Two, so I've been shoveling dirt all over it. Now you say it's alive. That's no way to treat a treaty."

The man who would be Regan said to the George Shultz man, "The President wants SALT Two back in the White House before the next press briefing. He's going to stick with the treaty until he meets with Gorbachev."

The George Shultz twin said, "I should have been consulted if he was going to change his mind."

"He didn't change it—it was the first thing that came to his mind. Come on, what's the difference if we go with SALT Two or we don't?"

"It makes me look stupid. I don't like to use something

as a bargaining chip which I say is dead and the President says is alive.''

The man in the grave was sweeping the dirt off the pages with a broom. ''Here's the treaty that you say isn't worth the paper it's printed on. The next time you bring one of these out here, get your signals straight. I have a bad back.''

The man who would be Shultz said to the gravedigger sternly, ''If anyone asks you about the last time you saw SALT Two, say it was alive and kicking and raring to stop World War Three.''

Rich Man, Poor Man

A report of the Joint Economic Committee of Congress indicates that the concentration of wealth in this country is falling into the hands of fewer and fewer people. The conclusion appears to be that the rich are getting richer and the poor are getting poorer.

I don't know why this should come as such a big surprise to anybody. A recent survey I took shows most of the wealth in the U.S.A. is now in the hands of real estate tycoons, and for the last few years, poverty has spread to Texas and Oklahoma oilmen. It is this disparity in earnings between real estate and oil that is leading to class warfare in the country.

A crude-oil wildcatter who was living in the Dallas Greyhound Bus Terminal told me, "It's not right that the real estate people should have it all and the rest of us be on our keesters. If you don't spread the wealth around, the oil people at the bottom of the pile are going to rise up and take their share by force."

"But didn't you oil fellows have all the money a short time ago?"

"We had some, but that was only because oil was selling for thirty-two dollars a barrel. At those prices we could afford to buy whatever was for sale. But when oil plunged to eleven dollars a barrel they took away our MasterCards."

"So from being rich you became poor overnight."

"What else? Don't let anyone tell you the rich always get richer. In the oil business the rich get poorer. There's nothing as sad in this world as yesterday's millionaire."

"And to think that at one time you had it all."

"I don't know if I had it all, but I had whatever was out there. We were such good customers at Neiman-Marcus that when my wife told them she couldn't afford to shop there anymore, they retired her Adolfo jersey so that no one could ever wear it again."

I said, "But one thing nice about being a poor oilman is that overnight you could become rich again."

"Not with those OPEC bums glutting the market. Every time one of them lowers the price, another American oil producer goes on food stamps."

I decided to seek out a real estate mogul who is getting richer. I found him looking out of his new tower office building which took up twenty acres of Central Park (he had gotten a variance from the zoning board).

"Is it true that people of your ilk are up to your eyeballs in hard cash?"

"We make a living."

"The oil people say you're filthy rich."

"What would you expect them to say? They're all poor."

"They were once rich. They say it's an outrage that people like you are gobbling up the wealth in the country."

"They should have gone into a business with some decent tax breaks."

"Do you believe it's good for society that millionaires like yourself have three houses, a yacht, and an airplane, while Texas oilmen are capping their wells?"

"I don't know why real estate people should have to do without the necessities just because oilmen don't know how the system works. Maybe we're rich, but did anyone ever ask how we got that way?"

"How did you get that way?"

"We did it the old-fashioned way—by using other people's money."

Avengers of the Word

THE thing I like about the citizen censors we now have in this country (and there are more of them all the time) is that they not only worry about what their own families are reading, but yours as well.

Buddy Bloonose, a block warden for the Reverend Abner Ick, is a frequent visitor to my house. He usually comes in through the kitchen window while I'm eating cornflakes. The other day he said to me, ''Mind if I check your library to see if you have any Secular Humanist literature stashed away?''

''Be my guest,'' I told him. ''But you're wasting your time. I wouldn't know a Secular Humanist book if it jumped up and bit me.''

''I can't take your word for it. My organization, The Avengers of the Printed Word, asked me to see for myself. We won't stand for filth in your house.''

''No problem there,'' I assured him. ''We burned everything The Avengers put on their blacklist. If you find anything that violates the teachings of the Reverend Ick, you can take it with you.''

''We're doing this for your own good,'' Buddy said.

''I know that or I wouldn't let you into my house.''

''Our job is to clean up America, and the only way to do that is to alert the people to dangerous reading.''

''Let me ask you a question. Where does the Reverend Ick get the time to read all the printed material he attacks on television?''

"He doesn't read it himself. He has Avengers doing it for him."

"Reading stuff for the Reverend must be a wonderful job."

"There's no fun in reading it. It's banning it that gives our followers a purpose in life. Every Avenger wants to ban Jane Austen."

"I didn't know Jane was on the Reverend's hit list."

"No one has filled children's minds with more sinful garbage. Thanks to the Reverend Ick, all the schools in the country have been notified."

"Buddy, I can see where your people would want to keep their own bookshelves clean, but why us? We don't even belong to your sect."

"Because if you read the banned books, you'll burn in hell. These are not my words but those of Reverend Ick, who is within an arm's throw of the Lord."

"Granted," I said, "but let's assume that the list of other distinguished book-burners does not match yours. This means I can't read anything."

"The Avengers' list is the only one to follow because it has been blessed on television by the Reverend Ick."

"Back to the question. If I'm not an Ick follower, why are you inflicting your philosophy on me?"

"Because the Reverend believes that if you don't throw out your books, you will be condemned to a fiery inferno in the afterlife."

"Does the Reverend really want to control our lives?"

"No. All he's trying to do is keep the Secular Humanists from capturing your soul."

"How can the Secular Humanists capture my soul? I've never met even one of them."

"The Secularists come into your home through the printed

word. Go into any bookstore and see how much mischief the devil is making.''

''You people really have a lot of work to do.''

''Book burning can be exhilarating if you know what you're looking for.''

''What can I do to make sure I don't buy a book I shouldn't?''

''Send one hundred dollars to Reverend Ick and he'll tell you how to become a born-again reader.''

Fly Away

I didn't know why the airlines were in so much trouble until I talked to a seatmate while waiting to take off from La Guardia airport.

He told me he had been President of East Chop Airlines before it went bankrupt.

''We were a very successful carrier,'' he said, ''and made a good living, not only serving the large cities but the smaller ones as well. We had an impeccable safety record and gave our passengers their money back if we were more than two minutes late.''

''One couldn't ask for anything more,'' I said as we moved up to the thirty-ninth position on the runway. ''Then what happened?''

"The government decided to deregulate the carriers. After that it was every airline for itself. At first deregulation seemed like a good idea because it is no secret that the public benefits from competition. As soon as we were deregulated, I cut out all flights to the smaller cities so I could use the planes to service the lucrative routes to California and Hawaii."

"That was a smart business decision," I added.

"It seemed that way until all the other airlines did the same thing. TLC Airways, United Cream, and the Flying Panthers not only chose identical routes but they also decided to leave at the same time. Even so, there might have been enough business for us except that an upstart company called Pizza Airlines announced that it would fly anyone from New York to Honolulu for $9.95."

We were now thirty-first in line on the runway.

The ex-airline president continued. "As might be expected, Pizza filled up every plane even though it was losing one hundred dollars a passenger."

"What did you do to meet the competition?"

"We cut back on maintenance. When we were regulated, we kept our planes in the hangars for seven days for an overhaul. After deregulation, we only let the mechanics work on them for fifteen minutes."

"That's enough," I said.

"We might have gotten into the black with the new maintenance schedules, except one of our laid-off whistle-blowers told the Department of Transportation we were cheating. So we were fined ten million dollars."

"That seems unfair," I said. "Since all you were trying to do was compete in a free market."

"To make matters more difficult, Reagan fired the air controllers, causing two- and three-hour delays on the runways, which burned up all our fuel before we could get into the air.''

''What was your answer to all that?''

''We chose to undercut Pizza Airlines and sell tickets to Hawaii for $4.50, which would also include a free week at a deluxe hotel and a rental car for eight days.''

''A very fair price.''

''So fair,'' he said, ''that I had to put East Chop Airlines into bankruptcy.''

''Why didn't you sell it to Pizza Airlines?''

''Because they went bankrupt too. So did TLC, United Cream, and Flying Panthers. Thanks to deregulation, everyone has gone bust except for the line we're flying on right now.''

''We're number one for takeoff,'' I said excitedly.

But then the pilot's voice came over the loudspeaker. He said, ''Ladies and gentlemen, I'm getting off the plane because I haven't been paid in over a month. You can take this flight and shove it.''

My seatmate said, ''I told you deregulation isn't what it's cracked up to be.''

The Constitution Busters

THE United States is celebrating the Two-Hundredth Anniversary of the Constitution. As part of the ceremonies the House of Representatives just passed a bill which would require the armed forces to become involved in battling drugs in this country.

It's been a long time since the military has been assigned the role of keeping domestic order, and I for one am glad we finally are going to use them for what they are trained to do—maintain law and order at home.

Selwyn Barnaby is not as sanguine about the provision as I am.

"Who wants tanks in our streets?" he complained.

"There won't be tanks in the streets," I assured him, "and if there are, their guns will only be pointed at the windows of the drug dealers."

"How will they know who the drug dealers are?" Barnaby asked.

"The Pentagon will set up a special branch of military intelligence. If the services are responsible for getting the dealers and pushers, they must gather an awful lot of information about our citizens."

"That's what I'm worried about. As soon as the military is given a police role in this country, it will open files on all of us, and then they will use them for other things besides finding dope."

"May I remind you," I said, "that this isn't Chile. Our

military will not spy on innocent people—only those who
are guilty.''

"By whose reckoning?"

"Barnaby, this is an emergency and we have to use every
weapon in our arsenal to beat the drug dealers. If this means
giving the military new powers, so be it.''

"But once you use the armed forces for anti-drug enforce-
ment, what is to prevent them from being assigned to other
police duties? One of the things I have always enjoyed about
living in this country is that we have never seen any troops
in the street.''

"You're overreacting. It is my impression that the services
will be expected to halt penetration of illegal aircraft into
the United States and monitor the U.S./Mexican border. So
it isn't as if the Marines are going to knock down your door
at four o'clock in the morning.''

"Speaking of knocking down your door," Barnaby said,
"did you know the House also passed a law making it all
right to introduce evidence obtained illegally and without a
search warrant as long as the officer was acting 'in good
faith.' ''

"What's unreasonable with that?" I demanded.

"Who knows when a cop is acting 'in good faith'?"

"Cops always act in good faith. They had their hands tied
for years because they couldn't do what they wanted to do.
But this is coming to an end. Once we see that illegal search
and seizure works in drug cases, we can do away with search
warrants once and for all.''

Barnaby said, "You really believe that don't you?"

"This is the way I see it," I told him. "The people of
this country have to be prepared to give up some of their
liberties, particularly during an election year. Do you know

what is responsible for the drug crisis? . . . The Constitution of the United States. There are so many loopholes in it that any narcotics dealer can crawl through it standing up. The only way to win the war on drugs is to fix the Constitution so that it no longer gives aid and comfort to the dope peddlers.''

''Which means?''

''I have to report this conversation to the Pentagon.''

''What are you going to report?''

''That you're soft on drugs, you don't want the military on the streets, and you have a thing about policemen knocking down your door in good faith.''

The Brothers Hunt

WHENEVER I have no one else to feel sorry for, I ache for the Hunt brothers of Texas. The reason I cry for them is because no one else will.

Nelson, Herbert, and Lamar are down on their luck, facing hard times through no fault of their own.

In 1980 the three brothers were worth over six billion dollars between them. But now they are barely worth two billion. Is there a sadder story in America today?

I am glad I wasn't sitting at the breakfast table the morning that the Hunt brothers found out they were broke.

"Gosh darn it, Bunker, I told you this would happen if you diddled in silver," Lamar said.

"You didn't complain about diddling when silver hit fifty dollars an ounce," Bunker snorted.

"Don't you snort at me," Lamar said. "The reason we're in such bad shape, Bunker, is that you never know when to pull out of a nosedive. We must have dropped two and a half billion because you swore that Americans would kill for silver."

"What's the big deal?" Bunker shrugged. "Anyone can drop a few bucks in the futures market."

"Why are we in so much trouble for just losing two billion?" Herbert asked. "Daddy left us a lot more than that."

"Because, Herbert," said Bunker, "it isn't just silver we're up to our belly buttons in. We're drowning in sugar. We bought all those refineries after the lady in Fanny Farmer told you there would be a sugar shortage. Do you know how much we're selling now? One teaspoonful a day."

"You're a financial genius, Herbert. What did the sugar cost us?" Lamar asked.

"Another billion," Bunker replied.

"Are we wiped out?" Herbert said.

"We're flat-busted," said Lamar. "I figure we're down to four billion, give or take some change."

"How can we be down to four billion? We still have oil wells," Herbert said.

Bunker answered, "We put up the oil wells to borrow money from the banks on the silver we gambled on, which we couldn't even sell with sugar on it. The oil wells wouldn't have made much difference anyway."

"Why, because we drilled too many dry wells?"

"No, Lamar, because we drilled too many wet ones. We

struck oil just when the price sank to nine dollars a barrel.''

"Bunker, you should not have lost my money," Herbert protested.

"When you were a kid you always cried about anything I did. It wasn't your money, it was Daddy's money," Bunker told him.

"Daddy would roll over if he knew you were choking on sugar," Lamar pouted.

"Oh, shut up," Herbert said. "How bad is it?"

Bunker scribbled some figures on a pad. "It looks as if all we've got left is two billion."

Lamar cried, "Who can live on that?"

"Two billion isn't even a safety net," Herbert declared.

Bunker replied, "We're going to have to make do, guys. There are lots of brothers in this country living on two billion dollars, and they don't complain. Remember, we're not always going to be in such sad shape. When lady luck smiles again, we'll look on these times as the happiest years of our lives."

Making a Buck

M UCH has been written lately about college graduates who are more interested in making a million dollars than serving their fellow men.

"There is a good reason for this," young Ernst Beltwood said. "If we don't make the million, one of our classmates will."

The senior Beltwoods recently gave a party for Ernst, who received his MBA diploma from the Wharton School at the University of Pennsylvania.

When I congratulated him, I said, "I have one word to say to you Ernst—plastics."

"Plastics have taken a downturn," he replied. "The only way I can make it in plastics is to become an investment banker and merge plastics with soybeans and get mine on top from a leveraged buyout."

"Then your only goal in life is to make a bundle?"

"Not necessarily. I would like to improve society. I'm still looking at the Peace Corps."

"That sounds good. What country do you want to go to when you join?"

"I don't want to *join* the Peace Corps—I want to be a paid consultant. A fellow I went to school with has just signed a hundred-thousand-dollar contract to advise the Corps on what languages people speak in different countries around the globe."

"What happens if you don't get a consultant's job with the Peace Corps?"

"I still want to do some community service. But it has to pay extremely well or they can forget it."

"Ernst, I detect in you a sense of wanting to climb the ladder of success very fast without paying any dues."

He was taken aback. "Ralph Lauren doesn't sell his Polo suits for food stamps."

"Why do you need to wear Polo garments so early in your career?"

"Because a company is not going to hire me at ninety-five thousand dollars a year if I don't dress like someone who can afford it. Would you begrudge me a few designer suits as I rise to the top?"

"No, I wouldn't. But if everyone who graduated from college was only interested in making money, this country would be in sorry shape. I should have thought your professors would have taught you that."

"Why should they? Our professors are making even more money than we are."

"How can that be?"

"They are all moonlighting as consultants for large American companies at enormous fees. And they're always looking for new business. One computer-firm recruiter showed up at my school to find a graduate for a big job in his company and the professor, who had been asked to recommend a student, took the position himself. He told me that in a flat economy it's every man for himself."

"No matter where we start the subject always keeps coming back to money."

"I notice that too," Ernst said. "My fiancée, Sarah, says that's all I ever talk about. She claims that as long as we've gone out, she has never mentioned money once."

"What does she talk about?"

"The house we're going to buy—how she's going to furnish it—whether we should have a live-in maid or one that will leave after dinner—what model Jaguar we should get—what shape the pool is going to be and what kind of caterers would best serve our needs for entertaining."

"She sounds as if she's got her feet on the ground."

"Young people today are no different than young people in the past. We want the same things that you dreamed about. The only difference is that we want it ALL and we want it by Tuesday."

"Who Are You?"

WHEN all the details of the Tax Reform bill are worked out, it looks as if business entertaining as we have known it will never be the same. Under the new rules you can still eat on the government for eighty percent of the meal—but you have to prove that you really did discuss business with the client. The conversation must be substantive and not just for goodwill purposes. If you try to deduct extravagantly without proof of the seriousness of the conversation, you will be fined.

This isn't like the old days when men and women took their spouses to dinner and did not hesitate to write them off as legitimate business contacts.

[257]

This scene has been repeated many times in one form or another:

"Who do you want me to be tonight?" Bea Hofstadter asked her husband Milton as they entered the Café de Paris.

"You can be Gerry Buckingham, President of the Bayou Kite Company."

"Why can't I be Ira Harris of Salomon Brothers?"

"You were Ira last week. We have to mix it up just in case the IRS does an audit."

Bea and Milton were seated and the headwaiter gave them a menu.

She said, "Can I go all-out?"

"Of course you can," Milton replied. "Gerry is a very important client. He buys thousands of spools of string each month. He has to be treated like a king."

"Do I have to talk business or can we just eat?"

Milton replied, "I think we ought to talk *some* business just so that the taxpayer doesn't think he's paying for our dinner."

"Remember the time you took me to Las Vegas and I was Clint Bronzestader of the Freepoint Cement and Weathervane Company?"

Milton said, "Will you be quiet. Somebody could be listening. If you keep talking like this, I'm not going to deduct you anymore."

"You're such a worrywart, Milton," Bea said. "I'll never forget the night you wrote me off as David Jaffe, your accountant, and then suddenly hid under the table."

"What would you have done if Jaffe walked into the restaurant just as I was paying the check?"

"So what? You were with your wife and he was dining with his."

"How could I claim to have dinner with him when he and his wife were eating alone in the same restaurant?"

"Maybe he was taking his wife to dinner and saying it was you."

"David wouldn't do that," Milton said. "He's too chicken. The reason I ducked under the table was that I was afraid when I sent him my bill for dinner, he would see I deducted him for a meal I never had with him. David doesn't have a sense of humor."

"Forget David. Where are you going to take me for our anniversary?"

"How about Bermuda?"

"That would be fun. Who am I as far as the IRS is concerned?"

"How about Norman Plankton of Plankton, Witchhazel Advertising? No one would say a word if I said I took him to Bermuda."

"I hate Norman Plankton and if I have to be him it will ruin my trip."

"Well, who do you want to go as?"

"If I'm going to be deducted for the whole business trip, I want to go in style. I'd like to be Lee Iacocca."

Milton protested, "What would I be doing taking Lee Iacocca to Bermuda?"

"You could always say you took him because he promised you a good buy on a Plymouth Station wagon."

The Thirty Year Gap

WHEN it comes to the Nobel Prize, you never hear about the person who came in second. This year the runner-up for the economics award was Professor Valentine Septable, who wrote the best-selling book *Japanomics—The Sony in Us All*.

Septable has been working on the theory that the Japanese are not thirty years ahead of America but thirty years behind.

It was this reasoning that led him to unravel the mystery of why the sun never sets on a Seiko watch.

To find out more about his school of economics I drove out to Septable's lab underneath the RFK Stadium.

The professor was taking the loss of the Nobel very calmly. "I may not have won the biggie, but I was voted Mr. Congeniality by all the other economists. That meant more to me than being able to buy a new blackboard."

"Even if you lost," I said, "your work is not to be sneezed at."

"I'm very proud of it. It took me five years to build this model." He pointed to the top of it, which looked very much like a Benihana restaurant. "This is where the U.S. was thirty years ago and this is where it is now. Over here is where the Japanese are now, which is where the U.S. was thirty years ago."

"But if they are that much behind now," I said, "why are they so far ahead?"

"Very simple," Septable replied as he showed me photographs plastered all over the model. They were pictures of American manufactured products from the past.

He asked me, "Do you remember how it was in this country thirty years ago? We made wonderful cars, radios, refrigerators, hot water heaters, and baseball mitts. Everything, including the mitts, seemed to work. The reason for this is that our workers knew what they were doing and management knew how to sell the product. We also had something else which has been lost, and that's QUALITY CONTROL."

"Where did it go?" I asked.

"Some say the Japanese stole quality control from us because we wouldn't pay them reparations for World War II. But this is not true. It was strictly our own economic decision that brought us down. Thirty years back the United States had two paths to follow. It could either stay where it was or move ahead and make everything out of plastic. We chose plastic. At the same moment Japan, which was not good at advanced technology, decided it had to stick with old stuff that wouldn't break. It didn't take long, as everyone's cars and appliances fell apart, for Americans to look eastward for satisfaction. It was then the Japanese realized that to become number one, all they had to do was stay way behind the U.S."

"If the Japanese are thirty years behind us, how do we persuade them to catch up?"

Septable said, "It's quite simple. The American managers who brought us to where we are today all went to the Harvard Business School. What we have to do is get the Japanese to send their kids to Harvard as well. Only when all the centers of industry in Japan are manned by Harvard graduates will the U.S. be able to compete with Japan again."

I could see why Septable was runner-up for the Nobel Prize.

"Who would have thought the solution to our trade deficit is to make our foreign competitors earn MBAs at Harvard?"

Septable said, "It's our only chance. We have to hope when they return to the Empire the graduates will screw up Japan as much as the Harvard Business alumni have screwed up the United States."

Alumni Giving

IT isn't easy to raise money for your school when you have a losing football team.

As Tuna University's leading alumnus fund-raiser I made a house call at Marvin Bromfield's the other day.

"As you know, Bromfield, we have a drive on for the new library and I've been assigned to find out what you will pledge to further the educational goals of your alma mater."

"One hundred thousand dollars."

"That's very generous of you. The school needs a library in the worst way."

"Library? I thought you said linebacker!" Bromfield yelled. "I don't give to libraries when we don't have anyone who can sack a quarterback."

"The chancellor is aware that the university is weak on the line, but you know the school's financial policy as well as I do—one year the money goes for books and the next three for athletics. We want our university to be a cathedral of learning."

"Tell the chancellor I want that for the school as well. But he'll never get it unless he fires the coach."

"Do you honestly believe Tuna U will be a better place if the coach is fired?"

"It will be if we find a decent replacement. Look, I'm not one of those fanatic alumns who is always yelling for a winning team, but I have priorities too. When I go out to a bar no one ever asks me how Tuna U's library is going to do against Notre Dame. I love Tuna and I say that if there is any money left over after we pay the players, then use it to buy books. All I ask is that you don't take it away from the boys breaking their butts for ole T.U."

I told him, "We've never shortchanged big-time football at Tuna and we never will. But we're still obligated to educate our nonplaying students. That's why we were hoping you would throw a few bucks into the academic pot."

"I don't ask for a Rose Bowl invitation every year, but you can't expect a Tuna alumnus to give to a school that is two and seven and going down fast."

"Nobody likes to be two and seven. At the same time, we can't shut down the entire institution just because we're having a losing season."

"Why not? It will give everyone a chance to reflect on where we're going as a serious university."

"What would you do if you were the head of Tuna?"

"For starters I would allow the players to cut back on

study time so that they can concentrate on their game plays."

"We'd like to do that too, Bromfield. But the conference insists on the team members keeping up their grades, and there is nothing we can do about it."

"Then the chancellor should pull us out of the conference."

"The chancellor feels the way you do. He's hurting because not only does he love T.U.—but his job is at stake."

"If he really loves the team, why doesn't he allow the alumni to give the players better cars? How can we have players who drive Fords go up against ones who drive Audis?"

"The chancellor believes cheap cars give our kids moral fiber?"

Bromfield said, "Hogwash. All he is doing is de-emphasizing football."

"Bromfield, I'm not supposed to tell you this, but we're after an all-American high-school quarterback who happens to be an A student. We can get him if we improve our library."

Bromfield took out his checkbook. "Why didn't you say so in the first place?"

They Didn't Do It

OR some time now I have been trying to find out who was responsible for the C-123 cargo plane that was shot down over Nicaragua. Everyone seems to be taking credit for it.

The White House folks say that the Reagan administration was involved.

"We don't approve of airplanes that fly over Marxist countries we have diplomatic relations with, but we're always willing to make an exception. If we can't violate the laws of Congress to wage a secret war, then we have no right to call ourselves the White House."

"Who helped you do the job?"

"The Abraham Lincoln Brigade. They fought on the loyalist side during the Spanish Civil War and they were aching for action again. What gets you mad is that Major General Singlaub says he did it all with his mercenaries."

"Who is General Singlaub?"

"He runs the Club Med for the Contras in El Salvador."

I went to see General Singlaub. "Are you involved with the plane that was downed in Nicaragua?"

"I didn't know a plane had been shot down, but we'll take credit for it anyhow."

"It was one of ours, not one of theirs."

"You mean one of mine. No plane flies over Nicaragua without my permission."

"Then the CIA had nothing to do with it?"

"They always brag about being part of a covert operation whether they are or not."

"Maybe I should ask William Casey. His footprints are all over Central America."

When I called and asked for Casey, I was told he wasn't there. "Where is he?" I inquired.

"He's on the Hill telling everyone that the CIA was up to its ears in monkey business in Managua. He's afraid someone else will get the points."

"You would think he'd want to deny it, since it is against the law."

"Denying covert operations gets you nowhere. Besides, we subcontract most of our work in Central America, and if it leaked out that we didn't do our own illegal airdrops, the press might think we're up to no good."

"In spite of what you're telling me, I assume you do have a cover story denying any involvement in this?"

"Our cover story is that the pilot of the C-123, whom we didn't know, took off from Miami, which we've never heard of, on a crop-spraying flight to Green Bay, Wisconsin. The plane ran into bad weather and to save fuel dumped all the guns and ammunition it was carrying over what he thought was Nashville. Unfortunately, some Alabama duck-hunters fired on the plane, forcing it down over Nicaragua."

"Is that the best the CIA can come up with?"

"It sounded better in the briefing room."

"Everyone claims responsibility for the C-123 plane, even Vice President George Bush."

"He's always loved covert operations."

I called. "Mr. Vice President. It's being bandied about all over town that your office is handling illegal arms smuggling to Nicaragua."

"I can't say no and I can't say yes."

"Why not?"

"I don't know whether it's a plus or a minus for my campaign."

"Why would the White House give you the assignment when it could inflict embarrassment on the office, challenge your credibility, and cause you nothing but grief and suffering?"

"They owe me one."

Dear Ms. Kelley

THE word on the street is that Kitty Kelley, Frank Sinatra's unofficial biographer, is now looking for another fascinating subject to write about.

Well, Ms. Kelley, this is to warn you that I'm not cooperating with you, and you're just wasting your time if you think you can do to me what you did to Sinatra.

I've told all my close friends not to talk to you, and this goes for Ava, Mia, Lauren, Jill, Victoria, Shirley, Angie, Dinah, and Walter Annenberg.

Unlike Frank, I do hold grudges, and if I read one word in your book about me going skinny-dipping with Madame de Gaulle in the fountains at Versailles, I sue.

You think, Ms. Kelley, that just because I am an outstanding public figure with a worldwide following you can steal my life story and appropriate it as your own. Well, you can't do it, and if I am unable to stop you, I have friends who can. What if I told you the entire Chilean Navy owes me a favor? If you have doubts, just write about the orgy we all had with the Bartles and Jaymes Brothers and see if someone doesn't shoot a torpedo up your word processor.

I believe in freedom of the press as much as the next man, Ms. Kelley, but there are certain things better left unsaid when writing a biography. And that includes the shouting match I had with Mother Teresa when I jumped the line in Wagshal's Delicatessen.

Ms. Kelley, you have no more right to include that than you have to say I was one of the great earlobe kissers of the sixties.

Having read your book about Frank, I am worried that you may be more interested in scandal than history. Like Warren Burger, there are plenty of skeletons in my closet. I've never claimed that I was a saint, but I did a lot more than fall off the gold chairs at the White House. Behind all this craziness was a man who knew how to make Phil Donahue cry "uncle."

I don't know why I'm even writing this, since the only reason you are interested in me is because my life sells books. Well, Ms. Know-It-All, just because I always took the fast lane doesn't mean I am in the public domain. Win or lose, I had a good time and you can check that out with the Mormon Tabernacle Choir.

The reason why I refuse to cooperate with you is because you can mess somebody up badly. You could take a little story about me stiffing a Vietnamese hatcheck girl and make it into a Gulf of Tonkin resolution.

Ms. Kelley, I can't stop you from writing the book, but I will do everything in my power to see that no one buys it. I have friends amongst the street people, and I'm going to see that all of them stretch out in front of a Walden bookstore until it closes for the night.

Don't think flattery will get you anywhere either. You can publish that I am the greatest unmined biographical subject in the country, and you can say that my married life was vivid and unforgettable, and you can imply that I was a womanizer, and wildly lavish with money. You can say I was complex and misunderstood, and it wouldn't bother me. But then you are going to have to write about my private life, and that's when you get to talk to my lawyers.

So the purpose of this letter is to make sure you understand that I will not cooperate with your biography even if it is a fully documented, highly detailed, penetrating love story that will capture the hearts and imagination of the American people.

After this warning, if you insist on going ahead with the project, my wife would like you to title the book, *I Did It* Your *Way*.

"Disinformation Please"

"THIS is the White House Office of Disinformation. Can we help you with any stories today?"

"What are you selling?"

"We have a good one about Gadhafi catching diaper rash from sitting on the desert floor for too long."

"How do I know that this is true disinformation?"

"It comes stamped with the Seal of the United States government."

"Can I think about it?"

"We can't hold it up. Marlin Fitzwater is going to plant it with *The Wall Street Journal*."

"You people have been putting out an awful lot of false stories about Libya. Aren't you afraid that people won't be able to distinguish between the truth and the garbage?"

"All we're doing is telling it like it is, and hoping that it plays in Tripoli. If you're not buying Libya, can we give you an exclusive briefing on South Africa? We have some great lies on all the Republican Senators who overrode the President's veto."

"That's not the kind of erroneous story I deal in."

"All right. What if I told you that the President was about to convince the Botha government to give up apartheid, when the U.S. Congress sabotaged the whole deal?"

"With all due respect, even the presidential speechwriters wouldn't believe that one."

"They're the ones who are passing it around."

"I don't think I want to mess with a South African fairy tale. Could you disinform me about the arms talks?"

"Gorbachev works for the CIA."

"You're kidding," I said. "This is probably the hottest disinformation story of the year. How come the President is still talking to him if he knows this?"

"The President doesn't know it. We made it up at lunch today in the White House Mess. We keep Reagan away from the disinformation crisis room as much as possible so he won't be caught in a credibility gap."

"Does he mind?"

"President Reagan doesn't like to be kept out of things, but he realizes that when it comes to lying, there are other people in the government who are so much better at it than he is."

"If I don't take the Gorbachev disinformation, is there anything else you can deceive me with?"

"I have something that was created from pure cloth and is hot out of the oven."

"That sounds up my alley."

"The latest disinformation we have on Central America is that Nicaragua has the bomb."

"THE bomb?"

"We're calling it A bomb. The reason for putting out the disinformation is we can now go back to Congress and ask them to give the Contras a bomb. You better take this one because we're going to release the disinformation to Evans and Novak tomorrow morning, and then it will be in the public domain."

"The White House owes the story to me," I said. "You people haven't given me a falsehood in weeks."

"You're number one on our 'A' leak list" he assured me.

"When we plant false newspaper reports, you are one of the first people we call."

"How does the White House Office of Disinformation want their stories attributed?"

"Just credit it to a high administration official who rides a horse and works in the Oval Office. When it comes to official deception, it's better for our credibility if we don't pinpoint the source."

Top Secret Cables

I⊤ isn't too much fun for an American diplomat to be stationed in the U.S. embassy in Moscow. When the U.S. kicked out fifty-five Russians, the Soviets withdrew all their house-keeping personnel from the American Embassy in Moscow, leaving over four hundred American employees to scrub the floors.

To show you what pain this caused, here are reprints of some of the top secret cables exchanged between the State Department and our brave people in Moscow.

TELEX TO:

U.S. EMBASSY, MOSCOW

Please advise exact status medium-range missiles, including number now on station as well as how many in reserve. Urgent

you also let us know whether Soviets intend to increase conventional troops if treaty is agreed upon.—Harlequin

STATE DEPARTMENT, WASHINGTON, DC

Toilet on fourth floor leaking. Have made it off-limits to all those below the rank of consul. Urgently need to talk to department water-closet expert with particular know-how in rubber plungers. Don't send any more new embassy personnel until toilet is fixed. Everyone here would rather have half-baked plumber than first-class CIA station chief.—Stick

U.S. EMBASSY, MOSCOW

President wants to know what was Politburo's reaction when Gorbachev returned from Iceland summit. Also, is hanging tough on Star Wars playing in Smolensk? Finally, how much grain will Soviets buy this year? Need information for G.O.P. fund-raising speech tonight.—Harlequin

STATE DEPARTMENT, WASHINGTON, DC

Sending this in code so someone in Washington will read it. Lower oven in the kitchen has funny smell. Experiencing severe frying pan shortage. Those who can't stand the heat are getting out of kitchen. Please advise Secretary Shultz that wives of American employees refuse to polish silver unless husbands do windows. Am unable to supply information the President requested because today is field day and the Ambassador is going to inspect our rooms.—Stick

U.S. EMBASSY, MOSCOW

We are not, repeat not, interested in your problems. We just received word here that Marshal Blini, commander of all Soviet Air Forces, wants to defect and live in U.S. Make immediate contact and give him asylum in embassy so we can wring him dry.—Harlequin

STATE DEPARTMENT, WASHINGTON, DC

All hands Moscow agree this not a good time to give Marshal

Blini asylum as we are short on sheets and pillowcases. Staff resistance to doubling up with a defector is growing. Suggest he stay on Soviet General Staff until housekeeping crisis is over. By the way, snack bar pizza machine broke down. Can we set up conference call with pizza engineer in U.S. to repair it? Morale still high since you sent chicken cacciatore in diplomatic pouch.—Stick

U.S. EMBASSY, MOSCOW

We are notified through Kremlin hotline that giant Soviet missile misfired and is now heading towards Malta. Find out exact position of missile and where it is expected to land. Also is it nuclear-armed? This is a priority message.—Harlequin

STATE DEPARTMENT, WASHINGTON, DC

Good news. Just found out what was wrong with pizza machine. There was a broken bolt that you can't see unless someone crawls underneath it. Am trying to get over to the Foreign Office to check out missile query. Can't leave embassy until repairman from Helsinki arrives to look at our washing machine. You know how hard it is to get one of those guys.—Stick

Winners and Losers

THE tax bill has been passed, and while no one understands it, every expert seems to be producing a "Who won—who lost?" column. What do taxpayers really think?

To find out, I decided to speak to a representative from each tax bracket affected by the legislation.

The first one I talked to was a poor person.

"How do you feel about the tax reform bill?"

"Very good," he said. "The poor people have always prayed for meaningful tax reform and are delighted it is finally here. We have continually maintained that once the tax system became fair, the poor would be willing to pay its share which, in our case, is nothing."

"Do you believe that if the poor lower class is not obligated to pay taxes, it will encourage many in the middle class to become poor?"

"On the surface it sounds like an incentive for the middle class. But there is more to being poor than not wanting to pay taxes—such as having rotten housing, eating bad food, and walking in unsafe neighborhoods. I hate to think that people would choose to be poor just to save money on their taxes."

"What are you going to do with the money you save by not paying taxes?" I asked.

"Invest in bonds, buy out Donald Trump, or take over CBS. There's no telling what a poor person is capable of doing when he doesn't have to give everything to Uncle Sam."

After speaking to a poor person I sought out a rich one.

"Sir, I would like to talk to you about the new tax reform bill."

He was very serene. "I pay all the taxes that I am obligated to pay, not to mention the fees I am charged by those who handle my money."

"I am happy to hear that. Do you see yourself a winner or a loser with the new tax law?"

"When it comes to taxes, rich people are never winners. We are always looking for ways to make the code more equitable. That's why we support so many experts and accountants— to ensure that we are paying our portion. After all, what is money if one can't share it with Washington?"

"So does that make you a winner or a loser?"

"This particular bill takes away many of the deductions that the rich have considered part of their life-support systems. But the wonderful thing about being rich is that whatever they do to you, you can always find a way of getting around it."

"Then what you are saying is that even if the rich start out as losers, they will eventually be winners."

He continued, "If there is any bitterness amongst the rich, it is because of the fact that in writing the tax reform bill, Congressmen and Senators abandoned the class which financed their way to power. The very people whose campaigns we donated to have set a torch to our tax shelters."

"You're taking it extremely well," I said.

"The art of being rich is to pretend that nothing bothers you."

The last person I spoke to was a middle-class taxpayer.

"Do you consider yourself a winner or a loser in the new tax bill?"

"At the beginning I will be a small loser, but eventually I'll be a big winner. The middle class is always a winner when it comes to income taxes."

"Do you honestly believe that?" I asked him.

"No, but I thought you'd like an upbeat note for the end of your column."

Cop a Plea

I F you have committed a white-collar crime, or are thinking of committing one, now is the time to do it. The reason is that the Justice Department has run out of gas and is willing to settle with anyone who seems to have gotten himself into trouble.

Trinka, a lawyer for the American White-Collar Criminal Defense League, told me that this is absolutely the best time to make my deal with the government attorneys.

"But I haven't done anything," I protested.

Trinka said, "They'll give you a good deal anyway. I have a client who flies around in a helicopter doing TV commercials telling everyone what a great country this is.

"He bilked his stockholders out of a bundle and was fined, given a censure, and suspended from playing squash for ten days."

"What's such a good deal about that?"

"The government agreed not to stop him from doing his helicopter commercials."

"But he manipulated stock. I didn't do anything. Why should I try to make a deal with the government?"

"This is the opportunity of a lifetime. Meese's boys will roll over for a white-collar criminal."

"Why is the Justice Department so easy on white-collar criminals?"

"Because they're pro-family. Almost everyone who commits a white-collar crime has a family. Do me a favor, let me go down and talk to them. I know that they are in a good mood. What have you got to lose?"

"I keep telling you I didn't do anything."

"Do you know Ivan Boesky? He violated all sorts of laws on the books. They stuck him with a one-hundred-million-dollar fine."

"That's a lot of money."

"To you that's a lot of money. To him it's less than what he puts in parking meters every day. Besides, now that he's turning state's evidence, there's a rumor the government is going to redecorate his house in Palm Springs, California."

"That's fine for Boesky—but I still can't figure out what's in it for me if I confess to committing a felony."

"It won't be a felony. We'll go and see the Justice people and if you act contrite, they'll knock it down to a misdemeanor and give you a seven-day Caribbean cruise on the *QE 2*."

"You're just saying that because you're a lawyer."

"I'm looking after your interests. I've never known white-collar-crime settlements to be so easy to get. We won't see anything like this again."

I was beginning to lose my patience. "But I haven't committed a crime."

Trinka said, "Then go out and commit one so that you

can take advantage of their sales. Let me plead for you now.''

"No way. Even if you could make a good deal with the feds, I don't want my name in the papers.''

"Did I tell you that if you commit a white-collar crime on Wall Street before Christmas, they give you a ticker-tape parade down Broadway?''

"But if I plead guilty to a white-collar crime which I didn't commit, won't the other white-collar criminals get mad at me?''

"Why should they when every American is entitled to equal plea bargaining under the law?''

Russkie Garage Sale

I live around the corner from the Soviet Embassy in Washing-ton. The other morning I saw a crowd in front of it and asked an FBI man dressed as a parking meter maid what was going on.

"It's a garage sale being held by the Russians who were booted out of the United States. You can get some great buys on Afghan wool potholders and Andropov ashtrays with secret tape recorders inside.''

I wandered over to one of the bridge tables. The Soviet Embassy employee said to me, "Can I interest you in U.S.

Navy submarine codes that have only been used once? They come in this beautiful Statue of Liberty key ring and can easily be hidden in a pumpkin.''

"No, thank you," I said. "I stopped collecting submarine codes after Admiral Rickover died.''

"Then perhaps I can whet your appetite with stolen blueprints of the Stealth bomber. They make extremely colorful wall decorations.''

I said, "I wouldn't know one stolen blueprint from the other. How can I be sure they're genuine?''

"Each and every one of them has been authenticated by Cap Weinberger. We Soviets do not deal in phony American blueprints. That's why we're being kicked out of your country.''

I told him I would be back. The next table featured microfilm of Reagan's Star Wars plan.

A Soviet Embassy lady manning the stand was selling microfilm which she had taken when she walked through the White House with a little baby under her arm. "All I had to do was say the baby was a Right-to-Life poster child and they let me photograph everything in the Oval Office.''

"Are you an expert on microfilm?" I asked her.

"No, but I know what I like.''

"Why are you selling them rather than taking them back to the Soviet Union?''

She replied, "If you are an American you get a fortune from Moscow for Star Wars material. If you are a Russian they tell you it's your duty to turn it over to the motherland for free. This is my last chance in America to make a buck.''

I wandered over to another table and saw a framed silver photo.

"Is that who I think it is?" I asked.

The Russian Embassy man smiled. "This is a genuine auto-graphed photo of the American spy John Walker. It is dedicated to me and says, 'Tovarich, I couldn't have done it without you.' "

"That is a very sentimental memento. Why are you unload-ing it at a garage sale?"

"I have hundreds of them. John gave me a picture every time he committed an act of treason. The only one I won't sell is this picture of John selling out his son to the FBI. It was taken from a bakery van by one of our best KGB photogra-phers at F-4 and one hundredth of a second."

"What is this book here?"

"It's the Bible Vitaly Yurchenko swore on when he promised William Casey that he would always be a loyal defector."

"How did you get hold of it?"

"I got it from Vitaly just before he boarded the plane for Moscow. He asked me to give it to Casey for old times' sake. When I tried to deliver the Good Book, Casey turned it down and said he didn't want a Bible that had been sworn on by a defector who couldn't keep his word."

"Is there anything else in the garage sale I might be interested in?"

"I have the White House text of what Ronald Reagan said to Gorbachev in Iceland."

"Which one?"

"What version do you want?"

French Fries

THERE are many methods of handling countries who train and harbor terrorists. One way is what Britain did when it broke all relations with Syria and booted their ambassador out of the country. The reason for this was that the Syrians were found to be knee-deep in helping a terrorist blow up an El Al plane. The British asked their NATO allies to support them in punishing the Syrians for their lousy behavior. Naturally, the French refused.

Why did the French turn the British down?

Once again it was a question of French pride.

Gaston de Boccador, a deputy French Minister of Duplicity, said, "It was either a question of honor or of selling the Syrians a half-billion-dollars' worth of arms. What choice did we have? We had to send a message to Damascus."

"What kind of message?"

"France doesn't hold grudges."

"My dear friend, there are bombs going off all over Paris these days. Doesn't that make the French angry at Syria?"

"You miss the point. If Syria knows who is responsible for the bombings in France, then she is the only one who can stop them. It would be a serious mistake to annoy a country who has such close links to the people who are trying to blow us up."

"There is something wrong here. Syria starts the terrorism and you have decided to be nice to her so she'll stop it. Haven't you people in France ever heard of blackmail?"

[283]

Gaston looked shocked. "France never pays blackmail. What we are doing is taking a 'special' role in the Middle East crisis. We can't play that role if we take Britain's side over Syria's."

"Have you ever heard of Georges Ibrahim Abdallah?" I asked.

"We are holding him in prison in Paris because he is a terrorist swine and a presumed murderer."

"Do you know that when he comes to trial, the French have assured Syria they will acquit him?"

"It isn't that simple. We will only acquit him if Syria promises us that the terrorist bombings in Paris will stop."

"Is that blackmail or isn't it?"

"No, it's smart thinking," he said. "We have to persuade Syria that we have good faith so she'll help us free our captured French hostages."

"Which Syria was instrumental in kidnapping in the first place. What happens when they release these hostages and then kidnap nine more?"

"We can deal with it," Gaston said. "France knows more about fighting terrorism than any country in Europe."

"How is that?"

"When someone insults us and slaps us across the face, we say, 'What do you want from us?' And when they tell us we give it to them."

"That will get you respect every time," I said.

"We like to think we're more practical than our NATO allies. When the Syrian Embassy got involved in trying to blow up a 747, the British kicked them out. And what did they get for it? Nothing but scorn from their friends in the Middle East. On the other hand, the French, by ignoring Syrian dirty tricks, will not only wind up with a very good trade business, but with a sympathetic ear in Damascus the next time the Syrians try to pull off another bombing.''

I said to Gaston, ''The French really seem to know how to handle terrorism.''

He agreed, ''We have to be weak or people will walk all over us.''

He's Hungry

Not long ago Attorney General Ed Meese declared that the Supreme Court does not make the law of the land. He urged his Justice Department lawyers to ignore the Court's rulings if they don't agree with them.

In fairness to Meese, his quarrel with the Supreme Court is not personal. There are many rulings he has no problem with as long as the Court agrees with him.

Quincy Wheelbright, an avid Meesewatcher, said, ''What I like about Ed Meese is that he doesn't look so much like a person who upholds the Constitution as someone who just ate it.''

I protested, ''That's a terrible thing to say about the highest law-enforcement officer in the land. Why would he eat the Constitution?''

''When you're hungry for power you'll eat anything.''

"Have you personally seen Meese eat the Constitution?" I asked Quincy.

"Yup, I saw him do it one day in the Justice Department cafeteria."

"You're kidding me."

"I'm sure it was him. The reason I remember it is that he was putting catsup on it—and Meese is the only guy I know who puts catsup on the Constitution."

"Did he eat it with a knife and fork or with his hands?"

"With his hands. He just ripped the First Amendment into shreds and then stuffed it in his mouth."

"Are you sure it was the First Amendment?"

"I'm positive. Meese had a helluva time swallowing it. One of his deputies—I think it was William Bradford Reynolds—kept handing him water to wash it down. I thought he was going to upchuck all over the table."

"Did he stomp out of the cafeteria?"

Quincy said, "He was about to when someone urged him to taste the Second Amendment. He liked that because it deals with the right to bear arms. Then he tried to eat the Sixth but he couldn't do it even when he dipped it in Tabasco sauce."

"Why didn't he relish the Sixth?"

"He said it was cooked up by bleeding hearts."

"Did he put anything besides catsup and Tabasco sauce on the Constitution?"

"Yes," Quincy said. "He sliced off the part which prevents the police from conducting an illegal search and smeared it with Gulden's. After tasting it he said to Reynolds, 'This one doesn't cut the mustard.' Then he spat it out."

"Meese hates anything with too many rights in it," I said.

Quincy said, "Did I tell you Meese choked on the recent Supreme Court rulings on separation of church and state?"

"No, you didn't. What happened?"

"He was digging in with both hands and suddenly his face got red and he gagged. Reynolds jumped up and gave him the Heimlich maneuver."

"Thank God for that."

"It came at an interesting time. Meese was just about to launch a lawsuit to get the Heimlich maneuver declared unconstitutional."

"Why?"

"Because he got word it was invented by a Secular Humanist."

I Am an American

IF Pat Buchanan has a strong suit, and I'm not saying that he does, it is his ability to test the patriotism of people he doesn't agree with.

Pat once said in a speech, "All newsmen should remember that they are Americans first and newsmen second. Those who don't feel that way should tell us so. We will know which TV stations not to watch and which newspapers not to buy."

Buchanan didn't spell out exactly what was required to be an American first, so I went to Dr. Buchanan's Americanism lab, where they physically examine you to determine loyalty to your country.

The technician handed me a specimen bottle and told me to fill it.

"Can you tell from this if someone is a good American or not?" I asked.

"Of course we can. If it turns blue, you're pro-Contra, and if it turns pink, you're pro-Castro. Now take off your shirt and pants. You can leave your shoes and socks on. What is your profession?"

"I am a journalist," I replied.

"Are you an American or a newsman?"

"Can't I be both at the same time?"

"Not easily. The Buchanan rule is that if a newsman reports about the President screwing up, he has no right to salute the flag. Blow into this paper bag."

"Then it follows that you are a bad American if you write that someone in the administration violated the law?"

"Dr. Buchanan wants you to know that everyone he served under violated the law—Lincoln, Franklin Roosevelt, Richard Nixon, and Spiro Agnew. There is nothing wrong with violating it as long as the President declares you a national hero."

"To prove his love of country must a newsman close his eyes to all the White House incompetents?"

"That's the big test. A patriotic newsman never says anything ill of someone who works for the President. Please stand on one foot and jump up and down."

I said, "Next question. Am I a good American or a bad American if I write about paying blackmail to terrorists for the release of hostages, and selling arms to Iran?"

"It's not a question of what is good for the hostages or Iran, but what is good for the Contras. When newsmen lose sight of what we're doing in the Middle East to help the anti-Sandinistas in Nicaragua, they put their loyalty to this country in doubt.''

''What about the money? No one knows where all the money from the Iranian arms sales went. It was supposed to go to the Contras but they claim they didn't get it. If newsmen ask about the money, will their patriotism be in question?''

''Buchanan does not believe that is a newsman's business. There is now a frenzied witch-hunt going on amongst the press because a few million dollars were misplaced. Every time a newsman asks where the Contra money is, he is hurting our Star Wars initiative.''

Under the Buchanan rules I could see why it was so difficult to be a newsman and an American at the same time.

''What can I do to prove my loyalty?'' I asked.

He said, ''You see this shovel? It originally belonged to Don Regan and he used it to clean up after the elephants went by. Follow Pat Buchanan around, and every time he stops to make a speech you do the same thing.''

The Big Deal

O NE of the major players in the takeover game is Marvin "the Shark" Arbmaker, whose brilliance at Wall Street's crap tables with loaded dice has not only captured the imagination of the American public but of the Securities and Exchange Commission as well.

Marvin was waiting with his lawyer outside the SEC enforcer's office to make his most important deal, after having just sold out his mother and all her friends in a hostile takeover.

I said, "The SEC wants you badly. Do you have any idea why?"

"They're mad at me because I'm greedy," he said.

"That certainly isn't illegal."

"They said I made one hundred million dollars by using inside information on the merger of Wilkie Tent Pins and Cyrus Cotton Balls."

"Why would they say that?"

"Clara Dooley, the chairman's secretary, moved in with me a week before the merger took place and told me what was going on. It was just pillow talk."

"Pillow talk is not inside information," Marvin's lawyer said. "Besides, just because the secretary of a major player is keeping house for him doesn't mean Arbmaker made a killing on her company's stock."

Marvin said, "The SEC always gangs up on anyone who owns more than three Mercedes-Benzes and a Har-Tru tennis court."

"That's not right," I said. "If it wasn't for guys like you and Ivan Boesky there would be no avarice in this country at all."

Marvin said, "Making money is my life. I have a house in East Hampton, a boat in Fort Lauderdale, and a treehouse in Nairobi. But I'd rather spend my weekends in the men's room of the World Trade Center getting inside information on a U.S. Steel takeover."

The SEC enforcer came out of his office and yelled, "Arbmaker, you've violated the law and we're going to make you pay for it! We're fining you one hundred fifty million dollars."

"I know my rights," said Marvin. "I'm allowed to make one telephone call."

"But," the SEC enforcer said, "your lawyer is with you."

"I don't want to call my lawyer—I want to call my broker. I need to sell all my stocks before word gets out on the street that you people are going to indict me."

"Okay, here's a quarter, but come back when you're finished."

After talking on the pay phone Marvin came back smiling and said to the SEC man, "Thanks for the tip. I should make two hundred million dollars on that one. What I like about the investment business is you never know where your next piece of insider information is coming from."

The SEC enforcer was livid. "It's not going to be that easy, Arbmaker. Besides the fine, we're tying a microphone around your neck and you're going to tape everyone you talk to for the next six months."

"That sounds like fun," said Marvin. "I might get some more hot stock tips that way."

"We're not wiring you so you'll make money!" the enforcer

yelled. "We want to get other dealers like you and make them pay for mocking the rules of the takeover game."

"I'll cooperate. I own a penthouse on Fifth Avenue, a private airplane at La Guardia, an island in Greece, and twenty Renoir paintings which I loaned to the Met. But the only real pleasure I get out of life is ratting on my friends."

The Crime of the Century

EVERYONE loves a good mystery, and it isn't surprising that the Iran-Contra caper continues to hold our fascination as one of the most bungled cloak-and-dagger crimes of our time.

"What do you make of it all?" I asked Sherlock Holmes in his Federal townhouse in Georgetown.

"It's very interesting, my dear Watson," Holmes replied, tamping down on his pipe. "The President promised that he would get to the bottom of this, and we know less now than we did when he said it."

"Do you believe that the President is happy because we can't get to the bottom of it?"

"He appears to be extremely happy."

"Holmes, what did Secretary of State George Shultz know and when did he know it?"

"That's the most interesting thing, Watson. For a secretary of state, Shultz didn't know anything at all. He didn't even know when Nancy's dog did doo-doo on the White House lawn. According to him no one on the President's staff spoke to him, and they only made decisions *after* he left the room. Scratch Shultz as a suspect."

"If it wasn't Shultz, could it have been Bill Casey?"

Holmes puffed on his pipe. "Casey has an ironclad alibi. He was home laundering money for Angola when the overcharges for Iranian arms were being washed in Switzerland. Besides, as CIA director, why would Casey know anything about what was going on in Iran?"

"By jove, Holmes, this is getting more difficult than I thought. What about the Marine chap, Colonel North?"

"A likely suspect," Holmes said, "but you forget one thing. He took the Fifth Amendment. You can't accuse a man of a crime if he takes the Fifth. We have to eliminate Admiral Poindexter on that count as well."

"Too bad. I was hoping North and Poindexter could give us a clue."

"Watson, we must ask ourselves who had the most to gain from the Iranians getting arms, and the Contras getting money."

"Imelda Marcos?"

"No, that's another case. The ones who had the most to gain in this whole affair were the press chaps."

"You don't believe the press was behind the whole thing, do you, Holmes?"

"I don't, but Pat Buchanan does."

"Well, fiddledeedee on him. He's just attacking the press so that he will get his name in the newspapers. If you want to know what I think, I see the hand of Richard Nixon in this whole business. I say we find the smoking gun and make him resign all over again.''

"Watson, I would like to think Richard Nixon was to blame, but except for the eighteen-and-one-half-minute gap on the tapes we have no evidence. It's true he does keep calling President Reagan, which indicates he feels guilty about *something*. But until Nixon gets up and declares that he is not a crook, we cannot consider him a suspect.''

"You're probably right, Holmes. I suppose the thing that bothers me the most is that although laws were broken, everyone involved has been called a national hero.''

"Perhaps I may have a clue, Watson. As you know, the key to the mystery is the secret numbered bank account in Switzerland. What do they give you, Watson, when you open a numbered Swiss bank account?''

"Depending on the size, Holmes: Tupperware, a coffeepot, a Cuisinart, a toaster, an orange-juice squeezer, and if you put in more than thirty million dollars, a microwave oven.''

"Precisely, Watson. Whoever opened that account in Switzerland was given one of those items and it is now in his possession. If we find it, we'll know who committed one of the most amateurish crimes of the century.''

"By jove, Holmes, you're right. Let's have a look-see. You go to George Bush's kitchen and I'll go to Bud McFarlane's—and then we'll go together to see what they're cooking upstairs at the White House.''

Inside the Beltway

WHEN the President lost his cool in an interview with *Time* magazine he said, "The letters coming in are in my favor. This is a Beltway bloodletting. Frankly, I believe that as the truth comes out, people will see that what we were doing was right."

CIA Director Bill Casey was quoted as saying that the Iranian affair was of interest only to people "inside the Beltway."

I have to assume that the entire country has no idea what the President meant when he referred to Beltway bloodletting, or what Casey meant when he talked about people "inside the Beltway."

Therefore I will take time to explain it.

For some years now reference has been made in Washington to people who live "inside the Beltway." It means those who are out of sync with the rest of the country. They are so involved in their little world of bureaucracy and pack journalism that they cannot hear what song America is singing. The Beltway phrase first cropped up on conservative talk-shows and is now used to jeer at those of a more liberal persuasion.

When you talk about someone who lives "inside the Beltway" you are saying that the person has lost all touch with reality. He is narrow-minded, ignorant, and won't stand up for the U.S.A.

Thus you have the President of the United States blaming

those who reside "inside the Beltway" for his troubles in Iran and Nicaragua, and the head of the CIA using the Beltway to cover up his role in the Rube Goldberg arms scandal.

First the facts. The Beltway is a concrete necklace sixty-six miles long, and encircles parts of Virginia; Washington, DC; and Maryland. Six hundred thousand vehicles are driven around it every day, including twenty-three thousand trucks loaded with spare parts for Israel which will eventually be shipped to Iran.

Several million people reside inside the Beltway. Most of them are law-abiding citizens except for a few who play golf at the Chevy Chase Country Club.

People who live inside the Beltway eat Kiwi fruit, prefer Reebok running shoes, and read 1.5 *Playboys* a month. Because of their Beltway life-style they tend to be more promiscuous than citizens in other parts of the country. Since they are squished together so tightly, they have no choice but to intermarry with other Beltway residents, which produces very thin blood.

However, it is not their home lives but their thinking that separates them from other Americans. Since most Beltway people work for the government, they are terribly suspicious about what their leaders tell them. Also, those inside the Beltway are gun-shy because they were the first ones Richard Nixon and his Watergate gang dumped on.

The present White House has no more use for the inner Beltway people than previous administrations.

So it was no accident that in his fury the President would use the phrase "Beltway bloodletting" to sum up exactly what he thought was going on in Washington.

President Reagan believes it was the knee-jerk reaction of the Beltway liberals that stopped the government in its tracks and ruined his chances of becoming the Ayatollah Khomeini's pen pal.

What do you do with people who live inside the Beltway? Several of Mr. Reagan's NSC advisers have suggested bulldozing the entire area and making it into a secret landing strip to handle future Ollie North flights to Iran.

Next Question

Now for some questions about the twelve-million-dollar Iranian misunderstanding.

Who in the White House knew what was going on in the Iran arms deal?

A U.S. Marine colonel and a teller in a bank near the White House.

Did the CIA know?

No, because all the arms were shipped in sealed wooden cases marked, DO NOT OPEN UNTIL CHRISTMAS. The CIA always honors requests like that.

The President said the arms hardly filled one airplane. Now it turns out it was bigger than the Berlin Airlift. What does one make of that?

Since the President didn't know anything about the operation, he was also in the dark about what transportation was needed to ship the weapons. He was under the impression you could put five hundred anti-tank guns under an airplane seat.

Although the President didn't know, did he suspect certain people of being involved in a shady deal?

From the start he has been suspicious of a lady who lives in a welfare hotel in New York City on thirty-seven thousand dollars a month.

Did the President ever meet anyone in the White House who roused his suspicions as to what was going on?

There was one occasion when the President was in the basement looking for his dog. He ran into a Marine officer who was sticking long-range nuclear missiles into Federal Express boxes. The President asked the Marine what he was doing, and the leatherneck replied, "I'm sending flu shots to my mother."

How were the arms paid for?

This was the brilliance of the operation. After the planes arrived in Tehran, an Iranian rug merchant sent thirty million dollars to a butcher in Tel Aviv, who took the money and deposited it in Karl Malden's American Express account in Morocco, where it was turned into traveler's checks and forwarded to the First National Chocolate Bank of Geneva. Then the traveler's checks were sent to retired General Singlaub, manager of the Club Med for Contras in Central America.

It all sounds very neat. So where did it go wrong?

A Syrian magazine in Beirut featured a story blowing the whistle on what was going on in Tehran. It told about former moderate NSC director Bud McFarlane's role in forwarding arms to Iran in exchange for hostages. The news of arms for hostages got George Shultz mad and he said that he would never launder the Ayatollah's money. This statement got Nancy Reagan mad because it showed once again that Shultz wasn't a team player.

What was the first thing that the people in the White House did after the story broke?

They shredded the evidence.

Why?

To save the country.

What was the second thing they did?

They blamed the press for smelling blood.

If the President didn't know about it, isn't he grateful to the press for telling him what was going on?

Not when his bile is up. So what comes next?

The White House is talking about throwing out the baby with the bath water.

That should solve it.

It has constitutional problems. If the President knows about the baby, he had to know about the bath water.

The Truth But Not the Whole . . .

Every time I believe my credulity has been stretched to its limit someone stretches it even more.

This time it was my confidential source at the White House who did the stretching. His code name is The Meeseburger.

"Do you believe the story that Colonel North of the NSC was the only person in the White House who knew we were smuggling arms to Iran and sending funds to the Contras at the same time?" he asked me.

"I not only believe it, I'm sorry I didn't think it up myself. Anyone who can run an under-the-table multimillion-dollar arms-smuggling ring in the White House can write a helluva yarn," I told The Meeseburger. "The movie rights are worth a fortune."

"Do you believe that Secretary of State George Shultz is a rat?" he asked.

"Do you want me to?"

"No, but I would appreciate it if you passed it on."

I asked The Meeseburger, "When did the President know George Shultz was a rat—before or after the arms shipments to Iran were okayed?"

"He found out afterwards—but we suspected something earlier when Shultz refused to take a lie detector test, which showed he wasn't a team player."

"Do you believe that the President knew about the arms to Iran but not about the money for the Contras?"

"What does the President want me to believe? After all, it's his movie."

"He wants you to believe that it was okay to send a few firecrackers to Iran as a goodwill gesture to the Ayatollah, but it was a bad idea to use the money from the sales to finance our brave freedom fighters in Nicaragua—especially if you get caught at it."

"Now can I ask about the law? Did anyone violate it?"

The Meeseburger's nostrils started quivering. "That's for the Attorney General to tell us after he conducts a thorough and complete investigation."

"Maybe. But he's the President's lawyer, and has a vested interest in protecting the White House."

"That won't stop the Attorney General from finding out who is behind this dastardly act, which took place in the White House within steps of Don Regan's office. I assure you the AG will pursue this case even if the evidence leads to George Shultz's bedroom."

"I'd still feel better if the AG took a drug test."

"You're being too harsh on the Attorney General. He may have some weird ideas about the law of the land, but he's hell on wheels when it comes to people who are running money through Swiss bank accounts from the White House basement. The AG will get to the bottom of it."

"Suppose it involves all the President's men sneaking around the laws of Congress?"

"You have to understand something. Nobody likes to violate laws passed by Congress. But what is the White House going to do if the lawmakers won't back up the President? Ronald Reagan has to have some flexibility in ignoring the law of the land, as long as he personally doesn't know what is going on."

"You've convinced me."

"Now, if you won't buy George Shultz as the heavy in this whole mess, would you consider Nancy Reagan's maid as the one who smuggled the arms to Iran?"

"Is that the direction you're heading?" I asked.

"The White House has to keep all its options open."

Immunity

THE key word for 1987 will be "immunity." Everybody will be asking for it, and whether you receive it or not could affect your chances of becoming President of the United States in 1988.

Immunity is what you can get if you have taken the Fifth Amendment and the government wants you to talk up a storm. In exchange for spilling the beans, you are immune from anything you say being used against you.

It is not only in the legal system where immunity is popular. People in all walks of life use it as a bargaining chip, especially children.

This is how it works:

Someone has stolen the entire rear end of the Monster Machine which three-year-old Adam Marks received for Christmas. The suspects are his brothers Jason, five; and Ben, eight.

The prosecutor, in this case their mother, Connie Marks, demands to know who did it.

Both brothers refuse to answer any questions. (They are too young to realize that by clamming up they are taking advantage of the Fifth Amendment, but they do know that confessing at this stage will get them nowhere.)

Mrs. Marks is serious. "Unless someone tells me in one minute where Adam's toy is you will go to your rooms for the rest of the day."

Jason and Ben hang tough because they sense that Mrs. Marks is bluffing. It makes no sense to send them to their rooms when they are the only ones who know where the Monster's rear end is. The brothers are aware that it is more important for their mother to stop Adam crying than to find out who took the missing toy part.

"The minute is up. Are you going to tell me or not?"

There is dead silence and a lot of staring at feet. The witnesses, suspected of committing a heinous crime against the youngest brother, are waiting for an immunity offer.

"If you tell me," Mrs. Marks says, winding up for her pitch, "where you hid the Monster Machine's rear end, I will not punish either of you."

Jason and Ben try to figure out if this is a valid offer or a trap.

"I don't know where it is," says Jason, "but if I did know, how could I be sure you wouldn't spank me?"

"I'll tell you how," Mrs. Marks says, "because after the Christmas I have just gone through, I don't have the strength to punish anyone."

The boys accept this as a valid assurance and take the immunity in exchange for their critical information. Thus the Monster Machine's tail is returned to its rightful owner, who stops crying as soon as he gets it and then kicks it across the room.

Not everyone approves of making deals with children who refuse to talk. They feel it encourages wrongdoers. There are many reading this who insist that Mrs. Marks should not have granted immunity to her sons but leaned on them heavily when they refused to testify.

To them Mrs. Marks replies, "People who are critical of my actions have never spent any post-Christmas time with their children. To get them to reveal the whereabouts of Adam's toy I was prepared to not only give the boys full immunity, but throw in a trip to Disney World at the same time."

He's Innocent

UNLESS I am presented with convincing evidence to the contrary, I have to go along with Kurt Waldheim's story that although he was a lieutenant on the staff of a Nazi general, he had no idea that any atrocities were committed in Greece and Yugoslavia from 1942 to 1945.

There is no reason at this time to question the fact that the former Secretary General of the U.N. was anything more than a translator for German General Alexander Löhr, who unfortunately cannot be with us today because he was hanged as a war criminal.

Despite unfounded accusations, it is my humble opinion

that Mr. Waldheim was a victim, as were most German officers of World War II.

I cannot verify it, but this is probably what happened:

Mr. Waldheim, then a bright young officer of Austrian birth, was assigned to General Löhr's staff. Löhr's job was to kill as many Yugoslavs and Greeks as he possibly could and solve the Jewish Balkan question once and for all.

But Lieutenant Waldheim never knew about any of this. He was under the impression General Löhr's mission was to keep the Yugoslav and Greek partisans from looting stores.

When Waldheim first arrived and presented himself to General Löhr, the General told him, "I need a translator."

"Jawohl," said Waldheim. "What would you like me to translate?"

"Shakespeare. I love to read Shakespeare in the original. It relaxes me after a long day on the battlefield." Löhr handed Waldheim a German copy of Shakespeare and said, "I want a new play on my desk every night."

"What about my fighting, sir?"

"Don't worry about fighting. Leave that for our boys in the field."

So Waldheim moved into an office three doors down from the General and started to translate Shakespeare.

Every so often someone would rush in and say, "We have five thousand Greek men, women, and children in trucks outside. What should we do with them?"

Waldheim would yell, "That's not my department! Can't you see I'm translating *Hamlet*?"

Or an SS sergeant would crash in and say, "Where are the freight trains for the Jews of Salonika?"

Waldheim would put his hands over his ears so he couldn't hear what the man was saying and run out of his office.

For three years Waldheim kept his hands over his ears and eyes, never once hearing or seeing anything that the Germans were doing in the Balkans. As long as he completed his Shakespeare translations, no one ever asked him to do anything for Hitler's war effort.

Probably one of Waldheim's great triumphs was translating *All's Well That Ends Well* while Löhr and his troops wiped out fifteen thousand Yugoslav partisans in the infamous Operation Black.

The fact that Waldheim appears in a photograph at a Montenegro airport in full uniform with other officers a few days preceding the operation in no way means that he was involved in it. He was just saying hello to old friends before he went off to his tent with his German-English dictionary.

Some people maintain that it is awfully difficult to serve on a Nazi general's staff in the Balkans from 1942 to 1945 and not know what went on. Kurt Waldheim was the kind of guy who could do it.

If he made any mistake it was not mentioning in his autobiography that he served in the Balkans as a translator of Shakespeare for General Löhr. The only reason I can guess for this omission is that he was ashamed he had no idea what happened in World War II.

Your Money or Your Life

Not everything that happened during the Iranian-arms fol-
lies was tragedy. There were some light moments and
they deserve to be noted. One of them is when the State
Department put the arm on the Sultan of Brunei for ten million
dollars to help the Contras.

The way they tell it in the State Department cafeteria is
that Assistant Secretary of State Elliott Abrams thought up
the notion of asking the Sultan to hand over a few bucks for
the anti-Sandinista campaign.

The Sultan is said to be the richest man in the world, and
there's so much oil in his country that Brunei children pour
it on their cereal in the morning. The Sultan, who is very
lonely, agreed to give the money provided Secretary of State
George Shultz would stop by Brunei and say hello.

"No problem," Abrams said. "Just deposit the ten million
in this numbered Swiss bank account, and Secretary Shultz
will be happy to have a cup of tea with you."

Now here is where things start getting funny. The Sultan
did as he was told, and the money was put into a bank in
Switzerland. But His Highness never got so much as a thank-
you note from the State Department. Every time the Sultan
saw the U.S. Ambassador to Brunei, he winked at him, but
the U.S. Ambassador did not wink back.

Finally, at a diplomatic reception, the Sultan said to the
Ambassador, "I know it isn't much money, but could I get
a receipt for my ten million dollars so that I can deduct it

from my income tax?'' This started bells ringing in the State Department.

Abrams had been getting stories from his buddy Ollie North, who opened the Swiss bank account, that no funds from Brunei had ever been deposited. But when Abrams checked, he found out that the money had not only been put in but taken out without anyone knowing about it. Ollie was either playing national hero or taking the State Department to the cleaners.

What worries people is not what happened to the money, but what will happen to American relations with Brunei. How can the Sultan respect the most powerful nation in the world when it doesn't know how to launder money to countries in the Third World?

Some people in Washington are also concerned about how the request to the Sultan was made. Did Abrams ask for the money in a nice way or did he say, ''Okay, Sultan, give us ten million dollars or your tall ship will never pass the Statue of Liberty again.''

Other people are unhappy that Abrams and Shultz may have started a precedent by leaning on oil-rich sultans to finance U.S. wars which Congress doesn't want to pay for.

And then there are those who insist that Abrams sold out the United States too cheap. One expert, critical of Abrams, said, ''Ten million dollars is peanuts to get from Brunei, and it sure isn't worth a stopover by Shultz.''

Another question is, why was the State Department using Ollie North's Swiss bank account? Why didn't the State Department have an account of its own in the bank across the street from the American Embassy in Bern? Then embassy employees could watch it in case a Marine Corps colonel or an Army general made a withdrawal.

Elliott Abrams spent months keeping a Colombian woman correspondent out of the United States because he claimed she was a Marxist, which she wasn't. Abrams was so busy making sure that she didn't get in that he had no time to devote to protecting the Sultan of Brunei's money. The whole thing is embarrassing, and officials at the State Department have decided that the only way to make it up to His Highness is for George Shultz to go back to Brunei and give the Sultan a brand-new bank account number if he promises to give us another ten million.

"Bull"

"WHAT are you doing under the table, feller?"

"I'm a little investor and I'm hiding from the big guys who are trying to kill me."

"There is no reason to hide from the big guys. What makes America great is that it doesn't matter what size you are, everybody has the same opportunity to make money on Wall Street."

He whimpered as little stock players are apt to do.

"But the big guy with one trade can change the price of any stock on the market, while the little guy can't even get his broker on the phone."

"It's true that the larger investors can get in and out of a stock much more quickly than you, but you have the advantage, while waiting, of watching Louis Rukeyser on TV. The Street respects the little guy because he doesn't go blindly into the market throwing his money hither and yon.''

"That's because as a little guy I'm investing in the future of America, while the big guys are buying and selling to make three cents on soybeans. They're shooting crap with the country's economy.''

I said, "You're being too harsh on the big guys. All they are trying to do is create some excitement in the market. Years ago there were a lot more little guys than big guys on Wall Street. It had a sluggish, boring pace. The volume was pitiful and neither Dow nor Jones was anything to write home about.''

"I enjoyed it,'' the little player said.

"But the big guys took over the game and suddenly the market is now a vibrant, healthy, heart-stopping game where billions can be made or lost in seconds. The market is no longer for weak men or women, and by God when you play it today you know you've been in a fight.''

"But how can the little investor be sure when to buy and sell his ten shares when the large investor is speculating with the teachers' pension fund?''

"It's not easy. The big guy counts heavily on rumor— any rumor. That's why he is called a professional. As a small investor you have to watch where the big fellow is going and follow him.''

"I don't mind following him, but how do I know when to turn back?''

"That is what separates the professionals from the amateurs on Wall Street.''

"What makes a professional?''

"Most of them are under thirty years of age, went to good business schools, and wear Burberry raincoats.''

"Do they know much?"

"No, but they have dandy Apple computers."

"What worries me is if one of their computers makes a mistake."

"Yuppies never make mistakes."

"I have nothing against the big guys playing against me on Wall Street. I just want to know what their game plan is so I won't get wiped out," he said. "I feel I'm in a poker game where I have two chips and the other guy has twenty thousand. What do I do now?"

"Maybe you should give your two chips to the big guys and let them shoot crap for you."

"But I like to invest my own money. It's fun to sit in the ground floor of a broker's office and watch the lighted stock prices flashing over my head. Besides, what gives the big guys any more qualifications to be experts than the little guys?"

"For one thing they go to better restaurants than you do and order finer wines. Secondly, the big guys rarely play with their own money, so they can be a lot bolder than the little investor. And thirdly, when you're tossing around billions of dollars, people figure you're either crazy or an expert."

"How can you tell whether a big guy really knows what he is doing?"

"You look at his portfolio and if it's gone up, he is a brilliant investor, and if it's gone down he's just making a market correction."

You Better Watch Out

SANTA Claus was aghast when he picked up his newspaper and read the headline: NORTH POLE SCANDAL—SANTA DELIVERS TOYS TO NAUGHTY CHILDREN.

The story read, "After condemning naughty children in the strongest terms and vowing he would see that they never got any toys, it turns out the North Pole was secretly supplying bad kids with everything from G.I. Joe helicopters to spare parts for Barbie Dolls. The world was rocked by the news that Santa would advocate one toy policy and pursue another."

There had been a leak, and Santa was furious. He called in Rudolph, chief of the Christmas staff, and wanted to know what he was to say when asked about the botch-up.

Rudolph said, "We'll tell them that by supplying toys you were hoping to win over all the bad kids in the world to our side so they would become moderate naughty children instead."

Santa was red-faced. "How could it have leaked out to the press?"

"I have no idea, sir. We've never had a leak from the North Pole before."

"Well I want to get to the bottom of this. If children think they can be good or bad and still receive the same presents, I'll lose my credibility. My first question is: Was I involved?"

"No, sir. You were in the dark, as always. But whoever released the story was trying to stab you in the back."

Santa said, "The first thing we have to do is find out who

is telling the truth. I suggest we all take toy lie-detector tests.''

"That is a good idea, sir. I assume you want all elves wired up?''

"I am also talking about the reindeer.''

"It's hard to get reindeer to pass a detector test, sir, because they always lie through their teeth.''

"I'm appalled that anyone could believe that I would negotiate with naughty children. Mrs. Claus said they mean to get me in the popularity polls, which show 99.5 percent of the public think I am doing a good job. Now people will say that if Santa knew about the naughty-child policy he was stupid, and if he didn't know about it he was a dummy.''

"That's why we have to protect the name of Santa Claus at all costs. Here is a list of the elves who had access to the naughty-children file. I have North, South, East, West, and Poindexter.''

"Who is Poindexter?''

"He is a reindeer who was supposed to give you intelligence on who was good and who was bad last year. It's quite possible the elves and the reindeer were working together.''

"How's that?''

"This business started after a certain moderate child named Archie Archibald, aged five, refused to go to bed and was holding his mother hostage in the kitchen. When the mother said he would not get any toys for Christmas, Archie put his head in the garbage compactor. At this point members of the North Pole, without your knowledge, offered Archie any toys he wanted in exchange for letting his mother go.

"Unfortunately the word got out that you were willing to give in to blackmail and that you were also sending a message to kids saying that it doesn't matter if you are naughty or nice at Christmastime.''

"Why wasn't I made aware of this change in my blackmail policy?"

"Because Mrs. Claus told us never to bring you bad news."

"But what do I do now when they ask me if I will continue delivering presents to bad children?"

"What you should say, sir, is that you have always been against giving presents to naughty children, but at the same time you had to do it so that the bad kids wouldn't jump ship for Toys-Я-Us."

Snow Job

DESPITE what the President said in January, this country doesn't need a Star Wars program—it needs a Snow Plow Initiative. All Mr. Reagan had to do was look out the window of his limousine to realize that the capital had been brought to a grinding halt without one Soviet missile being fired.

The idea of having enough snow-clearing equipment for Washington, DC, has always been a dream of government scientists, many of whom live outside the Beltway.

Werner Zamblowski, a leading voice for developing the Snow Plow Initiative, claims that it is not only feasible to produce such a system with present technology, but it is absolutely necessary considering the snow job the Soviets are doing on Moscow.

"The United States has the technical know-how to remove the snow from its streets," he said in his thick German accent. "It's just a question of getting the Congress to pay for it. To dump tomorrow we must be willing to invest in the future today. Our children and their children must never be snowed in. I see the day when not only our main streets, but our side streets will be plowed out from curb to curb. I see the day when we can push all abandoned cars into the Potomac. And I see the day when Washington's honorable mayor will actually be in town when the snowstorm comes."

Opponents of the Snow Plow Initiative believe SPI is unrealistic. Jarrell Jerryboam is opposed to it because he doesn't think snow removal in Washington has any future. "Once the first snowflake hits the ground," he says, "everyone in the nation's capital panics. It doesn't matter how many snowplows you deploy, they're only going to be blocked by people taking early leave from the Pentagon."

Jerryboam showed satellite photographs of the storm to prove that snowplows are not the answer to snow removal. "It takes more than equipment to deter snow. The truth is that there is no response to a Washington snowfall because the chance of human error is too great."

Secretary of Defense Cap Weinberger, caught in a storm on the George Washington Parkway, told reporters in an off-the-record weiner roast that Moscow has three times as many snowplows as Washington. These plows have a throw weight capable of clearing a six-lane highway from Pinsk to Minsk in less than an hour.

Asked why Washington is so short on trucks and bulldozers, and the Soviets so big on them, Weinberger blamed liberals soft on snow for drifting from one crisis to another. He told Ted Koppel, who happened to be on the parkway doing a snow-removal report, "We're paying the price for twenty years of salt and sand neglect."

I called the White House and asked where the President stood on a Snow Plow Initiative. A spokesman replied, "The President's dream has always been to leave a clean Washington behind when he finished his term. He plans to go on television next week and deny that any U.S. snow-removal equipment was sold to Iran. He will also announce that he is appointing a snow-removal commission made up of those responsible for the January disaster to recommend what Washington should do in case of a new storm. In an address to the nation, the President will express sympathy with those who suffered during the storm, and intends to read a letter from a little girl who couldn't go to school and pray because of the snowstorm and the Supreme Court. Finally he will cite a true American hero—a driver of a tow truck who was buried in an embankment for three days on I-66. When he was dug out, he was asked by the highway patrol if he had any message for the American people and he said, "Send me more snow!"

A Trojan Thou Art

S HOULD condom companies be permitted to beat the drum for their products on national TV?

I say they should.

I had a passing acquaintance with condoms long before they became an advertising issue. But our generation never called them condoms. They were Trojans. Even in those days brand name was everything.

The first thing we learned in the P.S. 35 schoolyard was that Trojans came three in a pack, and that you had better carry them at all times because you never knew when lightning was going to strike.

We looked upon anyone who carried Trojans as our role model, and believed as gospel everything he told us about his sex life. They were lies, all lies, but they certainly held our attention.

The toughest thing about Trojans was obtaining them from the drugstore. The attempt to purchase them has been drama-tized in every book and movie you can think of, and none of it is exaggerated.

On Jamaica Avenue it went like this: I entered and went to the soda fountain for a chocolate egg cream. Then I cased the store, waiting for it to be empty, or as near to empty as it could get. I read comic books until Doc Fiedler's counter was clear.

Doc Fiedler always kept the Trojans under the cash register next to the Feen-a-mint and Jergens lotion. I once peeked back there to see how they were stacked. Finally, after buying a small tube of Ipana toothpaste, I said, in a very high, screechy voice, "Oh, I forgot. I believe I'll have a pack of Trojans, for my uncle."

Doc Fiedler looked at me suspiciously. "You got a date with Jean Harlow tonight?" he asked.

"Maybe. Are these the real thing?"

As I think back, I'm sure Doc had trouble restraining a grin. He said, "You can have a money-back guarantee on all three."

I gave him fifty cents and stuffed the Trojans in a wallet, where they remained untouched for ten years.

Then they were discovered by my sister, who demanded to know what I was doing with them. I said that I had bought them for an emergency when I was twelve years old, but sadly for everyone, I never needed them.

As most sisters would do, she called me a pig.

Even in the forties some people didn't appreciate the importance of having protection at a moment's notice.

So far as I can tell, Trojans went into a decline after World War II and miracle drugs took their place.

In fact, folklore has it that if it hadn't been for schoolkids buying Trojans to impress their friends, the company might have gone under.

Now condoms are back, and they are trying to sell them on national TV. I don't believe that Doc Fiedler is still with us, but if he is, he doesn't have to worry about putting Trojans under the counter anymore. You can have a nice big display in your store window and no one could care less.

You would think now that Trojans are so popular, I'd stock up on them. But that isn't the case. The fun of buying them was sneaking to the back of the store and making my purchase before anyone caught me. Besides, what's the big deal of showing off to all my friends when they can see them for themselves next to the L'eggs display by the door?

I know that there are people who object to the sale of condoms on the premise that they lead to promiscuity. They have nothing to fear. Ninety-eight percent of all men who carried them in their wallets for forty years have never broken the seals.

Another Lie

THE dream of the Reagan administration was to have everyone in the government take a lie detector test. The President felt that the lie detector was the only way to keep public servants from leaking government secrets to the press. It also put the fear of God into those who weren't following the White House game plan.

Alas, the lie detector has fallen on hard times. Since Irangate, all the machines have been recalled because they are giving out false signals.

The retired detectors are being collected in a warehouse in Alexandria, Virginia, where they are guarded by Victor Veracity, who is the Deputy Director of the U.S. Department of Truth and Consequences.

"Why," I asked, "have you recalled so many detectors?"

Victor replied, "Because they reported that everyone attached to Irangate is lying. We know for a fact that the people who were involved don't lie, so it must mean that the machines are faulty."

"How could the lie detectors have gone so far off?"

"Each time we strapped up one of the major players in the Iran affair, he blew out every fuse in the Senate hearing room. Since the President's men are all Boy Scouts, we had to assume that the glitch was in the detector. Let me show you what is going on. I will ask this lie detector machine a question. 'When did you know we were selling arms and not Bibles to Iran?' Now I will respond to the question. 'Only after the Ayatollah Khomeini told me about it in a Tel Aviv discotheque.' Do you see where the needle went? Right off the board."

"And the machine wasn't even plugged in," I said.

"That's why we've recalled all the detectors. You can't trust them."

"What are you going to do now that you have brought back all the detectors?"

"We've established a course in remedial truth. It helps people involved in Irangate to realize that they have options. They can tell the truth, they can stick with their stories, or they can choose the boring way out by taking the Fifth Amendment."

"I didn't know the government could afford a remedial truth course with all the budget cuts."

"We established it for people who are up to their hips in Iran and Contra operations but are also interested in protecting the President."

"Can the lie-detecting machines distinguish between those

who are team players and those who are just interested in telling the truth to save the country?''

''We're very suspicious of people who use lie detectors to save the country. Even the CIA can't be trusted.''

Victor showed me a copy of *The Washington Post*. ''Look at this. The CIA is re-examining whether the Agency's covert operations in Nicaragua violated congressional bans against giving military aid to the Contras. This part may interest you. The first thing the acting director of the CIA did was to rule that since so many agents may have given questionable testimony regarding Contra operations, everyone can testify over again and change his testimony.''

''Are we to assume that because of Irangate the lie detector is no longer held in such high esteem as it was before?''

''The White House has only one goal in all the Iran-Contra hearings.''

''Which is?''

''To see that everyone involved in this dreadful mistake can once again look at himself in the mirror and not be ashamed.''

Wrong Number

I have in my hand the transcript of the last telephone conversation between Don Regan and Nancy Reagan.

Nancy: Don, can we talk?

Don: I told you never to call me at the office. What is it this time?

Nancy: I want to know why you don't send me flowers anymore.

Don: Because I'm trying to run the White House and you keep butting in with some crazy idea about the President and it's making my life miserable.

Nancy: I don't believe that I'm out of line by objecting to you sending Ronnie down the Snake River on a raft two weeks after his prostate operation.

Don: The President has a lot of admirers along the Snake River.

Nancy: You don't care about Ron. All you're trying to do is make an abrasive name for yourself.

Don: If you keep talking like that I'm going to put you on Hold.

Nancy: If you put me on Hold I'll sic my dog on you.

Don: Nancy, you have to stay out of the Oval Office. Women just don't belong there.

Nancy: Listen, worm, we had a very nice White House until you took over as chief of staff. Why don't you pack your bags and take the next thirty-nine-dollar United flight to Syracuse?

Don: Stick to baking birthday cakes and leave the business of running the country to me.

Nancy: Why don't you stuff your Touchtone in your ear?

Don: That does it. Now I am going to hang up on you.

Nancy: You wouldn't dare hang up on the First Lady. If you did you'd wind up as our next ambassador to Iran.

Don: The President has assured me that my job with him is safe. After the Tower Report he needs me more than ever.

Nancy: Why does the President need you?

Don: Because I am the only one who tells him what he said and why he said it.

Nancy: Ronnie doesn't have to know *anything*. All he has to do is be himself.

Don: Are you finished? I have work to do to save the country from the horrible mess we got it into.

Nancy: I want to know why you attacked me for supporting the President's appointment to communications chief of someone who happened to be a cub Nazi when he was ten years old?

Don: I didn't attack you—I attacked the East Wing of the White House where you work. All I said was that the East Wing was stupid, incompetent, and interfered in West Wing business.

Nancy: Do you know what I suspect, Donald Regan? You're trying to get me to resign as the First Lady so that you can have Ronnie all to yourself.

Don: It's not true. I know that the President respects you very much and it's my job to ensure that he never has to choose between us. In the meantime I think I'll hang up on you.

Nancy: Don't you dare hang up on me. I was talking to Ronnie last night and we thought it would be nice if you took a private office next to Michael Deaver's. In that way you'd still be near us and out of our hair at the same time.

Don: Nancy, may I ask you a personal question? Why are you calling me?

Nancy: It's no mystery that the telephone company wants us all to reach out and touch someone we love.

Dog Talk

EVERYONE I know has a dog. And each one of them believes that his dog is the most beautiful, intelligent pet in the world. What has me worried is that many of these people would rather talk to their dogs than to their friends.

Bernheim, who owns a big black labrador named Killum, invited me for lunch the other day to catch up on what I had been doing for the last six months.

As I entered the foyer, Killum jumped up on me and slobbered all over my sport coat.

"Down, Killum," Bernheim said. "Give your Uncle Artie a chance to walk around and get used to his environment."

"I'm not his Uncle Artie. I don't even know him."

"It's not a him—it's a her. Killum, tell Daddy what kind of day you had," Bernheim said, ignoring me completely.

I went into the living room and Killum followed me, sniffing my socks.

Bernheim messed up Killum's fur. "You love to sniff ankles, don't you?"

"I love to have my ankles sniffed," I said, hoping to make a good impression on Bernheim. He just turned to the dog and said, "After Uncle Artie leaves, we'll really have a good fetch."

"Is Killum going to stay with us the whole day?" I asked.

"Of course not. I'll put her out. Honey, put the damn dog out right now!" he yelled to his wife.

"Who wants her out? . . . Oh, I might have known. You've hated every dog we have ever owned."

"With reason," I replied.

"Killum," Bernheim said, "you're not amongst friends. Stay alert."

I was starting to get a little queasy.

Killum climbed up on me while I was sitting in the chair and had me by the shoulders.

"Good girl," said Bernheim. "Now give Uncle Artie a big kiss."

"Does anybody around here ever talk to human beings?" I inquired.

"Why do you ask?"

"Because most of your remarks have been addressed to the dog. I don't mind her being part of the conversation, but does she have to dominate it?"

"Watch what you say. Killum is very sensitive. You can tell that just by the way she puts her tongue in your ear."

"Can we talk about the stock market?" I asked.

"Of course—as soon as I get Killum to stop chewing on the rug. STOP CHEWING THE RUG," Bernheim yelled.

"Look, if I'm interrupting anything, I'll go," I said.

"Don't go. You're not in the way."

Bernheim's wife announced that lunch was being served. I got up.

"Come on, Killum, lunch is ready." Bernheim then said to me, "You don't have any objection if she eats with us, do you?"

"Objection?" I laughed falsely. "Why would anyone object to eating with a dog?"

Killum made a tour around the table, trying to decide where she was going to rest her head.

"So what's new?" Bernheim asked.

"Nothing much," I said. "I ran into Jimmy Hoffa the other day and he wants to turn himself in."

"Just a minute. Killum, if you want something to eat, ask for it. Marjorie, give her something to munch on."

"Where is she?" Marjorie asked.

"She's under the table," I said. "Chewing on my tattoo."

The Power Game

THE big question is, Who holds the power in the average American home? Until recently the answer was up for grabs. Now this has changed. Dr. Jungfreud, a visiting psychiatrist at Paneful University, told me, "The power in America rests with the person who controls the TV remote unit."

"Zap!" I said.

"Studies show that the man or woman who has the power to change a TV channel from bed is the one who will get the respect in the family."

"But all one is doing is selecting programs. That doesn't make you a god."

"It's not just controlling a TV set. The person who has his finger on the clicker is making a powerful statement. He is saying, in no uncertain terms, 'You mess with me and you'll never see channel 9 again.' "

I said, "Personally I don't care who holds the remote in our family. There are many nights when I've let my wife click it as long as she wants to. We've had no power problem except on the occasional evening when I have asked her, in a very nice way, to give the remote back to me and she has refused. I got really mad because she knew it was my turn."

"And what did you do when she refused to give back the remote?" Dr. Jungfreud asked.

"I told her she wasn't being fair, and that no marriage can survive if one spouse switches channels more than the other."

"Did your wife keep the remote?"

"She did for *I'll Take Manhattan* but I took it back when she dozed off during *People's Court*."

"Can you tell me how often you've let her use the TV clicker?"

"More than a lot of husbands I know."

"Yet you feel that when she holds the remote she has the upper hand?"

"Not all the time. But I think I should be consulted when she uses the 'mute' button during Dan Rather. She also changes programs without asking me. I'm for women's rights, but how many women in this country do you know who are up to operating a remote button on a nineteen-inch Sony?"

"On the other hand, they have come a long way since the fine-tuner was invented," Dr. Jungfreud said. "Frankly I think you are in a power struggle with your wife. Every time she grabs the clicker and goes by the *A-Team* you feel emasculated."

"Maybe you're right, but what do I do?"

"You both have to gain equal control of the channels. This can be done either with a remote TV marital agreement, specifying how much time a person will have to hold the clicker, or, if that doesn't work, by purchasing a second remote so that each of you will have your own in bed."

"I like the second idea better than the first. This will give me a chance to zap her *Wheel of Fortune* off the screen."

"And she can do the same to your wrestling. It will become a game, and there is nothing like a game to keep two people happy in the bedroom."

"Are couples all over America experiencing the same problem?"

"I am afraid they are. Most people don't even know they're at war when they're watching TV."

"The whole thing seems sick."

"No one ever told you that mixing remote TV with marriage would be easy."

A Talk With G

THE old man, known to us all as G, answered the door. He looked more fragile than when he ran our spy network— that was during the days when the cold war really counted for something.

G, now living a block from the Soviet Embassy in Northwest Washington, ushered me into the living room and offered me a cup of instant tea. Then he put two slices of bread out on the windowsill. He explained that the microwaves from the Soviet Embassy roof toast his bread a lot faster and cheaper than his oven. "I even cook my steaks that way," he said.

"What do you make of all this espionage activity?" I asked him.

"Big budgets and showboating. We must let Ivan know that we can hear every word he says, while he is doing the same to us. I'm not in the game anymore, but if I were, I wouldn't hesitate to stick my bugs up every commie pantleg in the country.''

"G, if you were running things, would you plant American girls on Soviet guards here in Washington so that the guards would show us their basement?''

"I would if I could find any American who would participate. But in my forty years with the Company I never found an American woman who would offer her charms to a Red Marxist-Leninist rat.''

"Not even for money?''

"Not even for money. I went to every madam between Park Avenue and Anchorage, Alaska, and they all said the same thing. 'We may be fallen women, but we're Americans first.' ''

"Since you couldn't get American women to compromise themselves with Russian government personnel, what *did* you do to garner important information from Ivan?''

"We did the next-best thing. We gave the Russian secretaries nylons and Hershey bars.''

"Could they be turned around for that?''

"No, but the Hershey bar almonds were really listening devices, and once the bar was consumed the secretary unknowingly was on our side.''

"G, will this mutual bugging hurt relations between the United States and the USSR?''

"I shouldn't think so. Both sides are very aware that their intelligence people have to make a living and look good with their bosses at home. What bothers me is why the U.S. did not anticipate that Ivan would bug our new embassy in Moscow.''

"Maybe it's because our State Department is dumb?''

[331]

"That's too obvious," G said. "There might be another reason. The Americans wanted the KGB to bug the embassy in Moscow so that they could pass on disinformation to the Soviets."

"That's possible, but wouldn't the embassy eventually run out of disinformation and then be stuck with leaking legitimate secrets?"

"Exactly," said G. "That's why it is so confusing. Somebody is doing something to someone, and we don't know the who and why of it because their side has enlisted women agents and our side is still paying off their people with Japanese watches."

"Your toast is done," I told him.

He took the bread off the windowsill. Then he said, "You know we've bugged their building in Washington up, down, and sideways. Every time I try to get the game show *Jeopardy* on television I hear the Soviet Ambassador's wife talking to Mrs. Gorbachev in Moscow. I'm sure it's them because Mrs. Gorbachev keeps insisting she wants her American Express card renewed."

The old boy was getting tired, so I got up to leave. "G," I said, "if we can't use lovemaking as a legitimate weapon, what would you suggest we do to find out what they're really up to?"

He said, "Garbage. The first thing any espionage agent does is go through his opponent's garbage. Sifting through the other chap's trash pail may not be as exciting as compromising him with a woman, but it's a lot neater."

Flirt With Her

M Y favorite AT&T advertisement shows a gray-haired man and woman head to head. The copy reads, "Flirt with her again. Call the U.K. She was your childhood sweetheart. The girl you always planned to marry. And even though so much has happened since you left London, since you left her side, you still carry a torch for her. Why not give her a call and tell her?"

I came into the Dalinsky house and Marian was throwing ketchup bottles at Harry, who was ducking behind the sofa.

"What's up?" I asked.

Marian said, "He just called his childhood sweetheart in London."

"I can't believe it, Harry. I didn't know you had a childhood sweetheart in England."

"I met her once at a pub," Harry said. "I wouldn't recognize her if I saw her now."

"Did you tell her on the phone that she was the girl you planned to marry?"

"You have to tell women something like that to make them feel better."

Marian threw a jar of mustard at him.

"Harry, what on earth are you doing calling your childhood sweetheart after being married for forty-seven years?"

"I was reading an advertisement in this magazine and it said you could call the girl of your dreams for sixty-four cents. I figured I owed Mathilda a tinkle. There is nothing between us anymore except a lot of wonderful memories.''

The sugar bowl came sailing across the room.

''Why didn't you marry Mathilda if she was such a good childhood sweetheart?'' Marian shouted at Harry.

''She wasn't my type. Served me tea day and night until my stomach swelled up. She might have had the looks, but she repeated herself a lot.''

''Hold it,'' I said as Marian was about to spear Harry with a floor lamp. ''I want to know what Mathilda said when you got her on the phone.''

Harry said, ''I told her it was her childhood sweetheart calling and she said, 'Hello Fred.' ''

''English girls never get their men's first names right.''

''Then,'' Harry continued, ''I told her that I still carry a torch for her.''

''That must have pleased her,'' I said.

''I'm not sure because at that moment Marian took the palm tree out of the planter and shoved it down my pants.''

''It sounds as if Marian didn't appreciate the AT & T advertisement.''

''The phone company has a nerve to suggest that happily married husbands call their childhood sweethearts and tell them they're still carrying a torch for them,'' Marian said.

I said, ''The phone company has been doing some weird things lately. I wouldn't be surprised if they ran an ad soon suggesting that divorced people call their ex-spouses up and yell at each other. Did the call cost you a lot?''

''It cost me more than you think. Marian got on the line and told Mathilda what she had missed for the last forty-seven years. It would have been cheaper for me to fly over and have tea with Mathilda at the Savoy.''

War Is Hell

I didn't know how serious the Japanese trade war was until I turned on the shortwave radio and heard Tokyo Rose. For those of you who missed World War II, Tokyo Rose was an outstanding enemy disc jockey who broadcast propaganda for the Japanese. Many believe that World War II would not have been as much fun without her.

Rose's voice had hardly changed over the years. She said, "Hello, Mr. and Mrs. American Consumer. Your brainless leaders have started a trade war with Nippon that they cannot win. Before it's over they will rue the day they thought they could challenge the productive might of the sacred Imperial Empire.

"Your leaders started this war, Americans, but it is you who must suffer. Just let me tell you what the Japanese Joint Chiefs of Hitachi plan to do to defend their exports. We are going to fire our twenty-five-inch TV sets across the bow of every American living room.

"Our super VCRs are now programmed to intercept and scramble all NFL football games. No one will be safe from our high-speed laser CDs. How does that grab you, American dogs? If you want war, we'll give you war. For every tariff you lay on Japanese goods, we will retaliate with a duty of our own.

"To show that we mean business, Japan will no longer honor its green warranty cards. Yes, you will be stuck with billions of dollars of Japanese products, and your warranties will be useless. We are also talking about the ninety-day, no-questions-asked, money-back guarantees. The Geneva Convention says that all green warranty cards are void in time of a trade war.

"American consumer, you cannot dump on the Japanese without facing the consequences. What if I were to tell you that a fleet of our ships is now headed for San Francisco, and our salesmen will sweep across the Silicon Valley with hundreds of thousands of semiconductor chips? In one week there won't be an intelligible American chip left on the West Coast. Tell your mad leaders to give up their futile war against the Japanese nation before we unleash our elite Seiko brigades and bring Timex to its knees.

"American fools, we possess many billions of yen. If you continue your trade policy, there is nothing to prevent a Japan Airlines 747 from dropping them out of the sky down Paul Volcker's chimney in the Federal Reserve Bank building.

"Americans, your situation is helpless. If you want to know how helpless, check it out on our new hand-held Sony calculators.

"One more thing. I'd like to address myself to those U.S. citizens who bought Japanese microwave ovens for their kitchens. I could warn you about those ovens—but in a trade war everything is secret. So instead I'm going to sign off. As we say in the land of the Rising Sun, 'Have a nice Day of Infamy.' "

Latkes for Dollars

I was walking down the street when I saw my friend Alan Guimond coming toward me with a wheelbarrow.

"What are you doing, Alan?"

"I'm buying up every wheelbarrow I can get my hands on. With the dollar the way it is, everyone will need a wheelbarrow to go to the store."

"You're joking, Alan. The dollar has never looked better."

"I don't joke about wheelbarrows," he replied. "The tipoff came to me when the Van Gogh painting was sold at auction for $39.9 million. I said to myself, 'Alan, if that's what they're paying for sunflowers, you better get into something more comfortable.' "

"What is really going on?" I asked.

Alan replied, "There are too many dollars bouncing around, and not enough things to buy with them. The guy who bought the Van Gogh decided he'd rather have one picture of yellow sunflowers than 39.9 million pictures of George Washington. He has made it impossible for anyone to buy a Van Gogh for five million dollars again. That is why you're going to need a wheelbarrow to go to the supermarket."

"It doesn't make any monetary sense."

"It was all a game," said Alan. "We printed billions and billions of Eurodollars and petrodollars and just plain old-fashioned American dollars and kited them into the air. As long as they stayed up there no one paid attention. Well, they're starting to float down and people want something besides a pretty treasury bond to hang on their walls. And while they're looking for something to purchase with their money, they are going to have to buy a wheelbarrow."

"How many people can afford Van Goghs?"

"No matter," Alan said. "Everything else is out of sight as well. Have you seen the houses they are buying these days? Improved lean-tos go for a half million, and remodeled outhouses for a quarter of a million. When á $50,000 house now sells for $900,000 you know there is going to be a big demand for wheelbarrows. Look, I'm not making much of a profit on them. I have put money where my mouth is. I'm selling a $150 wheelbarrow for $800."

"Is that reasonable?"

"It's more reasonable than paying $39.9 million for a painting by a guy with a chewed-up ear."

"What is the answer?" I asked.

"We have to find something to substitute for dollars."

"What do you suggest?"

"Latkes. I am advocating we get off dollars and go on the latke standard."

"What are latkes?"

"They're potato pancakes that have ethnic significance. The reason they are better than dollars is if you can't find anything to buy, you can eat them. But the strongest case for the latke is that the Japanese hate them."

"What is to prevent the latke from becoming as weak as the dollar?"

"The people's faith in it. As Americans lose confidence in the dollar, they have to turn to something. Why not a potato pancake, which goes especially well with pot roast?"

"You couldn't have come along at a better time. I was going to use my life savings to go to a Broadway show.

Now I'm going to put them in latkes. One more question. If inflation is getting so bad why didn't the President tell us about it?''

''He forgot.''

Meals for Wheels

"**W**HEN I make a mistake, I make a doozy.'' Thus spoke Senator Lloyd Bentsen. The mistake the Texas Senator was talking about was his idea of inviting lobbyists to have breakfast with him once a month for ten thousand dollars—toast and marmalade included.

The donor would not only get to eat with the Senator, but he would be asked advice on trade, taxation, and anything else the lobbyist wished to bring up. It sounded like one whale of a deal. But when it leaked out what Mr. Bentsen was charging for breakfast, the Senator was forced to close down his diner.

I don't want anyone to get the impression that Senator Bentsen is the only one selling access to the power-brokers who prowl the Hill. The opportunity of getting close to one's senator for a price has become Washington's biggest business.

I was having breakfast with Senator Pogie at the Madison Hotel the other morning. Since Pogie is a junior senator it only cost me six thousand dollars.

The Senator was a gracious host. "Do you want some more corned beef hash?" he asked.

"No, this is fine," I assured him.

"You can have all the grits you want," he told me. "Say what they will, Pogie never stints on his Meals for Wheels Program. Would you like to know how I intend to vote on the pork barrel bill?"

"Am I permitted?"

"Your breakfast entitles you to three questions or three English muffins, whichever comes first."

"Can I ask what you plan to do with all the money you are raising from lobbyists?"

"Lobbyists need love too. But just because I listen to their stories doesn't mean that I'm obligated to vote in their favor, although I must say, most of them make excellent arguments for their cause. Have a waffle."

"I'm stuffed."

"Do columnists have any legislative problems I can help with?"

"I can't speak for George Will, but I don't have any. There is talk that the Japanese and South Koreans are thinking of dumping a lot of cheap foreign columns on the United States. But I'm not worried. When it comes to cheap columns, we American journalists can hold our own."

Two men passed by the table and one of them said, "Hello, Senator. How goes it?"

Pogie went red and mumbled, "I don't believe it. Liverheels refused to give to my political action committee and he now has the nerve to walk by and say hello to me."

"If he doesn't contribute he has no right to pretend that he knows you."

"Of course he doesn't. If he can say hello to me for free, why should other lobbyists pay for the privilege?"

"Do you know what I think? The guy with him is a client and Liverheels is trying to impress him by saying hi. It makes me mad when he gets a free hello."

Pogie said, "Don't worry about it. Just because someone says hello to me doesn't mean he owns me. Here, put this maple syrup on your French toast and then you'll know why I run the best political breakfast club in town."

"You really care about your constituents' appetites, don't you?"

Pogie said, "I call them as I see them. But if you say that I'm wrong and you want to add a few bucks to my election kitty, I'll be glad to look at it again on instant replay."

Make Your Bed

Earlier this year *Time* magazine devoted a cover to the breakdown of service in the United States. Nobody seems to be able to get anyone to help them anymore.

"There is a simple reason for this," Frankie Melnick told me as we stood at the airport check-in line, watching an airline attendant take thirty-two minutes to prepare one luggage tag.

"What is that?"

"All the trouble started a generation ago when the youth of America, the ones who now have us by the throat, were permitted to grow up without making their beds."

"Why did we allow it?"

Melnick said, "Because of the wars. Men went off to fight, and when they were asked what they were fighting for, they couldn't think of anything to say, so they answered, 'I am doing it so that my children will never have to clean up their rooms again. Our kids are going to become doctors and lawyers and investment bankers, and paid-up members of the Democratic and Republican parties, and they are not going to be distracted by household chores.' "

"I recall saying the same thing to my kids," I said as we inched slowly toward the ticket counter. "I remember years ago holding one of my children in my arms and saying to him, 'I will see to it that you will never have to hang up your clothes as long as you live.' I kept that vow—or, let's say, my son kept it for me. Whenever his mother or I yelled at him, he replied, 'If I have to think about my room, I won't have time to think about the human condition.' "

Melnick continued, "We did it because we loved them. But the message that they got was, 'If you want to lie down in your bed, there is always a dear person in your life who will make it up for you. This is not because that person necessarily loves you, but because she can't stand walking by every day looking at it.' "

"Do you really think," I asked, "that service has broken down in the United States since we let the kids have a free ride in their bedrooms?"

Melnick said, "You could make a case for it. The non-bed-makers are screwing up the entire government today because they never had to use a laundry hamper. The retail business is filled with people who are so homesick that they still dump their pants and skirts on the floor. There are millions of men and women in their prime who have never figured out what to do with a hanger.''

We moved up a foot in line. ''I assume that the attendant trying to fill out the baggage tag never had to make up his bed.''

''It's worse than that,'' Melnick said. ''The pilot of our plane didn't have to either.''

I told Melnick, ''I'm happy to say that we have been very strict parents in our family. Neither my wife nor I will tolerate a dirty room.''

''How do you do it?'' Melnick asked.

''We make the kids keep their doors closed so that we never see what is on the other side.''

The man standing behind us said, ''You don't necessarily have to be neat to do well in your profession. My son is now a surgeon, and he never made a bed in his life.''

''Who fixes the sheets for him just before he operates?''

''His mother.''

A Reasonable Discussion

HUSBANDS in bedrooms all over America are catching hell for Gary Hart's bad judgment.

"I really don't care what Gary Hart did," my wife said the other night.

"When you say you don't care that means you care a lot."

She shook her head. "He is a grown-up candidate and he probably thought at the time what he did would help his election."

"Gary didn't do anything."

"Of course he didn't do anything," she answered. "He was running a day-care center for *Miami Vice*."

"Women always think the worst when a married man goes out with a single woman."

"Not me. I say when the wife is away what are friends for? Let me ask you a question. If you were home alone for the weekend what would you do?"

"I'd paint the kitchen," I replied. "I love a free weekend because it gives me a chance to get all my household chores done."

"I expected you to say something like that. Suppose it got in the newspapers that you went out with a beautiful semi–movie actress?"

"I would deny it. The question is not what I'd say but what you'd say," I told her.

"I would say that whatever you said was good enough

for me. And if it's good enough for me then it should be good enough for everybody.''

"You're a trouper," I said.

"Then I'd find the girl and scratch her eyes out.''

"What happened to your stiff upper lip?''

"I'm saving that to bite your arm off.''

"I don't like where this conversation is going. Gary Hart was the one who got into a jam. Why do I have to take the flak?''

"Because you two have a lot in common. It would be just like you to take a boat ride to Bimini and stay overnight.''

"Not true. I hate Bimini. Besides, I don't like to sleep away from home.''

"What puzzles me is that with Gary Hart's enormous political campaign debt he could find a free Saturday in Washington.''

"There is no law saying a person in a tough presidential campaign can't relax for a few days in his home.''

"Yes, but he should have changed his name before he made his phone calls.''

I protested, "That's excessive and terribly unfair. Besides, you can't judge everybody by the former Democratic frontrunner. The difference between Hart and myself is if anyone called me in Washington I would put her on hold for the entire weekend.''

"I'm sure. What about all your boyfriends? Would they behave the same way?''

"Certainly. I don't have one friend who doesn't find philandering ugly and unseemly and something that must be avoided at all costs.''

"Then I suppose none of them are having this conversation tonight with their wives?''

"I hope not. Are you finished with this congressional hearing?"

"Yes," my wife said. "But I think you ought to be warned that if you so much as open the front door for an Avon Lady, I'll throw all your clothes out in the street."

No Comment

THE only thing we can do now is learn from Gary Hart's experience. These are the rules that any presidential candidate should obey.

Do not go on a picnic with someone named Donna.

Do not go down a dark alley with a person named Rice.

Above all, do not take anyone back to your house after dark to show her the improvements you made in the ceiling.

Never sail to the island of Bimini when the customs shack is closed.

If a woman wants to work in your campaign, tell her you're all filled up and have no room for even one more volunteer. Do not—repeat—do not telephone and ask her to join you for a strategy meeting to discuss how to get the singles vote.

Don't autograph your book to an individual who is liable to show it on an airplane to her fellow passengers.

There is no such thing as a free weekend. It can cost a presidential candidate a lot, particularly if he gets lonely and goes over to his best friend's house to have a quiet dinner for four.

Just because nothing happened between you and an unmarried woman does not mean that *nothing* happened. It did happen if it gets reported in the press. Therefore the only ones who should be allowed to visit you on the weekends when your wife is not there are the plumber and the Orkin Man.

It is absolutely essential that the candidate never say to the press, "If you think I'm a womanizer why don't you follow me and see for yourself?" The reason for this is too obvious to explain.

During a tough presidential campaign do not play cards with anybody named Bill—especially if he knows a lot of attractive people in Miami.

If you have ignored all of the above and the press takes after you, then you have to do the following:

Call a press conference and deny anything that you are accused of. Tell them you are guilty of bad judgment but you are clean as the driven snow. Offer a reward to anyone who can prove otherwise. (If for some reason there is a danger of losing the reward, cancel the press conference and go into a "No comment" mode.)

Attack all press stakeouts as un-American and beneath the dignity of a political campaign. Say you don't care for yourself but you worry about the American farmer and people who are on Social Security.

If that doesn't work, admit you were guilty of something or other and if you had it to do all over again you would go to a Baltimore Orioles doubleheader and order a hot dog instead.

The question of your presidential qualifications may come

up. If it does, insist you are a better presidential candidate now than you were yesterday because you weathered a crisis. Point out it takes a strong man to repulse the kind of attack you have been under. Declare that anyone can walk in the front door of his house and walk out the front. But it takes a man with great vision to go in the front door and come out the back.

Finally, if nothing else works you can always say, ''I made mistakes, but they were mistakes of the Hart.''

The Last Laugh

BENNEDY Berasimov, the Soviet Foreign Ministry spokesman, was described by the Reuters News Agency as finding the U.S. Marine scandal at the American Embassy in Moscow very humorous.

Well, Bennedy Berasimov, you may be laughing now, but you're not going to be laughing for long.

The truth is that the Marine incident was our setup job to snare Russian nationals into an American plot that would make the Soviets look foolish in the entire cloak-and-dagger world.

First of all, Bennedy Berasimov, you should learn a few things about our armed services. You cannot seduce an American Marine unless he *wants* to be seduced. When you sent your KGB agents, doused in Evening in Moscow perfume, through the halls of the U.S. Embassy, you made a mistake. Your female spooks were told to steal code books, top secret cables, and as many blueprints as they could possibly stuff into their peasant blouses.

As part of their assignment, the KGB ladies were ordered to commit sexual transgressions with our Marines in the name of Mother Russia.

What you didn't know, Bennedy Berasimov, and what you are probably finding out for the first time as you read this, is that we had your game plan all the time. Our Marines had instructions not to resist the overtures of your spook women. All the time your spyniks thought they were compromising our gyrenes, we were taking Polaroid shots of what was going on. What you did not realize, Bennedy, is that each Marine was ordered to "lie back, close your eyes and think of America" if things got tough.

This is what really happened, Bennedy Berasimov, that fateful night when all hell broke loose at the embassy. At midnight three of your women came to the gate and said they were from the Bolshoi ballet and wanted to defect. They asked if they could party at the same time.

Our Marines knew it was a plot, particularly when one of the women inquired if she could borrow a diplomatic pouch to put her tutus in.

Following instructions, one Marine called his superior and asked what he should do. An officer said, "Give them your sharpshooter medal. We must not lose their confidence."

As distasteful as it sounds, the Marines partied with the women. After everyone had had a bottle of wine and a dance, one of the women said, "Could we see the code room?"

The Marine again called his superior. "Show it to her," the officer replied. "Let the Russians think the U.S. has nothing to hide."

Another one of the girls told our Marines, "I have a mother who is very poor, sick, and aging. The one thing she wants before she dies is a State Department burn bag."

Well, we're not dumb, Bennedy Berasimov, so we gave her a burn bag that was full of shredded confidential memos. As for your third KGB heroine, we cooked her goose too. Her wish was to bug the new embassy building from top to bottom. We were ready for that one and loaned her the pliers and wire.

So, Bennedy Berasimov, the Marine Corps saga may be funny to you, but the Americans are the ones who are doing the chuckling. Your Kremlin party girls got very little for their sexual favors—code books, some top secret cables, and the U.S. Order of Battle for World War III. There wasn't enough stuff to fill the Ambassador's out basket.

What lulled you into a false sense of security, my Russian friend, is that you thought our Marines would rather make love than war.

The big joke, Bennedy, is that after all your dirty tricks we came out on top. You went to a lot of expense and time bugging every inch of our new two-hundred million-dollar embassy, never dreaming that after you wired it, we were going to tear it down. Ha, ha, ha, ha.